Holographic
Reprocessing

Holographic Reprocessing

A Cognitive-Experiential Psychotherapy
for the Treatment of Trauma

Lori S. Katz

Foreword by Seymour Epstein

Routledge
Taylor & Francis Group

NEW YORK AND HOVE

Published in 2005 by
Routledge
Taylor & Francis Group
270 Madison Avenue
New York, NY 10016

Published in Great Britain by
Routledge
Taylor & Francis Group
2 Park Square
Milton Park, Abingdon
Oxon OX14 4RN

Printed in the United States of America on acid-free paper
10 9 8 7 6 5 4 3 2 1

International Standard Book Number-10: 0-415-94757-X (Hardcover)
International Standard Book Number-13: 978-0-415-94757-X (Hardcover)
Library of Congress Card Number 2004023338

Library of Congress Cataloging-in-Publication Data

Katz, Lori S., 1963-
  Holographic reprocessing : a cognitive-experiential psychotherapy for the treatment of trauma / Lori S. Katz.
     p. cm.
  Includes bibliographical references and index.
  ISBN 0-415-94757-X (hardback)
  1. Psychic trauma—Treatment. 2. Cognitive-experiential psychotherapy. I. Title.

RC552.P67K38 2005
616.85'21—dc22
                                  2004023338

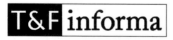

Taylor & Francis Group
is the Academic Division of T&F Informa plc.

Visit the Taylor & Francis Web site at
http://www.taylorandfrancis.com

and the Routledge Web site at
http://www.routledge-ny.com

To Aaron

Contents

Foreword

SEYMOUR EPSTEIN, PH.D.

Practitioners of the three major psychotherapeutic orientations, cognitive behavioral therapy (CBT), psychodynamic therapy, and experiential-humanistic therapy, until recently were satisfied to go their own way. They were comfortable with their own approach and had little interest in adopting procedures used in the other approaches, which they considered less successful than their own. Those who practiced CBT viewed the psychodynamic approach as speculative, unscientific, unnecessarily concerned with historical information, and ineffective, and practitioners of psychodynamic therapy viewed CBT as shallow and mechanistic and effective only for the treatment of some limited problems. Both groups regarded the experiential-humanistic approach as too subjective and fanciful to be taken seriously, whereas the experiential-humanistic practitioners considered the other two approaches as having an excessively negative view of human beings and not sufficiently appreciating an innate growth force in people that can be released by appropriate conditions, such as the establishment of a relationship of unconditional positive regard.

Responding to the challenge from some distinguished psychologists (e.g., Eysenck, 1953) who believed that psychotherapy was no more effective than no treatment, a great amount of research was conducted to evaluate therapeutic outcomes for different kinds of psychotherapy. The results from these studies were encouraging in one way and discouraging in another. The encouraging finding was that it was unequivocally established that psychotherapy is more effective than no treatment. The discouraging finding was that the success rate of all schools of psychotherapy is much less than had been anticipated. Of further interest, and much to the surprise of the practitioners of the different approaches, except for a few specific disorders, such as panic disorder and obsessive-compulsive disorder, all forms of psychotherapy have about the same success rate (Luborsky, Singer, & Luborsky, 1975). The result was that many practitioners became aware of the limited value of their own approach, and accordingly developed a new respect for other approaches that had been demonstrated to be just as good as theirs. This realization fostered an interest in constructing an integrated approach that includes procedures from all approaches.

But how is such an integrative approach to be accomplished? Several answers to this question have been proposed and preliminary attempts have made to implement the proposals. One kind of integrative approach is empirical eclecticism. The most effective procedures for treating specific disorders are selected from among the various schools of psychotherapy (e.g., Lazarus, 1992). The advantage to this approach is that it allows practitioners from different orientations to share a common repertoire of procedures to draw from in treating designated problems for which the procedures have been demonstrated to be effective. Another approach is to construct an integrative theory that can provide a common conceptual basis for all psychotherapeutic orientations. The advantage to such an approach is that a single coherent theory is scientifically preferable for reasons of parsimony, extensiveness, and triangulation than a number of more specific theories for treating particular kinds of problems. An advantage of this approach over empirical eclecticism is that it can suggest coherent combinations and arrangements of procedures that are theoretically meaningful. Although several attempts have been made to develop such a theory (e.g., Norcross & Newman, 1992; Prochaska & DiClemente, 1992; Wachtel, 1977), the challenge remains to construct one that is sufficiently inclusive and compatible with other theoretical views to be widely accepted. A third way of constructing an integrative therapeutic approach is by identifying common factors across different therapeutic orientations (e.g., Frank, 1961; Goldfried & Padawer, 1982; Strupp, 1973). This approach has been encouraged by the finding that specific techniques are less important than had previously been assumed, and that establishing an effective therapeutic working alliance, an inherent aspect of all orientations turned, out to be one the best predictor of outcome.

Dr. Katz's Holographic Reprocessing (HR) falls in the category of an integrative theory of psychotherapy based on an integrative, global theory of personality. The personality theory that influenced the development of HR is one that I introduced a number of years ago (Epstein, 1973). The theory, which is called cognitive-experiential self-theory (CEST), has been considerably developed since then and has been supported by an increasing body of research (for a recent summary of the theory and research, see Epstein, 2002). It integrates important aspects of learning theory, cognitive science, psychodynamic theory, and humanistic-phenomenological theory. As a result, it is ideally suited for providing a coherent theoretical framework for the three basic therapeutic orientations.

Among the most relevant assumptions of CEST with respect to HR is the assumption that people process information by two different systems: experiential and rational. The experiential system is an automatic learning system, the very same system with which nonhuman animals have adjusted to their environments over millions of years of evolution. As it operates preconsciously and automatically, people are not normally aware of it. However, under certain conditions, such as the occurrence of unbidden distressing thoughts and conflicts between the heart (the experiential system) and the head (the rational system), they can not help but become aware that some aspect of their mind is operating in a way that is different from their conscious thinking. In addition to operating automatically and preconsciously, the experiential system operates in a manner that is imagistic, holistic, effortless, rapid, intrinsically highly compelling (experiencing is believing), and intimately associated with emotions. It connects events by association, contiguity, similarity, and reinforcement. Because the influence of the experiential system normally occurs outside of awareness, people mistakenly believe that their emotions are a direct response to external events, rather than realizing that it is their interpretations of the events in their experiential system that mediates their emotional reactions. Change the operation of the experiential system and it will change not only how people think and behave but also how they feel.

In contrast to the experiential system, the rational system is an inferential reasoning system that operates in a manner that is conscious, verbal, analytic, relatively slow and effortful, and affect free. Rather than accepting the outcome of its processing as self-evidently valid, it requires justification via logic and evidence.

The two systems operate in parallel and are interactive. The interaction works in both directions, with each system influencing the other. Of particular importance with respect to adjustment is the continuous influence of the experiential system on the rational system and on all forms of behavior, including conscious reasoning, which, of course, is just another kind of behavior. The nature of the influence, including the degree to which it is adaptive versus maladaptive, is determined by the content of the schemas in the experiential system, which are primarily generalizations from emotionally significant past experience. To the extent that these schemas are compatible with a person's current situation, they are adaptive, and to the extent they are not, they are maladaptive. Thus, a major assumption in CEST is that people's past experience automatically and outside of awareness continuously influences how they interpret events and therefore how they think, feel, and behave. It is therefore concluded in CEST that problems of maladjustment lie primarily in the domain of the experiential system.

So much for the presentation of the most relevant aspects of the integrative global theory of personality called CEST. The important question for present purposes, of course, is how it relates to HR. As a graduate student Dr. Katz obtained her doctoral degree under my supervision. She therefore was well acquainted with CEST. She was sufficiently impressed with it to apply its principles to her clinical work both before and after she obtained her degree. By treating many clients and guided by the principles of CEST, she gradually developed HR

Although Dr. Katz's book is subtitled, "A cognitive-experiential psychotherapy for the treatment of trauma," she states that the trauma she is concerned with is not limited to the one identified by the Diagnostic and Statistical Manual of Disorders-IV (DSM IV, APA 1994) as posttraumatic stress disorder (PTSD), which involves a threat to life or limb of such magnitude that it cannot be assimilated into the existing personality structure. Rather, she is concerned with the maladaptive behavior resulting from a wide variety of emotionally distressing experiences that occur in everyday life, such as threats to self esteem and to relationships. Thus, HR has far greater applicability than is apparent from the title.

Dr. Katz has succeeded, like few others and perhaps even like no other, in developing an approach to psychotherapy that is highly integrative, systematic, flexible, and well-grounded in theory. It is integrative in two ways. First, it freely utilizes procedures from all three major orientations (CBT, psychodynamic, and experiential-humanistic), and it combines the use of the procedures in a synergistic manner. Second, in accord with the assumptions in CEST that behavior problems reside primarily in the experiential system, that producing enduring behavior change requires changes in the experiential system, and that there are three ways of producing such changes, Dr. Katz uses all three ways in a systematic and integrative way. She has borrowed from all other schools of therapy as well as devised her own innovative procedures for implementing these three ways, which are to use the rational system to influence the experiential system, to provide corrective emotional experiences within and outside of the therapeutic situation, and to communicate with the experiential system in its own medium through the use of fantasy, imagery, narratives, emotions, and bodily reactions.

As HR is highly systematic, it can readily be taught to others. Dr. Katz carefully describes the various stages through which HR normally progresses, from initially establishing a therapeutic alliance to finally building and testing newly acquired patterns of behavior in the real world. The center piece of her theory of therapy is the innovative construct of an experiential hologram, which is a representation of a traumatic event that results in various ways in which the hologram produces maladaptive manifestations of itself in everyday life. Dr. Katz thoroughly describes the different components of experiential holograms including how they can be identified and reprocessed. It is not always necessary to reprogram each separately, as the defining characteristic of a hologram is that each of its parts contains all the features of the whole. Thus feedback operates in both directions, from the whole to each of its components and from each of its components to the whole.

Although HR is highly systematic, this does not mean it has to be rigidly implemented. Rather, a highly flexible approach is favored, for there are many ways in which the same principles of CEST can be applied in each of the stages of HR and in detecting and influencing each of the components of experiential holograms. Moreover, the stages themselves do not have to proceed in an invariant order, for it is suggested that exceptions be made for different clients.

As to grounding in theory, the use of the procedures in HR can all be explained in terms of the principles of CEST. As a result, HR is highly cohesive, both as an integrative theory of psychotherapy and as an integrative therapeutic process.

In conclusion, HR provides a highly integrative approach to psychotherapy that has a great deal to offer at both the theoretical and applied level to psychotherapists of all persuasions.

References

American Psychiatric Association (1994). *Statistical Manual of Disorders–IV*. Washington, DC.

Epstein, S. (1973). The self-concept revisited, or a theory of a theory. *American Psychologist, 28,* 404–416.

Epstein, S. (2002). Cognitive-experiential self-theory of personality. In T. Millon & M. J. Lerner (Eds.), *Comprehensive handbook of psychology, Vol. 5: Personality and social psychology,* Hoboken, NJ: John Wiley.

Eysenck, H. J. (1953). *Uses and abuses of psychology.* Baltimore: Penguin Books.

Frank, J. D. (1961). *Persuasion and healing.* Baltimore: Johns Hopkins University Press.

Goldfried, M. R., & Padawer, W. (1982). Current status and future directions in psychotherapy. In M. R. Goldfried (Ed.), *Converging themes in psychotherapy* (pp. 3–49). New York: Springer.

Lazarus, A. A. (1992). Multi-modal therapy: Technical eclecticism with minimal integration.. In J. C. Norcross & M. R. Goldfried (Eds.), *Handbook of psychotherapy integration* (pp. 231–265). New York: Basic Books.

Luborsky, L., Singer, B., & Luborsky, L. (1975). Comparative studies of psychotherapies: Is it true that "Everyone has won and all must have prizes?" *Archives of General Psychiatry, 32,* 995–1008.

Norcross, J. D., & Newman, C. F. (1992). Psychotherapy integration: Setting the context. In J. C. Norcross & M. R. Goldfried (Eds.), *Handbook of psychotherapy integration* (pp. 3–45). New York: Basic Books.

Prochaska, J. O., & DiClimente, C. C. (1992). The transtheoretical approach. In J. C. Norcross & M. R. Goldfried (Eds.), *Handbook of psychotherapy integration* (pp. 300–334). New York: Basic Books

Strupp, H. H. (1973). On the basic ingredients of psychotherapy. *Journal of Consulting and Clinical Psychology, 41,* 1–8.

Wachtel, P. L. (1997). *Psychoanalysis and behavior therapy: Toward an integration.* New York: Basic Books.

Preface
What is Holographic Reprocessing?

The author developed Holographic Reprocessing (HR) (Katz, 2001, 2003) by integrating academic knowledge with observations from direct clinical experiences. But what *is* Holographic Reprocessing? It is (1) a treatment for trauma, (2) a method of conceptualization, (3) an integrative approach, and (4) a process of change.

HR Is a Treatment for Trauma

Trauma, as defined in the *Diagnostic and Statistical Manual of Disorders-IV* (APA, 1994) under the diagnosis of Posttraumatic Stress Disorder (PTSD), is an external event, either witnessed or experienced that involves actual or threat of death or serious injury to self or others and evokes fear, helplessness, and horror. These events may include being attacked, raped, tortured, or witnessing murder. However, HR assumes a broader definition of trauma and focuses on the underlying emotional violations, which may be an aspect of the aforementioned events or may be incurred from interpersonal mal-treatment such as the trauma of humiliation, emotional neglect, or demeaning criticism. There may or may not be a threat of death, but there may be a threat of loss of love, self-esteem, or feeling emotionally safe. The response may or may not include fear, helplessness, or horror, but may include responses of self-blame, shame, feeling alone, alienated, and unloved. Trauma given this broader definition could manifest as symptoms consistent with a clinical diagnosis, or it could manifest in a pattern of unfulfilling relationships and poor self-esteem.

More important than the type of external event or the emotional response to the event, HR is concerned with how the event has been processed. There seems to be two distinct scenarios. In the first scenario, trauma causes a rupture in a person's conceptual system rendering the event to remain "frozen" or unassimilated. This is consistent with Horowitz's (1986) conceptualization of PTSD. Clients typically have fragmented, disorganized, or partial narratives, memory loss, and recurring nightmares and intrusive thoughts.

In the second scenario, trauma has been accommodated into a person's conceptual system and it forms the basis of limiting or negative beliefs, schemas, and perceptions about the self, others, and the world. A victim may perceive herself as bad, flawed, unworthy, or unlovable, and others and the world as unsafe, unloving, restrictive, or threatening. These perceptions set in motion emotional, cognitive, and behavioral dynamics where a person unconsciously replicates similar types of events that reinforce the limiting world view. HR is not designed to help people integrate trauma as per the processing of the first scenario, but rather HR is a treatment for the second type of processed traumas that impair a person's self concept and social functioning. HR is a method of reprocessing an already accommodated event.

HR Is a Conceptualization

HR provides a simple way to understand and map the complex repeating patterns, or reenactments, that are often found in clients with trauma histories. A core violation (the type of underlying emotional trauma) and associated emotional and behavioral responses are identified. These tend to be very consistent and replay themselves in relationships. Thus, each incident represents the whole pattern. In this way, the parts contain information about the whole. When a client shifts her perception regarding one of these incidents, then she is likely to shift the whole pattern. This is similar to a hologram, where the whole is contained in the parts. An incident of the reenactment as well as the whole pattern is termed an "experiential hologram" (Katz, 2001). (This will be explained in more detail in chapters 3 and 4.) Because of the interconnected quality to these patterns, they are a unique construct.

HR Is an Integrative Approach

HR allows for the expression of inhibited emotions and combines the holistic processing approach of EMDR, the identification of a repeating dynamic as in psychodynamic therapy, the constructivist approach of narrative therapy, cognitive reframing of cognitive therapy, and creative elements such as fantasy used in expressive-arts therapies. HR combines a variety of techniques used in therapies such as Cognitive-behavioral therapy, Psychodynamic therapy, and Experiential therapy, to identify the recurring patterns, alter them, and to encourage new behaviors. HR also offers several unique techniques, developed by the author, such as some of the coping strategies, "experiential discovery," "mapping experiential holograms," and "reprocessing." Each of these will be explained in detail in the text.

HR Is a Process for Change

One procedure used in this therapy is called "reprocessing" (Katz, 2001) which facilitates a change in clients' perceptions of a traumatic event, themselves, and others. It is through this perceptual shift that they are able to gain insight and release constricting negative affect. Reprocessing uses a non-arousing method of "exposure" or revisiting of the event. Clients remain anchored in their current aged self (who is safe and in the therapy office) and imagine that they can observe what happened to the younger version of the self. From the observer vantage point, clients can broaden their perception of what happened. With imagination, they can step into the scene as their current self to remove or confront the perpetrator, and offer empathy and understanding to the younger version of the self. "Younger version" refers to any past event. This technique is not exclusive to childhood events.

> For example, after Edward completed reprocessing of being gang-raped he stated, "I was an 18-year-old kid and now looking back at it as a man, I realize that the 18-year-old really couldn't have done anything about it. Looking at it as a man, I can see that the kid was really helpless . . . He couldn't have fought them off. It wasn't his fault."

In reprocessing, fear and arousal are intentionally minimized. Because reprocessing produces low distress, the risks of sensitization, retraumatization, and dissociation are greatly reduced. Therefore, reprocessing is a safe and relatively comfortable procedure. Edward stated that at first he was hesitant about doing a reprocessing procedure. He felt somewhat reassured by the fact that this author as his therapist was "going with him" so he "didn't have to do it alone." After his first reprocessing session, he stated that he was surprised that it "wasn't that bad!" He requested to do two more reprocessing procedures on the same event. At the end of the third procedure, he reported feeling a tremendous relief including feeling less ashamed and less blamed.

Reprocessing may facilitate the reduction of low self-esteem such as shame, blame, guilt, alienation, and negative emotions such as hurt, anger, fear, and frustration. It may re-establish a sense of safety, empowerment, security, trust, and self-acceptance. It may help clients grieve losses and complete undelivered communications to the younger version of the self who

trauma, to perpetrators, and to lost loved ones. Examples
unications are: "good-bye," "you're going to be okay," or "I'm
you!" Detailed descriptions of the techniques of reprocessing
ed in chapters 11 through 13.
also a process for couples therapy, family systems, and a way to
con. ptualize recurring themes of reenactments in socio-cultural histories.

Why *Holographic?*

The author is often asked how she came to use the "hologram" as a model
for this therapy. About 10 years ago, she noticed consistent patterns in her
clients' stories. They seemed to repeat similar types of traumas in their lives
and also seemed to react with a consistent set of emotional and behavioral
responses. But these were not merely a series of reenactments. These patterns seemed interconnected and somehow organized in such a way to lend
themselves to consistency and reinforcement.

A client could talk about one event and in a basic way, the other significant relationships in her life could be "reconstructed." For example, one
client described a pattern of being cornered, constricted, and feeling
"trapped." No wonder she also had a response of wanting to "run away"
(e.g., leave relationships, move, quit jobs, run outside, etc.) Observing this
pattern, it was hypothesized that she experienced a traumatic event where
she felt "trapped." Lo and behold, she was raped as a teen-aged girl. What
upset her most was being pinned down, feeling helpless, and most disturbing to her was "feeling trapped." In other words, one event embodied the
information consistent with the whole pattern. Each replication reinforced
the system. Her responses inadvertently perpetuated the pattern. This dynamic pattern became evident, but there didn't seem to be a way to describe
these partterns. Serendipitously, the author came across the book, *The Holographic Universe* (Talbot, 1991) and she thought, "That's it!" The patterns observed in her clients are "holographic." From that day forward, the
process of articulating Holographic Reprocessing began. (A full description about holograms and how they relate to these recurring patterns is
discussed in chapters 3 and 4.)

This book is intended for practitioners and other care providers who
conduct psychotherapy with a variety of clients including those who have
experienced trauma, broadly defined. It covers both the theory and practice
of HR, and with an emphasis on techniques it is particularly useful to therapists (e.g., psychiatrists, psychologists, social workers, and counselors), looking to incorporate an efficacious treatment option into their practice. Many
case examples are provided to illustrate the therapy. Contraindications of
HR and common barriers to its practice are also addressed.

Author's Note

The pronouns used in this text (e.g., he/she, his/hers) alternate between male and female throughout the book to represent both genders. The case examples provided are based on real clients' stories. Their names and identifying information have been changed to protect their confidentiality. Although, the information was changed, I still grappled with including such personal examples. When possible, I asked clients how they felt about having their story included in this book. Some were flattered and others felt it was an opportunity to "make a difference," but without exception, each was pleased to be included. It is with great respect that I share their stories.

Acknowledgments

First of all, I want to thank my clients as they are the ones who have taught me about healing. I marvel at their courage and fortitude. I feel privileged to know each and every one and I am grateful to be able to serve those who served in the military. I am also thankful for my students as their questions, observations, and clinical experiences have helped me articulate and refine my thinking. In particular, I am grateful for the input of Dana Lasek and Lisa Grencavage (who encouraged the first attempts at articulating Holographic Reprocessing), Lori Wicker (who contributed case examples), Lise Flores, Tammi La Tourette, Lynn Rossi (who contributed case examples), Shoshanna Shea, Heather McIsaac (who suggestions helped define the components of the experiential hologram), Claudia Avila, John Haung, Omar Alhasoon, and Serina Carson (who critiqued this manuscript). I am especially grateful to my mentor Dr. Seymour Epstein who has influenced, critiqued, and inspired my thinking and writing for the past 18 years. Finally, I extend thanks to my professional colleagues, to the editors at Routledge, and to my family and friends: Beatrice and Donald Katz, Paul Katz, Karen Katz, Jack Yanoff, Judy Solomon, Nancy Schwartz, and Ariel Hubbard for their unwavering encouragement and support.

CHAPTER 1

Overview of Holographic Reprocessing

> This chapter provides an overview of Holographic Reprocessing (HR). It begins with a case example that illustrates some of the main tenets of the therapy. The rest of the chapter describes the general theory and practice. This chapter prepares the reader for the rest of the book.

Case Example: Rescuing the Tiny Heart

This example highlights some of the techniques used in Holographic Reprocessing such as the rational versus experiential system distinction, identifying repeating patterns in relationships, using coping skills to tolerate and manage affect, and using reprocessing to help the client shift her perception of the event and release negative affect such as guilt and self-blame.

Kelly was a 33-year-old Caucasian female. She stated her goal for seeking psychotherapy was to be able to cultivate a romantic relationship that would lead to marriage. She felt that she had a tendency to "push people away in general and men in particular." She admitted that people find her abrupt, even harsh, and was aware that this was inhibiting her from achieving success in the arena of intimate relationships.

Kelly was bright, attractive, and articulate. She had earned a degree in finance and held a managerial level job in a large corporation. She was also active in sports and had several casual friends. From all appearances, she seemed to be a highly successful, independent, and competent individual.

She shifted in her seat and assumed a rather critical demeanor. She began asking me a series of questions. After all, she was an educated consumer and wanted to be sure that she was not wasting her time. She focused on my credentials, the extent of my clinical experience, and stated outright that she was not sure if I would be able to help her. I responded by giving her the requested information, and we discussed the general process of psychotherapy. Silently, I hypothesized that coming to therapy must be very difficult for her. I thought that she wanted to be "in control." I interpreted this as a defense or compensating strategy, but for what? I wondered what possibly was making her feel so "out of control." Was admitting that she was "unhappy and less than perfect" triggering an emotional sensitivity, an unresolved emotional conflict or fear?

The likelihood that she would engage in therapy seemed to me tenuous at best. I knew she was looking for a reason to discontinue this process by discrediting the therapy and the therapist. If I only had this one opportunity to connect with Kelly, what could I give her that could be beneficial? How could I let her know that it was safe to be here and that I would do my best to understand her? I knew appealing to her rational mind would only give her fodder for further criticism. I had to appeal to the part of her that was in pain, wanting help, and desperately feeling alone. I knew this part was being protected and guarded by her intelligence and quick wit. I needed to by-pass the "armed guards" of her rational mind. I had an idea . . .

I asked if I could tell her a story. I did not have a story prepared and was not at all sure what I was going to say. However, it was necessary to shift the conversation away from a rational discourse, and storytelling evokes imagery, emotions, and associations—a perfect combination to reach her experiential system. She listened as I described a fairy-tale like story of a tiny heart that wanted to love. This precious heart was kept in a steel box—hard and cold on the outside but lined with soft purple velvet on the inside. It was locked in this box by an evil force and was then hidden in a big stone castle surrounded by a moat filled with sharp-toothed alligators that would "snap" and by clever guards who could "outwit" any approaching visitors. The description, of course, was about her, her presenting problem, and her defenses. The story continued. A young female warrior (the part of Kelly who sought psychotherapy) made a vow to rescue the heart. This warrior effortlessly maneuvered through the defense system of the castle, but then had to contend with the "evil force." She thought that confronting the evil would be terrifying and had to muster all of her courage to continue forward on her quest. But in actuality, she saw that the force was really just a cloud of fear and it dissolved when she had the courage to confront it. Finally, she could reach the tiny heart which was so small and timid as it had shrunk from undernourishment. She opened the lid of the box and set it free. The tiny heart grew bigger and stronger. As it emitted an endless amount of love to the world, the castle began to transform. The cold stone melted into a beautiful warm palace complete with white marble columns and a fresh water pond. Visitors, including a prince charming, were invited to the palace and welcomed to stay.

Kelly liked the story. It was admittedly laden with positive suggestions about her being "courageous to continue forward in her quest" and reassurances that her fears would "dissolve" and, ultimately, she would be successful. The final image of a warm welcoming palace appealed to her stated reason of why she was seeking therapy. The story was constructed on what I believed she was telling me about herself and her desires. The intention was simply to let her know that I heard her. If there were parts that were incorrect, or did not resonate with her, I trusted she would either verbally or nonverbally indicate this to me. She seemed to feel understood and her demeanor softened. We discussed the distinction between the "rational" and "experiential" systems (which will be explained in detail in chapter 2) in terms of "her head and her heart." She stated that she tried to run her life according to her "head" (seeking achievement, doing what seemed logically good for her rather than following what she truly desired) and it was her "heart" (emotional needs) that felt ignored. She hoped therapy would help her "listen to her heart" so she could learn how to have better relationships. She was willing to explore the underlying feelings that could lead us to clues about the "evil force" which trapped her heart. By the end of the first hour, she was hopeful and agreed to meet for weekly therapy sessions.

In subsequent sessions, by listening to themes in situations where she was having interpersonal conflicts and by using experiential techniques such as associating to images, body sensations, and feelings, we identified a very consistent pattern in her relationships. She tended to feel ignored and neglected, demanded attention in ways that offended others, and then felt "guilty and ashamed." Others avoided her because she seemed "harsh" which only magnified her feelings of being alone. Not only was this pattern evident in her romantic and current work relationships, but it was also consistent with the relationship she had with her mother. Her mother admitted that she tended to ignore Kelly because she was so "competent and independent." In HR, this pattern is called an "experiential hologram." (A complete explanation of experiential holograms is the topic of chapter 3.) The outcome of this hologram was that it prevented Kelly from forming and sustaining close relationships.

We had been working on ensuring a foundation of coping skills to help her identify, tolerate, and manage affect (e.g., relaxation skills) throughout our therapy sessions. We agreed that Kelly had an adequate level of mastery of these skills and was ready to proceed forward—ready to explore the content of the origins of her experiential hologram. During one session, she stated she was feeling guilty and ashamed. She was asked if she remembered a time when she felt that way before. By asking questions to help her focus on the feeling, she was able to associate to a memory. By the shrinking of her body posture, I knew that she knew what these feelings were about. She was embarrassed, but we had established a solid rapport and she had developed sufficient trust that it was safe to share what she had just remembered. She stated that she was responsible for a sexual encounter she had with her stepfather. She was 9 years old, but blamed herself for being old enough to know better and that "it should not have happened." No attempts were made to "argue" her out of this belief as she admitted that she knew in her rational mind that she was "just a child" but experientially, continued to feel the guilt and shame. In HR, her statements are accepted as *her truth given her perspective* of herself in the situation. We did a holographic reprocessing procedure where she revisited the traumatic event remaining anchored in her current-aged self and from the vantage point of an observer. From this vantage point, she was able to see a different truth.

What was revealed was that when Kelly was 9 years old, she did flirt and invite certain attentions from her new stepfather. She saw that her mother got attention this way and figured it would make her special and loved by him as well. However, she did not expect to have a sexual encounter with him. She felt violated and hurt by his actions and had assumed it was her fault. She also assumed his subsequent rejection of her was also her fault. In the reprocessing, she saw that the 9-year-old girl was really innocent. She was lonely, neglected, and merely wanted attention and affection, all normal desires of 9-year-olds. Now that she is in her thirties herself, she realized that it was the 38-year-old man who should have known better. At an emotional level she realized that it was not the child's fault and thus, it was not her fault. She was able to shift her perception of the scene, imaginally deliver communications to both her stepfather and her younger self, as well as release the feelings of guilt and shame. After the reprocessing she reported feeling lighter and having a deep sense of relief.

Additional therapy sessions addressed her interpersonal relationships, specifically to encourage empathy for herself and toward others. She also learned more effective ways to get her needs met. We developed a set of "counter-images" to help her break old patterns and encourage new behaviors ("counter-images" are explained in chapter 14). A year later, Kelly called to schedule a session. She had needle-pointed a "therapy in session" sign for my door. She wanted to tell me in person how dramatically her life has improved since her therapy. She stated she is a "softer person" now. She feels her feelings and is more forgiving toward herself and others. She reported that her personal and professional relationships had significantly improved.

Holographic Reprocessing

Holographic Reprocessing is a cognitive-experiential approach to psychotherapy (Katz, 2001, 2003). It is based on Epstein's Cognitive Experiential Self-Theory of personality (CEST) (For review of the overall theory of CEST and its supporting empirical research see S. Epstein, 1991, 1994, 1998). CEST is a dual processing theory, which states that we have two systems for processing information: the rational and experiential systems. (These will be explained in greater detail in chapter 2.) Suffice it to say, that the rational system processes information logically and linearly, while the experiential system processes information emotionally and by associations. Both systems provide necessary and adaptive functions. The experiential system in particular, can help facilitate the retrieval and reprocessing of information that may otherwise be difficult to access or alter. HR uses the principles of CEST to access information about the cognitive, emotional, and behavioral tendencies that lead to the replication of situations that replay aspects of a previous trauma as well as to alter those patterns.

In HR, a pattern of reenactments is described using the hologram as a model. A hologram is a projected three-dimensional image that appears to be suspended in space. What is particularly interesting about holograms, is that the image is produced on special holographic film where by the whole image is embedded through out the film (details are explained in chapter 3). This creates a phenomenon where the whole is contained in the parts. In terms of explaining a repeating pattern of certain experiences, each cycle of a reenactment contains information consistent with the whole pattern of experiences. Although the experiences are certainly real, they also serve as a backdrop for clients to project their beliefs about themselves, others and the world. Just like a hologram, these beliefs appear to be supported by these experiences, when in fact the client contributes to their creation. In other words, the "experience is holographic," and thus, it is termed an "experiential hologram" (Katz, 2001).

Experiential holograms are holistic, integrative, and unique in terms of existing constructs. Experiential holograms are more than a schema, belief, expectation, self-fulfilling prophecy, sensitivity, or script, although all of these constructs may be useful parts of what is activated by an experiential hologram. These constructs are largely cognitive and only part of the holographic picture. What is also activated is an experiential reaction including affect, sensations, and associations. The model of an experiential hologram is intended to more closely explain human experience, as it is assumed that experience itself is processed in a complex array of cognitions, affective reactions, sensations, and associations (Epstein, 1992).

Each holographic reenactment cycles through the six components which will be discussed in chapter 4. Distinguishing these various components gives clients and therapists a user-friendly way to explain complex behavior. It also creates a template so that presenting problems can be understood in a holistic fashion. For example, a client may present with symptoms of social avoidance. Although this may be a problem in its own right, it may also be a part of a larger problem that encompasses a repeating pattern of feeling rejected in relationships. To address social avoidance without contextualizing it within the broader experiential hologram would be missing vital information about the source of the problem.

Once the experiential hologram is articulated by the client and therapist, the therapy shifts to focus on a series of techniques to "reprocess" the experience. Reprocessing facilitates adaptive perceptual changes of the situation, so that the client has a broader understanding of the event and has an increased feeling of emotional peace or "completion" with the experience. Reprocessing may include a non-arousing revisiting of the event. The client remains anchored to the here-and-now by remaining their current aged self, and imaginally reviews the event that happened to the younger version of the self. This technique is not limited to events that occurred in childhood. Any past event would have happened to a younger-version of the self. Using imaginal rescripting (similar to Smucker & Neideree, 1995; Smucker & Dancu, 1999 who use it for adult survivors of child abuse) clients can: (1) shift perceptions, (2) release negative affect, and (3) complete communications with perpetrators or the younger version of the self who experienced the trauma. If a traumatic event is not remembered, reprocessing may focus on a different event that replicates the experiential hologram. If the client or therapist feels that reprocessing a particular traumatic event would be too threatening, they may choose a less threatening event. However, they may choose to reprocess the more difficult event when the client is ready.

Following a discrete single episode trauma such as an accident, crime, or natural disaster, there may or may not be a life pattern of recurring similar events. Yet, if a person is seeking psychotherapy, there is most likely an emotional blockage associated with the trauma. Depending on the presentation and the nature of the problem, it could be handled with the same techniques of reprocessing including a non-arousing revisiting of the event with the goals of: (1) shifting perceptions about the event, (2) returning to safety, (3) imaginally completing communications, and (4) releasing and integrating constricted affect.

After completing the reprocessing phase, therapy shifts the focus to the establishment of new behavior patterns. Imagery may be used to elicit client's perceptions about being in problematic situations. Client and therapist create new images to counter the old images. These are rehearsed using imagery. New behaviors and ways to approach situations are encouraged and tested with behavioral experiments.

Other Therapeutic Techniques

In the context of HR therapy, several other techniques may be incorporated into the therapy such as exposure, Prolonged Exposure, cognitive, experiential, and psychodynamic techniques. Each of these will be briefly mentioned. The descriptions are in no way intended to be comprehensive, but are rather an acknowledgment of some of the useful therapeutic techniques that can be easily integrated with HR.

Exposure Therapy

Exposure therapy is beneficial to treat phobias (Hermesh, 2003) that can develop in response to trauma. Techniques such as Systematic Desensitization and Flooding are used to decondition an intrinsically neutral stimulus that has been conditioned to elicit a fearful response. For example, a client who was raped in a park developed a phobia of all parks and any grassy area that had any park-like features. These techniques, in conjunction with an HR reprocessing procedure, helped the client extinguish her fear of parks. The exposure changed her association of parks from being dangerous and threatening to being relaxing. The reprocessing helped her complete unresolved feelings of shame, self-blame, and anger.

Prolonged Exposure

Foa and Rothbaum's (1998) Prolonged Exposure technique has been proven to be beneficial to treat aspects of trauma. This technique is particularly helpful when clients have a fragmented narrative of their trauma which lacks details, organization, and sequencing. These clients typically have never articulated their entire story either through writing or talking. They may be overly focused on one frightening detail or may have amnesia for significant portions of their story. Prolonged Exposure helps them elaborate, integrate, and contextualize the traumatic event within the larger narrative of their lives. Prolonged Exposure may be practiced in conjunction with cognitive techniques such as those presented in Cognitive Processing Therapy for rape victims (Resick & Schnicke, 1993) and a cognitive model of PTSD (Ehlers & Clark, 2000). This technique can also be practiced before utilizing HR's imaginal rescripting techniques.

Cognitive Therapy

Cognitive therapy offers techniques to identify and shift negative thoughts or "negative appraisals" associated with having experienced trauma. Negative appraisals can lead to a host of maladaptive outcomes by perpetuating negative emotions and behaviors. For trauma survivors, negative appraisals may lead to the persistence of symptoms consistent with PTSD (Ehlers & Clark, 2000). Examples of negative appraisals are: "nowhere is safe" and "I attract disaster." These may lead to further appraisals associated with negative emotions such as anger "others treat me unfairly," fear "disaster will surely happen again" or guilt "it was my fault." Negative appraisals may contribute to dysfunctional strategies such as "If I think about the trauma, I will go mad, so I better use the strategy of drinking alcohol to avoid thinking." Cognitive therapy identifies these negative appraisals paying particular attention to the parts of someone's trauma story that elicits the most distress. These parts are called "hot spots" or "stuck points" and usually lead to problematic behavioral and cognitive strategies (Resick & Schnicke, 1993). Negative appraisals are identified and discussed, and then an alternative interpretation is offered. Techniques for altering these appraisals include reframing, behavioral testing, cognitive restructuring using thought records or confronting negative appraisals using logic. Although HR clinicians tend to use experiential techniques to access and modify experiential holograms, these cognitive techniques also play an important role. They are used to help "set the stage" for reprocessing by encouraging new ways to think about their experience.

Experiential Therapy

Experiential therapy is particularly useful to connect with emotions associated with a trauma through an acknowledgment of physical sensations and bodily awareness. Techniques such as "focusing" (Gendlin, 1981) help clients become aware of what they are feeling. For example, when clients experience a "felt sense" or a "moving forward," it signals that an emotional experience has been recognized or released. These techniques are applied during the "experiential discovery" stage of HR therapy.

Psychodynamic Therapy

Psychodynamic therapy, in simplistic terms, identifies the meaning associated with thoughts, feelings, and behaviors by bringing into awareness that which has been repressed. This is particularly helpful in eliciting information about experiential holograms which are in essence a repeating psycho-dynamic. Techniques of this therapy include associations, interpretations, and an exploration of what is personally relevant and significant to the client.

In conclusion, HR embraces a variety of psychological techniques and approaches. It is a highly integrative model designed to have a broad appeal that can be incorporated into a variety of therapists' current practices. There are aspects of this model that are similar with aspects of each of the above therapies. The intention is that HR will augment, not necessarily replace, current therapies by providing a broad integrative framework where a variety of therapeutic techniques are applied.

Overview of the Book

This book is divided into two sections: theory and practice of HR. The first five chapters discuss the theory and give background information about HR. They cover information on CEST, holograms, experiential holograms, the specific components and common types of experiential holograms, and theoretic distinctions between various types of therapies that use exposure.

The remaining twelve chapters outline the specific way to practice HR as well as additional applications of this model to couples, family, and socio-cultural issues. Although a linear structure is being presented, this is intended as a guideline rather than a prescription. As practicing clinicians know, clients present with "pressing needs" often including crises, life changes, relationship or job problems, relapses, or a variety of issues that require flexibility in the practice of therapy. With this qualifier in mind, the following is a description of the stages of HR.

The practice of HR includes three stages: (1) Safety, (2) Discovery, and (3) reprocessing. There are two tasks or steps to accomplish within each of these stages. The three stages and six steps are as follows:

I. *Safety*

Step 1. Establishing a therapeutic alliance
Step 2. Ensuring a foundation of coping skills

II. *Discovery*

Step 3. Engaging in experiential discovery
Step 4. Mapping the experiential hologram

III. *Reprocessing*

Step 5. Reprocessing the experiential hologram
Step 6. Establishing new patterns

In the Safety stage, the first step for the HR therapist is to establish a therapeutic alliance. This includes developing rapport, normalizing, and educating the client about common reactions to trauma, and gently diminishing resistance. In this step, distinctions about the rational and experiential system are presented as a model to explain the dual processing system of CEST (see chapter 2).

Second, the therapist reviews techniques to reduce anxiety and increase self-efficacy (e.g., relaxation techniques, affect tolerance, and mindfulness). These are necessary foundation skills and it is recommended that each client has an individualized "feelings plan" that outlines various ways to handle difficult emotions, triggers, and nightmares. In this stage, it is important to assess for the safety and stability of the client before moving forward into the next stage of therapy. For some clients, safety and stability are the focus of the entire course of therapy. In other words, not everyone is able to move past this stage, nor is meant to. Another scenario may be that a client is progressing well in therapy but then a stressful event occurs and the client may need to return to a focus on safety and stability. In other words, the goals of therapy have to match the goals and abilities of the clients.

For example, Kara had complex PTSD with a history of self-injury, suicide attempts, difficulty getting along with people due to her poor boundaries, impulsivity and rage, and problems with the law. For her, maintaining a contract of no-injury, keeping her appointments, reducing rageful or inappropriate outbursts, and increasing positive activities such as attending AA, going for a walk, and cleaning her room were significant accomplishments for therapy. She did not have a mastery of coping skills and had difficulty tolerating and managing intense emotion. Therefore, given her abilities at the time of therapy, it was inappropriate to attempt procedures such as "experiential discovery" or "reprocessing."

In the Discovery stage, the therapist inquires about clients' emotions, physical sensations, and images to facilitate the retrieval of emotionally relevant events. A theme or pattern related to a painful event (the core violation) and the characteristic emotional and behavioral responses become evident. This is identified as the "experiential hologram." The next step is "mapping" the six components of the experiential hologram to bring further insight and definition to the repeating pattern. A drawing of a pot on the stove is used as a template to visually organize or "map" the components. This process and the template is provided in chapter 10 along with several examples.

Once the experiential hologram is defined then the goal is to "reprocess" it. The specific steps to reprocessing, the techniques to ensure minimal arousal, and how to overcome barriers are outlined and explained in detail in chapters 11 through 13. To briefly summarize the technique: First, the client discusses what happened in the event. Then, the client is asked to broaden its context (e.g., who was there, how old were the participants, and what were their agendas?) Next, the event is "revisited" through imagery in a nonarousing, safe manner utilizing the observer vantage point and having the client remain anchored in her current-aged self. Once in the scene, the client can imaginally rescript the scene such as removing the perpetrator and comforting the younger version of the client.

Reprocessing addresses the unresolved emotional issues that can result from trauma, including single and multiple episodes. Examples of these issues are: (1) a loss of personal power (e.g., feeling like a victim, an easy target, and unable to be assertive); (2) decreased self-esteem (e.g., feeling unworthy, unimportant, or bad); (3) constricting affect (e.g., self-blame, guilt, shame, anger, and fear); and (4) unresolved grief due to the loss of a loved one (e.g., death, abortion, and abandonment from a parent). Specific examples are outlined in the book. Also, contraindications, and barriers to reprocessing are discussed.

The final step in HR is to establish new patterns in relationships and to identify new life goals. Specific behaviors are discussed and practiced to reinforce more flexible and adaptive ways of approaching life.

Chapter Summary

While providing an overview of Holographic Reprocessing, this chapter prepared the reader for the rest of the book. It began with a review of HR and introduced the concept of experiential holograms. It also discussed how other therapeutic techniques are complementary to the practice of HR. Finally, it presents an outline of the six steps of practicing HR: (1) the therapeutic alliance, (2) coping skills, (3) experiential discovery, (4) mapping experiential holograms, (5) reprocessing, and (6) new behaviors.

CHAPTER 2

Rational and Experiential Information Processing Systems

This chapter discusses the two systems of processing information, the rational and the experiential systems as proposed by CEST. The implications for psychotherapy and their utility with clients are discussed.

Case Example: I Must Be Crazy!

> *The following is an example of how a client may* know *what to do in a situation but may actually* respond *in a completely opposite way! This example illustrates the two processing systems of CEST.*

Miranda was a forty-two-year-old African American woman. She requested therapy because she quit her job and has been "sick to her stomach" ever since. Miranda has been divorced for more than 7 years. Her former husband, who has since remarried, has full custody of her three children. Leaving her children and trying to fend for herself during the past 7 years has been extremely difficult for Miranda. She has lived in three different states and has held eighteen different jobs. Instead of living with relatives or in a boarding house, for about the past six months, Miranda was living in her own apartment and working at a good-paying job. She thought her life was finally in repair. Until one of her "episodes" happened again.

Miranda began to cry. She stated she felt nauseated. We spent some time focusing on breathing and re-establishing feelings of safety. She stated matter-of-factly, "I know you are going to think I'm crazy . . . Well, I am crazy. It was completely illogical that I quit my job. I needed that job and it was a good one too. Who is ever going to pay me that kind of money again?

Now, I might lose my apartment and then what will I do? I am totally out of control. I know this sounds strange . . . but for no reason, I just started shaking and felt like I had to run away. I couldn't stand to be around people so I just got up and left. I know I should have called my boss to let him know why I left. I could have made up an excuse or something, but I didn't and now I am too embarrassed to return."

Miranda was most upset about the fact that she perceived her behavior as "not making sense." On the one hand, she could intelligently report good problem solving skills (e.g., that she should have called her boss to excuse herself). However, on the other hand, her physical and emotional responses motivated her to behave in ways that countered her logical mind. Since she could not explain this seemingly irrational behavior she concluded that she was "crazy."

She did not know that she was suffering from Posttraumatic Stress Disorder (PTSD) and felt great relief to realize that she was experiencing typical and even normal symptoms of this disorder. She was also relieved to learn that we have two systems of processing information, the rational and the experiential system. Her observation that rationally her behavior did not make sense was certainly correct. However, experientially, it made perfect sense. She was responding to triggers that reminded her of being raped by her boss 8 years ago.

Rational and Experiential Systems

Epstein's Cognitive Experiential Self Theory (CEST) states that we have two systems for processing information: the rational system and the experiential system. These two systems have been well supported in laboratory research and are widely illustrated in real-life phenomena (for reviews see Epstein, 1994, 1998).

The distinctions between these processing systems are illustrated in the following example. Let us assume that Daniel is making a decision to buy a car. He likes the look and feel of one particular model (car A), but then reads several reports that another model (car B) has been proven to be considerably safer. His "heart" desires car A, but his "head" knows that car B is a safer and better rated car. The rational system processes the facts whereas the experiential system processes the personal experience. Which would be the most likely car that Daniel would choose? Before answering this question, further information about the two systems will be presented.

The rational system operates in a manner that is linear, logical, and analytical. It is conscious, deliberative, intellectual, and operates through the use of abstractions, logic, and inferences. For example, the rational system processes information such as A + B = C, or if A meets this condition, then

B is true. It is slow to process information, just as it is slow to articulate a thought, but if presented with convincing data, the rational system is quick to change.

The experiential system operates in a distinctively opposite manner. It processes information at a preconscious level, through automatic associations. It is primarily nonverbal, affect-oriented, and holistic. Compared to the rational system which processes abstractions, the experiential system is concrete. For example, the experiential system processes information at "a gut level" or "a vibe." It is responsive not only to direct experience but also to experience rehearsed in fantasy, vicarious experience, images, metaphors, and stories. It is quick to process information, such as a "first impression" but slow to change.

For example, if someone was raped in an elevator, regardless of rational knowledge that elevators are no more dangerous than many other places, experientially, elevators have become dangerous. The environmental cue of elevators will continue to trigger the experience of the rape until the experience is processed and integrated into the person's experiential system. Until then, elevators will continue to provoke anxiety, despite rational knowledge, and they will most likely be avoided.

In summary, we have two systems for processing information. Each system has its unique advantages and disadvantages and, therefore, they are best used in a constructive, supplementary manner. Thus, in the above example of purchasing a car, the most desirable solution would require the weighing of information from both the rational and experiential systems. The intellectual knowledge of the car's safety record would have to be considered together with how secure or insecure one feels when driving the car.

Mistakes and Errors

There are advantages to having two processing systems in that information from both systems can be used to determine the most wise and adaptive decisions. However, they can also conflict with each other as was demonstrated by the example of Miranda. Epstein and colleagues have demonstrated in a series of studies that people make consistent non-optimal decisions based on the input of these two systems (see Epstein, 2001). Two of these errors will be presented as will their implications when treating issues of trauma.

The Ratio-Bias Phenomenon

Epstein and colleagues conducted a series of experiments demonstrating a ratio-bias phenomenon. In these experiments, people were told that they could win a prize if they blindly picked a red jellybean from a bowl that

Table 2.1 Comparison of the Experiential and Rational Systems.

Experiential System	Rational System
1. Holistic	1. Analytical
2. Emotional: Pleasure-pain oriented (what feels good)	2. Logical: Reason oriented (what is sensible)
3. Associationistic connections	3. Cause and effect connections
4. More outcome oriented	4. More process oriented
5. Behavior mediated by "vibes" from past experiences	5. Behavior mediated by conscious appraisal of events
6. Encode reality in concrete images, symbols, metaphors, and narratives	6. Encodes reality in abstract words and numbers
7. More rapid processing: Oriented	7. Slower processing: Oriented toward delayed action
8. Slower to change: Changes with repetitive or intense experience	8. Changes more rapidly: Changes with speed of thought
9. More crudely differentiated: Broad generalization gradient; Categorical thinking	9. More highly differentiated: Dimensional thinking
10. More crudely integrated: Dissociative, organized into emotional complexes (cognitive-affective modules)	10. More highly integrated
11. Experienced passively and preconsciously: "We are seized by our emotions"	11. Experienced actively and consciously: We are in control of our thoughts
12. Self-evidently valid: Evidence	12. Requires justification via logic and "experiencing is believing"

Adapted from: Epstein, S. (1991). Cognitive-experiential self-theory: An integrative theory of personality." In R.C. Curtis (Ed.), *The relational self: Theoretical convergences in psychoanalysis and social psychology.* New York: The Guilford Press. Reprinted with permission of The Guilford Press.

contained red and white beans. They could choose between two bowls: a bowl with 1 red jellybean and 9 white ones or a bowl with 10 red jellybeans and 90 white ones. When participants were asked how they would behave if given this choice, everyone stated they did not have a preference for either bowl and would not pay for the option to choose rather than have their choice determined by a toss of coin. This response is consistent with a rational processing of the information as both bowls offer the same probability of drawing a red jellybean.

However, when participants were placed in a real situation with the opportunity to win money for each red jellybean drawn, a significant number of people chose the bowl with 10 red jelly beans. People were even willing to pay for the privilege to choose from this bowl (Kirkpatrick & Epstein, 1992). The extent of this phenomenon was tested by allowing people to choose from a bowl with a probability advantage (1 red jellybean out of 10 jellybeans) or a bowl with a numerosity advantage (between 5–9 red jellybeans out of 100 total jellybeans) (Denes-Raj & Epstein, 1994). Most adults chose non-optimally from the numerosity advantaged bowl, although this bias held only to a certain extent since almost no one chose when the ratio was 5% (5 red jellybeans out of 100).

These experiments show that when information was presented in an abstract verbal representation, people responded rationally. However, in a real life situation, their selections violated their rational understanding when they made the non-optimal choices. All were aware that selecting 5–9% over 10% was irrational. Despite their rational understanding, they nevertheless found the influence of the experiential system was more compelling than that of their rational system, but only up to a point. It is, in a way, similar to people having phobias (e.g., of mice or heights) even though they rationally know their phobias are irrational.

The ratio-bias phenomenon is a good example of the way the two systems influence each other. The experiential responses are often more immediately compelling, but the rational system sets limits of acceptability. Of course in other situations in which the influence of the experiential processing operates out of consciousness, the rational system may fail to set limits because it is unaware that there is anything that needs to be controlled.

In terms of psychotherapy, rational knowledge is therefore not enough to affect rational behavior. This is an important distinction for both clients and therapists. Clients may rationally know what they "should" do in a situation, but this does not determine how they will behave when they are presented with a real situation. As in the case of Miranda, she could rationally discuss what she could have done, but when she was in the situation and experientially felt threatened, her behavior was to run. Therapists may fall into a similar trap of thinking that a rational conversation with a client leads to rational behavior. Those who want "to give a quick fix" by giving sound, rational advice soon find out that this is rarely an effective strategy.

The Global–Evaluation Heuristic

This "error" refers to the tendency for people to make global evaluations of others based on a holistic impression (e.g., someone is either a good or bad person) rather than evaluating specific behaviors or attributes. This heuristic is particularly important as it may potentially bias decisions such as when hiring an employee or when jurors are deciding on a defendant's fate.

Epstein and colleagues conducted a study to test this heuristic in terms of the processing systems of CEST (see Epstein, 1994). They used a vignette adapted from a study by Miller and Gunasegaram (1990). In this vignette, three friends are told that if all three toss a coin that comes up "heads" they will each receive $100. The first two toss a "tails" but the third friend, Smith, tosses a "heads." Participants in the study were asked to rate how each friend would feel. Most rated that Smith would feel guilty and the other two friends would feel angry with Smith. In an alternate version with reduced stakes (i.e., less money), participants gave reduced ratings of their emotions. When asked if the other two friends would be willing to take Smith to Las Vegas and share their winnings from gambling, most participants responded, "No, because Smith is a loser." The responses were similar from the perspective of how the participants themselves would feel and how they believed most people would feel. However, when asked from the perspective of a completely logical person, most participants stated that a logical person would realize that the coin toss was arbitrary and would therefore, not hold it against Smith. Furthermore, a logical person *would* invite him on the vacation to Las Vegas.

This study demonstrates that people are aware of the two systems of processing information. It also demonstrates the tendency to overgeneralize when judging others on the basis of good or poor outcomes regardless if the person has any influence on the outcome and regardless of rational knowledge about the situation.

In terms of issues related to trauma and abuse, this heuristic poses many problems. First of all, it is problematic when it comes to judging perpetrators of abuse. Perpetrators may be well thought of by other family members, employers, colleagues, or society. Who would believe that such a "good" person could do such a "bad" action? Survivors may be hesitant to report crimes of abuse for fear that nobody will believe them, or even worse, be punished for making a negative accusation of an otherwise positive person. Many clients have reported that they were fired, demoted, sent to live with a relative or at a boarding school, ridiculed, harassed, or threatened after they attempted to verbally or legally report the actions of a perpetrator. Clients have also reported incidents where their perpetrators were protected, not prosecuted, and, in one case, an offending supervisor was actually promoted to a higher position.

Second, this heuristic is problematic when judging the survivors of abuse. Victims of abuse are often blamed for somehow having caused the incident, just like Smith was blamed for tossing a "tail." For example, the abuse may be attributed to the behavior of the victim such as: she asked for it because of the way she dressed, walked, talked, looked, etc., or because she was out at night, on a date, drinking beer, asking for a raise, asking for extra credit at school, babysitting, etc. Or the trauma can be attributed to negative characteristics of the victim such as: she's a whore, has poor judgment, is a trouble-maker, etc. despite rational knowledge to the contrary.

The third problem of this heuristic is that victims of abuse judge them-selves according to this same bias. They may reason that because they were abused, then they are therefore, bad or deserving of the abuse. This error is particularly common among survivors of child abuse. Since their perpetra-tor (e.g., their parent, sibling, babysitter, or other relative) is usually some-one the child loves, it seems only natural to "make sense" of the abuse by evaluating themselves as flawed. These survivors report that they feel they are "stupid, dirty, shameful, damaged, and generally unworthy" again de-spite contradictory objective evidence. For example, three intelligent cli-ents with high GPA's, honors and awards, two with master's degrees, and one with a PhD, all reported that they were "stupid" because why else would they have stayed in abusive relationships? Also, many other clients suffer from chronic patterns of self-sabotage because they feel that they don't de-serve to succeed since their global self-evaluation is that they are unworthy and damaged.

CEST and the Implications for HR Psychotherapy

There are several implications of CEST in HR and the practice of psycho-therapy. Specifically, CEST is helpful in (1) explaining conflicts and nor-malizing client's experience, (2) locating unresolved emotional issues which are the source of experiential holograms, (3) explaining how lasting change is produced in the experiential system, (4) explaining how the rational sys-tem facilitates change in the experiential system, as well as (5) how the ex-periential system facilitates change in itself. Each of these will be discussed below.

CEST Helps Explain Conflicts

The colloquial distinction of "the head versus the heart" exemplifies the two systems of processing information. Indeed, clients may say, "I know I should do one thing" (such as break up with a partner, take a job, confront one's mother, stop an addictive behavior) but choose to do the opposite (such as stay with the partner, not take the job, avoid one's mother, and continue using an addictive substance). Clients may protest that they "can't help it" as they cannot explain their seemingly irrational behavior. Often trauma survivors, like Miranda, feel "crazy" for acting in ways that are not consistent with their rational assessment of their current environment. Their rational mind knows what should be done, yet they do not behave in rational ways. Why not? The answer is that their experiential system is automatically influencing their behavior outside of their awareness. They may be unconsciously responding to an uncomfortable or painful experience from the past or may be anticipating an uncomfortable or painful experience in the future. Why would anyone want to change if he or she is anticipating being in discomfort or pain? Explaining the conflict in terms of the two systems (1) helps validate and normalize clients' experience and (2) leads to discussions about exploring the underlying associations that are influencing their behavior in the experiential system.

CEST Helps Locate Unresolved Emotional Issues

Understanding the operating principles of CEST can also be helpful in locating unresolved emotional issues and the resulting experiential holograms. Through the use of associations via emotions, physical sensations, images, or fantasy, it is possible to reveal underlying blockages by accessing the available information from the preconscious state. This is revealed by (1) following the client's affect, (2) focusing on internal cues such as breathing and bodily sensations to heighten or bring awareness to the emotion, and (3) asking about associations such as memories, images, stories, and metaphors. Based on psychodynamic principles, difficulties in present day events are associated with earlier events. Not surprising, these usually occur in childhood.

The following example is adapted from Epstein (2001):

Robert exhibited a life-pattern of ambivalence about getting married. Recently, the woman he had been going with for several years gave him an ultimatum. She demanded that he either pronounce his intention to marry her or she would leave him. Robert loved her dearly, but he did not feel ready for marriage. He had always assumed he would settle down and raise a family, but somehow whenever he came to the point of committing himself, something went wrong with the relationship, and he and his partner parted ways. At first, Robert attributed the partings to failings in his partners, but after repeated reenactments, it occurred to him that he might be ambivalent about marriage. Since this made no sense to him, he decided to seek the help of a therapist. The therapist instructed and trained Robert to vividly imagine being married and coming home to his wife and children after work. When he had the scene clearly in mind, he was asked to carefully attend to his feelings. To his surprise, he felt irritated and burdened when his wife greeted him at the door and the children eagerly began relating the events of the day. The therapist then instructed Robert to imagine another scene in which he had the very same feelings. His mind turned to his childhood, and he had an image of taking care of his younger siblings when his parents went out for entertainment. He deeply resented having to take care of them and of not being able to play with his peers. The result was that he learned to dislike interacting with children at the experiential level, but had never articulated this at the rational level. As an adult, although Robert believed in his conscious, rational mind that he wanted to get married and raise children, in his experiential mind the thought of being in the company of children produced unpleasant vibes.

In Robert's case, he was not able to access his feelings in his rational mind. However, through associations of images and feelings, he was able to access the emotional blockage that prevented him from making a commitment to marriage. Further therapy enabled him to confront and resolve these feelings.

Associations via the experiential system is an efficient means to retrieve information about traumatic memories. Research has found that traumatic memories seem to lack a verbal narrative context in the rational system (van der Kolk, 1994). Traumatic experiences seemed to be encoded in the experiential system at the somatosensory level in the form of physical sensations and visual images (van der Kolk, 1994; van der Kolk, Burbridge, & Suzuki, 1997). Because there has been a halting of the processing of these experiences, they remain at the experiential level without the abstraction of a narrative context. Thus, retrieving information about a traumatic experience can be facilitated by directly activating the experiential system. In the case of trauma survivors, current difficulties are associated with memories from the trauma and oftentimes to events that occurred before the trauma. In many cases, how trauma is incorporated into the experiential system is largely determined by a pre-trauma experiential hologram.

Lasting Change Requires Changes in the Experiential System

CEST provides a broad model that can account for many different therapeutic techniques with the assumption that all therapies can work if and only if they touch the experiential system. Any therapeutic change must have an effect on the experiential system. Otherwise, psychotherapy results in a mere intellectual exercise. This appears to hold true across all therapeutic modalities.

CEST Explains How the Rational System Can Be Used to Change the Experiential System

The advantage of working with the rational system is that it is quick to change with the presentation of logic, facts, or new data. However, insight in the rational system is helpful only to the extent that it facilitates experiential change. If the problem involves a distortion or an overgeneralization that is persistent in the experiential system, then rational knowledge in itself will not change the problem. Rational knowledge, however, can enable or facilitate new experiences that help resolve the problem. It can do this by correcting or reframing distorted perceptions of events, acknowledging more adaptive responses, or indicating what kinds of new experiences are likely to produce constructive changes in the experiential system. For example, if the problem is feeling that all authority figures are overbearing (an inappropriate generalization based on experiences with one authority figure, such as an overbearing parent), then insight is helpful as a way to identify and bring awareness to the distortion, and, thereby set the stage for therapeutic change. The following are three ways the rational system can facilitate change in the experiential system:

1. In Cognitive-Behavioral Therapy, change can be explained in terms of CEST. Clients are instructed to identify the automatic thoughts and implicit beliefs associated with a negative feeling. Therapists teach clients how to use the rational mind to confront the underlying thoughts and beliefs and learn to substitute more constructive thoughts. This process helps clients alter their thought patterns and behaviors, thereby altering the associated experience of negative emotions.

2. Therapy as well as life experience can give people insight to their maladaptive patterns. This insight may come with the realization that changing the patterns can allow them to have corrective and healthier experiences. Insight in the rational system provides self-corrective feedback about the self. The awareness about a habit or pattern reminds the person to make new choices. But insight alone does not necessarily result in the change.

3. The rational system can be useful to shift perceptions about an event. Questions such as "What else could explain the situation?" helps clients reframe or reinterpret a perception. HR encourages discussions that broaden the context of a situation to facilitate multiple explanations of one event. These strategies help clients think about the situation differently and therefore, experience a situation differently.

CEST Explains How the Experiential System Can Facilitate Change of Itself

The experiential system normally changes with repeated experience, but it can also change from an emotionally charged single experience. Affect facilitates learning in the experiential system. The strength of that learning is influenced by the emotional intensity of what is experienced. Both imagined and lived experience can be effective in facilitating change in the experiential system.

There are two ways to generate these experiences: (1) through an emotionally corrective relationship either with the therapist or with someone else, and (2) through the construction of therapeutic experience via imagery, fantasy, and in-and-out-of office exercises. Each will be briefly discussed.

Emotionally Corrective Relationships

In therapy, there is often an attempt to produce a positive relationship where the therapist provides Rogerian "unconditional positive regard." Clients may experience their therapist as the nurturing parent they never had, and for the first time in their lives, may feel safe to share their stories and explore their feelings. The sense of safety, trust, and validation from this relationship may generalize to other relationships.

However, a positive therapeutic relationship, in and of itself, may not be insufficient to effect change because clients may encapsulate, instead of generalize, the unconditional therapist and either believe that the therapist is the only one who could ever understand them, or the therapist is discounted as not a "real person" because he or she is being paid.

An emotionally corrective relationship with someone outside of the therapy is also a potential agent for change. For some people, a loving, nurturing relationship may be enough to heal emotional wounds, dislodge emotional blockages, and transform unhealthy thought and behavior patterns. However, for most people, relationships provide the context where past emotional issues are triggered and replayed leading to both partial healings and reinforcing of old patterns. There are several barriers to healing from relationships in general: (1) it is not likely that someone will attract perfect unconditional love, (2) it is likely that minor conflicts or disagreements will be interpreted according to the difficulties of the past, (3) it is likely that the relationship will be sabotaged by responding to unresolved issues of the past instead of to the actual person, and (4) it is likely that both participants will be simultaneously responding to their own past emotional issues further confusing any attempts to communicate or reconcile issues. Thus, significant relationships tend to be a complicated mixture of loving and irritating features and most likely healing some patterns and replaying and reinforcing others.

Therapeutic Experiences

The second way experience can change the experiential system is to either have spontaneous therapeutic (or corrective) experiences in everyday life, or to construct them as part of a therapeutic exercise. The following are two examples of spontaneous experiences that were therapeutic: Dave is asked for his opinion when he has a history of being ignored, and Sue has a positive experience of presenting her ideas in front of a group when she has a fear of public speaking. These experiences may be effective in producing change by encouraging the likelihood of reinforcing behaviors such as Sue volunteering to speak in front of a group again. However, spontaneous experiences are not predictable or reliable.

In therapy, corrective experiences can be constructed. A few examples are (1) using imagery to create a positive scenario (such as imaginal rehearsal of giving a successful presentation), (2) using fantasy to represent emotional aspects of the self and imagine how they may be resolved, and (3) using role-playing techniques to practice communication or new coping strategies.

Chapter Summary

This chapter discussed the research and therapeutic implications of the theory of CEST. Research on CEST demonstrates that we have two systems of processing information: the rational and experiential systems. There are unique advantages and disadvantages of both and are best used in a supplementary manner. Experiments demonstrating why rational people make irrational decisions were reviewed. This knowledge explains how seemingly irrational behavior makes sense when understood from the experiential system. Finally, how the knowledge of the principles of CEST can inform HR psychotherapy was discussed (e.g., how it can be used in building rapport, diagnosing, and reprocessing unresolved emotional experiences). These later concepts will be further discussed as they are applied throughout the book.

CHAPTER 3

Holograms and
Experiential Holograms

This chapter explains holograms and experiential holograms in greater detail. Topics such as how experiential holograms are activated and reenacted are discussed.

Case Example: Women Leave Me!

This case illustrates how an "experiential hologram" is triggered and replicated. It shows how a client tried to defend against but inadvertently recreated the very outcome that he most dreaded.

John was a 25-year-old Hispanic college student who was studying accounting. He came to therapy because he was feeling depressed and had thoughts of "wanting to give up." His symptoms met the *Diagnostic and Statistical Manual IV* (APA, 1994) criteria for Major Depression. It was not the first time he had experienced these symptoms. When he was age 19, he was hospitalized for depression and attempted suicide by drinking alcohol and overdosing on barbiturates which he obtained from a friend. He might have succeeded in his attempt if his father had not come home early from his business trip. Following the hospitalization, John was referred to an alcohol treatment program. He stated he really was not an alcoholic and the program was "a waste of his time." He attended group therapy for a few sessions but then quit. He was also put on antidepressant medication but stopped taking it after four months. Previous to the suicide attempt, he was enrolled in a junior college. But after the attempt, he dropped out of college and started working in a retail store. He was doing well and was given more responsibilities. He discovered he had a "knack with numbers." At age 24, he decided to return to college to study accounting.

I wondered if he had some insight as to why he has had two bouts of depression, both occurring when he was in college. I asked an open-ended question about what he thought was going on. John said, "She left me." "Who left you?" I inquired. "Amber." Amber was a 21-year-old student he had been dating for the past 3 months. This was very distressing to John who was now tearful. He continued, "They always leave . . ." "Who always leaves?" "Women . . . Women always leave. No matter what you do. I really thought Amber was different. In the beginning, she was so great. I never would have fallen for her, but I really thought she was different. Now, I know it's hopeless. No matter what you do . . . they'll always leave."

John had a pattern of women leaving him. This started when he was 5 years old. His mother left him and his father to pursue a modeling career in Europe. She called on several occasions over the course of a couple of years, always promising to come home, but she never came back. Apparently, she remarried and is living somewhere in Europe. John was essentially raised by his paternal grandmother. He was very close to her and was devastated when she died of cancer when he was age 14. During his high school years, he described himself as being "introverted but did well in school." He had a few friends and tended to socialize in groups with women rather than dating anyone in particular. He "experimented" with alcohol and drugs and had a few incidents of getting into trouble such as the time he and his friends vandalized the girl's bathroom and was suspended for 3 days. He graduated with his high school class. He and his father agreed that he would live at home for 2 years, attend a junior college, and then he would transfer to a university and live on his own.

In junior college, John met Maria. He stated it was the first time he had fallen in love. He stated he would have "done anything for her." He was completely devoted to her and willing to marry her. However, they were both 18 when they met and, after dating for a year, she told him that she felt too constricted in the relationship. She wanted to spend time with her girl-friends and go out to parties. John was very jealous and insecure. He questioned her and demanded that she call him any night she was not with him. Sometimes he would call her several times during an evening. Maria got frustrated with him and stated she never wanted to see him again. This was the precipitating event for his first bout of depression and suicide attempt.

Fearing that he would be hurt again, John avoided committed relationships for the next 6 years. He would ask women for dates, initiate sexual relations, but would not follow through with a relationship. He pretended that he cared about the women and would keep seeing them as long as they were meeting his needs. He knew he was hurting many women in the process but he did not care. Any slight rejections of his advances fueled his anger toward women. He had an experiential sense (i.e., a gut feeling or an inner knowing) that women were dangerous, not to be trusted, and would eventually hurt him. He dreaded this outcome and experienced it as a great source of pain.

Then John met Amber. She was from South Africa and came from a mixed ethnic heritage. Something about her seemed different. She was more open and vulnerable than the primarily Hispanic women he had dated. She seemed like someone who would need him and, therefore, someone who would stay with him. Amber had a history of being with controlling boyfriends. Amber at first felt safe as a result of John's sense of caring and attentiveness. He described how they both felt they had met their soul mates. However, when Amber wanted to spend some time with her friends, John's fears were triggered and the associated emotional and physical sensations became activated. His response to the anxiety evoked by her request was to try harder to please her. Eventually, she felt smothered and controlled by John and left the relationship. Most likely, Amber also had expectations, associations, and responses from her past that were triggered by this relationship, which contributed to recreating her expected outcome of feeling controlled and dominated.

We identified that John was responding to and inadvertently recreating his experiential hologram through: (1) his choice of partners and (2) his controlling behaviors. Therapy for John focused on identifying his experiential hologram, then shifting his perception of being unlovable and destined to be abandoned every time he makes an emotional connection with a woman. During a reprocessing procedure he saw that his mother's choice to leave was neither his fault nor a statement about him. He also realized that his own anxious behavior pushed his girlfriends away and again their leaving was not proof of his perceived personal truth that he was unlovable. In fact, he saw that both Amber and Maria actually did love him but chose to leave the relationship because John's unresolved issues stifled the relationship.

Holograms

To thoroughly understand experiential holograms, it is important to understand holograms. A hologram is a three-dimensional image that appears to be suspended in space. It is produced in the following manner: A single laser beam is split in two. One beam is bounced off an object to be photographed and aimed toward special photographic film. The other is a reference

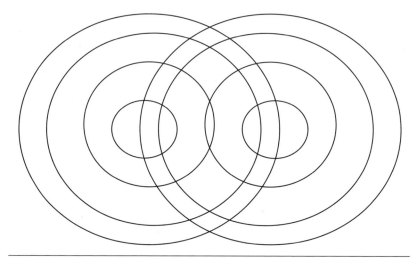

Fig. 3.1 Concentric circles depicting an interference pattern. Holograms are created when an image is embedded within an interference pattern on holographic film.

beam that is bounced from a mirror toward the film. When both beams meet on the surface of the film they collide, resulting in an interference pattern that is recorded on to the film. This is like dropping a pebble in a pond and then dropping a second pebble in the same pond. When the two pebbles hit the water, a series of concentric circles is formed; where the circles overlap is the interference pattern. The photographic film records this interference pattern and the image is embedded within the pattern.

Let's say the object to be photographed is an apple. Regular film would produce a flat two-dimensional picture of an apple. Cut the film in half, and only half of the image remains. In contrast, holographic film would produce a three-dimensional image of an apple that appears to be projected into space. However, what is particularly interesting is that if the holographic film were cut in half then the whole image would still be produced. In fact, if only a small piece of the film was broken off, the image of the whole apple would still appear to be projected from that piece of the film, although the resolution may diminish. The key point is that each part of the film contains information about the whole apple.

A second feature that is unique about holograms is the way they can organize themselves in layers of embedded holograms that together form a system. Ken Wilber (1983, 1982) discusses a hierarchical unity within systems by indicating that each level has its own structure within a more comprehensive structure, such that each whole is also a part of a larger whole. For example, a finger is a whole unto itself as well as a part of a greater whole, the hand. Similarly, the hand is a whole and is also part of a greater whole. In order to maintain integrity within the system, each part carries consistent patterns, or isomorphic themes, that run throughout the layers of the system. Von Bertalanffy's (1968) general systems theory discusses how different layers within a system organize themselves in structurally consistent ways. He uses the concept of isomorphism to explain structural consistency within and between the layers of a system. Thus, each layer of a system, although unique unto itself, contributes to the integrity of the increasingly greater wholes.

The model of a hologram is one of the featured elements in the theory of HR because of three unique qualities: (1) the whole is contained within each part, (2) each part is a whole unto itself as well as a part of a greater whole, and (3) it has a consistency that brings integrity to the entire system.

Experiential Holograms

The hologram is used as a model to explain the phenomenon of a pattern of reemerging experiences in people's lives. These patterns have at their core an unresolved violation (e.g., neglect, severe criticism, betrayal, or being threatened) and associated cognitive, behavioral, and emotional responses. Each complete reenactment is a whole experience unto itself as well as part of a greater whole (i.e., the pattern of experiences), and each experience contains information that is consistent with that whole pattern of experience. The reenactment as well as the pattern is referred to as an "experiential hologram" (Katz, 2001).

Laveman (1994) coined the term "complex structural replication" to describe how an individual's internal structure is isomorphic to his or her external expression. Although, in one particular moment (i.e., when someone is laughing at a joke), it may appear that the experiential hologram is not present because it is not being overtly expressed. However, over time there is consistency that recreates certain patterns or themes of experiences. Given the opportunity, over time and across various situations, the isomorphic themes of a person's life will be outwardly expressed.

For example, Evelyn has an experiential hologram of being invalidated and has experienced several incidents of the same type of event. If analyzed, certain responses to one of those incidents leading up to the event and occurring after the event could be identified. If a different incident was analyzed, the same responses would most likely be found. In fact, the entire dynamic is typically very consistent (the six components that make up one of these units will be discussed in detail in chapter 4). In other words, an experiential hologram is a fundamental unit that is replicated and repeated through time. Every event of being invalidated constitutes a whole experience as well as part of a theme of invalidating experiences. Each experience has the same basic structure or identifying "fingerprint" that can be traced back to a formative event. Thus, any one experience of invalidation can be analyzed as it represents the whole theme of experiences.

Each event of an experiential hologram is also associated to each other and organized in a system where the whole is contained in the parts, and each layer of the system is similar to or isomorphic to the basic unit. Just as holograms can be organized into a system where each level has its own structure within a more comprehensive structure, experiential holograms are also organized in a similar manner. Similar experiences are organized in such a way that each layer of a system is broader and more inclusive. These layers become the basis for lower and higher order postulates about the self, others, and the world. A lower order postulate might be "my mother doesn't respect me." A broader postulate might be "my family doesn't respect me." A broader layer yet may be "women don't respect me" or "anyone in authority doesn't respect me" with the broadest layer being, "nobody respects me."

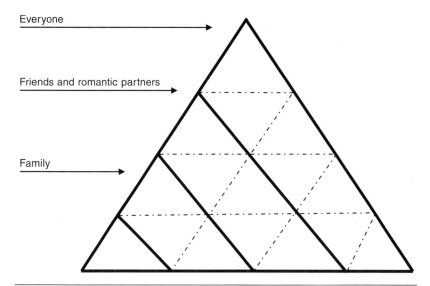

Fig. 3.2 Triangles depicting an organization where the whole is contained in the parts. Each small triangle represents an experience. The larger triangles represent broader and more inclusive levels of the experience. For example, one small triangle may represent an experience of rejection. However, multiple experiences may lead to a conclusion that a certain group or a certain situation leads to rejection. As rejection is experienced in more situations, the conclusions broaden (e.g., from only feeling rejected by family, to include feeling rejected by romantic partners, then adding close friends, and finally, feeling potentially rejected by everyone.

The implication is that occurrences of these incidents are not merely encapsulated events but rather have an accumulative effect especially if the incidents occur across a variety of domains.

Broader layers of these postulates may extend beyond personal experience and may encompass a theme that runs through multiple generations of a family or a theme that runs through the history of a society or culture. A person, family, or culture may or may not be aware of the origins of the core violation, and yet the hologram continues to be powerful and highly emotional at each of these layers. This topic is further discussed in the chapter 16 about family and socio-cultural holograms.

Implications for HR Psychotherapy

To review, an experiential hologram is the occurrence of a core violation and the emotional and behavioral responses associated with it. Several occurrences may contribute to increasingly broader generalizations about the self, the other, and the world. Given that each occurrence is linked or associated to one another, then the scope of the problem has grown quite large. However, instead of having to reprocess every incident of emotional trauma because of their association, reprocessing one or a few incidents helps shift them all. Although reprocessing any incident would impact the whole, it seems that reprocessing formative events yield the most dramatic results. The entire structure of an experiential hologram can collapse by reprocessing formative events upon which the experiential hologram was derived. If reprocessing a formative event is not possible either because of repression or being too threatening, a related or similar event can be chosen.

Also, some clients may prefer to reprocess specific events that occurred later in life. For people with multiple traumas, the client and therapist may choose which events they may want to reprocess and, in addition, they may also want to reprocess a formative event. For example, Thelma had experienced two rapes: one as a senior in high school, and the other in her second year while serving in the U.S. Army. Both incidents were reprocessed as she felt "a part of her was stuck" at each of the events. We had identified that she had a theme of being neglected and taken advantage of and a compensating style of caring for other peoples' needs to the neglect of her own. In both of the rapes, she knew the perpetrators and had agreed to be alone with them because she believed she was being "helpful." Although she felt significant relief after reprocessing the two rapes, we also reprocessed an event of herself as a young child who took care of her mother's emotional needs while her own needs were neglected. This last reprocessing helped to dislodge the whole pattern.

Holism and Holography in Medicine

The notion that treating one aspect (or in this case reprocessing one event) can affect the whole follows a holistic model of healing. This is not new or unique concept, by any means. Several medical practices embrace a holistic approach such as Chinese practices of acupuncture/acupressure, and herbal medicine, Indian *aruveda* and *chakra* systems, Japanese *reiki*, Native North and South American shamanism, and Western medicine practices of homeopathy and chiropractic, as well as health practices such as Yoga, Tai Chi, and Pilates to name a few. "Holistic healing methods always treat the person as a whole. They do not work specifically on an impaired organ or malfunctioning system, but on the whole person with the aim of mobilizing the body's own healing powers to restore the organism to a state of equilibrium" (Dougans & Ellis, 1992, p. 27).

Furthermore, in some systems, the whole is represented in the parts such as in the hands, feet, ears, eyes, tongue, and spine. An imbalance in the body may be diagnosed or treated by addressing the corresponding "problem area" in the above places. This notion is used for diagnosing such as in pulse reading, iridology (the study of the eye), and "reading" the coloration and texture of the tongue and fingernails. It is also used for treatment such as in the practice of reflexology and acupuncture/acupressure. For example in reflexology, an area in the hand or foot could be massaged to help a corresponding area in the digestive system.

If someone received acupuncture for pain management, the practitioner might place several thin needles on specific energy spots throughout the body. A certain spot on the ear may be activated (along with other spots) to help relieve pain in the knee! The ear is connected to the knee via energy networks called "meridians." There are 12 main meridians that may start at the fingers and end at the toes. Energy known as "Chi" flows through these meridians representing every major organ. There are more than 400 acupuncture points dotted along these meridians. The acupuncture practitioner may stimulate points along the meridian via thin needles to either unblock "stagnant energy" or bring more energy to a weaker area. Balancing each meridian brings balance to the whole person.

Holism and Holography in Memory

A holistic model of memory is an intriguing and controversial topic that provides a possible explanation for how experiential holograms are retrieved and reprocessed. In very simplistic terms, as an experience occurs, multisensory neural inputs are coded simultaneously. The information is processed by a neural network that can be reinforced and modified over time (McFarlane, Yehuda, & Clark, 2002).

Talbot (1991) presents evidence that the brain uses holistic and holographic principles to encode and retrieve memories in neural networks. This aspect is considered controversial and although there is evidence supporting it, there is also evidence to support contradictory theories. Nonetheless, it is worth mentioning in this text. The simultaneous firing of neurons may create the interference patterns upon which memory is encoded. Using holographic principles, vast amounts of information from countless experiences can be stored in the brain just as many holographical images can be stored on a single piece of holographic film (e.g., information of 50 bibles could be stored on a one square inch of holographic film (Talbot, 1991)). Memories are retrieved much like multiple holographic images can be retrieved depending on the angle in which the two laser beams strike the surface. Pribram (1971) and Peitsch (1981) believe that experience is processed holistically and encoded throughout the brain (or throughout a network) rather than limited to one specific area. This was also found to be true in vision such as demonstrated in an experiment where 98% of a cat's optic nerves were severed and yet the cat could still perform complex visual tasks (Pribram, 1969).

If experience is indeed encoded holistically, then the activation of any part of an experience facilitates the retrieval of the whole experience. To explain, an analogy of a string of holiday lights will be used. Each light on the string represents an event or a cycle of the experiential hologram. When the string is "plugged in" all of the lights on the whole string light up. Each light is also connected to a multitude of interlocking or multi-branched strings of holiday lights as the network of neural inputs. Some of these branches have specific functions such as activating or inhibiting a stress response. Nonetheless, the lights related to a particular type of experience would light up together. What lights up are the images, emotions, sensations (including smell, sounds, touch, and taste), thoughts, and behavioral reactions associated with a particular type of experience. Because each part contains information about the whole experience, a trigger of any of one reaction fires the whole network. A smell of pumpkin pie may retrieve a memory of Thanksgiving, or a smell of alcohol may retrieve a memory of abuse.

Similar to the dots along a meridian, if each occurrence of an experiential hologram is imagined to be a dot along a network of similar experiences, then reprocessing one or a few instances of experiential holograms (unblocking stagnant energy) addresses the whole network and brings balance to the whole person.

The model just proposed seems to be for systems that can function properly (there may be an energy blockage but the network itself is intact). However, McFarlane, Yehuda, and Clark (2002) propose a biological model of

PTSD where there is a disturbance in the neural networks themselves. In simplistic, non-scientific terms there seems to be a sort of short-circuit in the network that reinforces itself over time and renders a person to have incomplete processing with involuntary recollections, and an activation of a stress response without the inhibition to shut it off. A person with this type of dysfunction may not be a good candidate for reprocessing and certainly not a good candidate for exposure therapy as it would be prudent not to reinforce an already sensitized system.

Formation of Experiential Holograms

Two scenarios are offered to explain what happens when a traumatic experience is either not completely or poorly processed. In the first scenario, the traumatic experience does not fit with previously existing schemas and it remains "frozen," or only partially processed. This is consistent with a theory of PTSD (Horowitz, 1986) where the experience is not integrated into the person's conceptualization system. This may occur if the traumatic event shattered a person's assumptions or basic beliefs about the self and the world (e.g., the belief in invulnerability and the belief in a just world) (Lerner, 1980; Janoff-Bluman, 1992) rendering the person in a heightened state of confusion and vulnerability. Horowitz (1986) explains how repetitions, including nightmares and intrusive thoughts, are attempts to integrate or assimilate the frozen or partially processed experience. This manifests as fragmented memories or partial memories that are non-sequential and disorganized (Foa & Riggs, 1993; van der Kolk, Burbridge, & Suzuki, 1997). This scenario may also be consistent with McFarlane, Yehuda, and Clark's (2002) biologic model for PTSD.

The second scenario is that the event has been processed or integrated into the person's conceptualization system, but in order to accommodate and make sense of the event, the person developed new schemas, perceptions, and beliefs (e.g., personal truths) about the self, others, and the world (Horowitz, 1988). This scenario is consistent with the formation of experiential holograms. Clients develop expectations that the world is a hostile environment where others will treat them in ways consistent with the trauma (Briere, 1992). They are likely to interpret other's responses as being consistent with this assumption and to behave in ways to either compensate or avoid, yet these behaviors are also likely contribute to the replication of similar events in the future. Experiences that are isomorphic to the original event validate clients' internal processes such as perceptions and expectations, and reinforce behaviors that increase the likelihood of future replications. Replications reinforce the system leading to the self-evident conclusion that "this is the way life is." It is no wonder that clients like John (the example at the beginning of this chapter) feel that they are "doomed."

Activating and Reenacting Experiential Holograms

An experiential hologram is typically reenacted in the context of a relationship. When activated, the emotional and sensory associations are triggered, as are related expectations, beliefs, schemas, and sensitivities. These associations may have an adaptive function to protect people from various types of danger. They serve to alert people to mobilize and prepare themselves to cope with familiar difficult situations. However, experiential holograms are also maladaptive if they reflect a limited or distorted view of reality and are the source of rigid response dispositions. In other words, experiential holograms may have adaptive features but are mainly maladaptive because they keep people from flexibly and constructively responding to present circumstances.

In response to a perceived danger, a person will mobilize a protective response, or a compensating or avoiding coping strategy, which has reduced anxiety in the past. These coping strategies are similar to Epstein's (1998) concept of compulsions, which are responses that are used to minimize the discomfort brought on by sensitivities. The strategies may have had an adaptive functioning in the past (to avoid pain, survive, be loved, or get attention); however, they tend to be inappropriate or rigid in the present. Compensating and avoiding strategies are not only inflexible but they attract others to engage with them in ways that actually facilitate the recreation of the expected unfavorable outcome. Returning to the case of John, his compensating strategy of "smothering" and being overly-attentive actually pushed his girlfriends away and created the dreaded outcome of being abandoned. These responses lead to the replication of the experiential hologram. Although he may be motivated to defend against a reenactment of his experiential hologram, at the same time he is likely to be unintentionally recreating it.

Relationships also provide opportunities to rewrite or "rescript" experiential holograms. Each individual contributes to creating certain situations consciously and unconsciously that mimic the isomorphic themes of his or her life. The context is often co-created by the participants of a relationship and it triggers the firing of each individual's experiential holograms. Laveman (1994) states that because the individual is a whole and a part of the context, then change can occur as the individual alters his or her perceptions. This becomes very clear in couples therapy where each member of the couple reenacts experiential holographic themes in the context of their relationship, and the relationship itself can become the medium for therapeutic change.

Since unresolved aspects of the past are re-created by holograms in the present, they provide people with an opportunity to modify the holograms in adaptive ways. For example, if John gains insight that it was his own behavior that made "women leave him," maybe next time, John will choose to be more understanding of his girlfriend's needs. HR therapy provides a structure to easily understand a complex pattern of emotional and behavioral responses. With this understanding, people can shift limiting perceptions of themselves and others and choose new responses that are more likely to lead to positive outcomes in their relationships.

Chapter Summary

In summary, this chapter reviewed holograms, experiential holograms, holistic processing, and how experiential holograms are activated and recreated in relationships. Not only are personal truths triggered and activated in relationships, but the very strategies that may have developed to protect and guard against re-experiencing the core violation are usually the ones that inadvertently lead to the recapitulation of it. For those who lack insight into their holographic patterns, the dreaded outcome serves to reinforce not only the personal truths but also seems to strengthen the use of ineffective strategies. This may seem counter-productive and even illogical, but as Epstein and his colleagues demonstrated (see description in Epstein, 2003), when the experiential system is activated, it can override the logic of the rational mind. So instead, of attempting new coping strategies, they try the old ones more fervently. They learn to believe that the reason they reexperience the same interpersonal patterns is because "this must be the way I am, or the way the world is." However, HR therapy gives people an opportunity to gain a new awareness and understanding of their holographic patterns in the safety of a therapeutic relationship.

CHAPTER **4**

Six Components
of an Experiential Hologram

This chapter identifies and outlines the six components of experiential holograms. Each component is explained in detail. Some commonly reported experiential holograms are offered as examples.

Case Examples

The following are two examples illustrating the six components of an experiential hologram. The components are labeled in the example, and then they will be discussed in detail in the text.

Lucy's Experiential Hologram: Neglected and Ignored

Lucy is a 41-year-old Caucasian woman. She has never been married and rarely dates. She has a few friends that she has known for over ten years and has a medium-sized family. However, she complains that these relationships are not satisfying because her friends and family members are "inconsiderate, selfish, and neglectful." She states that she continues these relationships because she values loyalty and honors the ties of friendship and family. She assumes that the way to love people is by being attentive and caring. For example, she initiated a family reunion picnic in the summer and then was deeply disappointed when only three family members attended. When her efforts are not reciprocated, she assumes it is because she is not loved. She feels unwanted, ignored, and unlovable. This wears down her self-esteem and she believes that nobody will ever love her. She engages in behaviors such as "stuffing her feelings" by overeating. She continues to reach out to these same relationships because she believes "at least they are something." This pattern can be described as the following:

> Lucy feels lonely. → She wants to connect with others so she reaches out to family and friends (who are similar to her neglectful parents). → They don't follow through and she feels ignored and neglected. → She feels she is unwanted, ignored, and unloved. → She tries harder to be attentive and caring. → She withdraws and overeats to avoid her feelings. → She feels lonely.

Lucy's Experiential Hologram

Core violation: Ignored and neglected
Personal truth: I am unwanted and unlovable. Nobody cares or attends to me.
Compensating strategy: Be attentive and caring to secure relationships
Avoidance strategy: Withdraws, overeats
Residual negative emotions: Lonely
Acquired motivation: To be wanted and to secure relationships

Alex's Experiential Hologram: Betrayed

Alex is a 23–year-old African American woman. She stated that she tended to feel lonely, empty, and sad. She longed for a romantic relationship as she felt this would quell her empty feelings. One night, Alex decided to go to a bar to seek romantic attention. She flirted with the men and tried to be enticing. She found someone who seemed interested, so she started a conversation with him. They seemed to hit it off and she felt her loneliness dissipate. He bought her a drink and she watched as he played a game of billiards. He appeared genuinely interested in her so she agreed to go home with him. At his home, she stated she was having a nice time until he initiated sex. She expressed that she was not ready, but he forced himself on her anyway. In attempting to fight back, she was choked. He refused to let her leave so she ended up staying the night. In the morning, he forced sex on her again. He then blindfolded her to drive her back to her vehicle that was parked in front of the bar.

Although Alex was angry with him, she was mostly angry with herself for trusting him. Her core violation was a sense of betrayal. She has a history of feeling betrayed by people she loves and trusts. They either present themselves to be different than they really are, or they make promises that they never intend to keep. After feeling betrayed, Alex would feel used and angry with both the perpetrator and herself. She stated, "I'm stupid!" "I'm nothing, just a piece of dirt to be trampled upon." To compensate she would seek revenge and as a result has a history of inappropriately "fighting for her rights." As she put it, "people can't trample on me!" Although, the conclusion of many of her life's stories is that she does feel "trampled upon." For example, she lodged a complaint at her workplace and threatened to file a lawsuit against her boss and the business because one of the coworkers made a sexual advance toward her. Instead of getting support and help from her boss and the other coworkers, she alienated them. Alex stated that she feels that she cannot trust anyone and, if there are trustworthy people in the world, that she cannot trust herself to detect them. She believed the only safe thing to do is to avoid people. She declined social invitations and generally avoided contact with her friends. This strategy worked for a short time, while she would regroup from an incident of betrayal. However, eventually she would feel lonely, empty, and sad.

Alex feels lonely → she flirts to get attention from inappropriate men → she is betrayed and she feels "trampled upon" → she feels vulnerable, stupid and powerless → she compensates by "fighting for her rights" or by being "sexy" → she can't trust others or her judgment of others so she avoids social contacts → she feels lonely.

Alex's Experiential Hologram
Core violation: Betrayed, trampled upon, taken advantage of.
Personal truth: I am a vulnerable and stupid target. I am powerless to men.
Compensating strategy: Be tough, fight for my rights, and use sexuality to feel powerful with men.
Avoidance strategy: Withdraws, avoids social contact.
Residual negative emotions: Lonely, empty, and sad
Acquired motivation: To secure a loyal and trusting romantic relationship with a man.

Both women have experienced these patterns multiple times in their lives. Not only are the associated emotional and behavioral responses triggered by actual events, but also by memories, fantasies, and dreams. This is because these thoughts activate the experiential system. Thus, a memory of a painful experience can trigger the circuit of associated thoughts, feelings, and behaviors.

This serves to reinforce the patterns to the point that people believe their holograms are their only reality and the destiny of the rest of their lives.

Overview of the Six Components of an Experiential Hologram

There are six components of an experiential hologram. A seventh component was included which was the *emotional response* to a core violation.

However, almost all clients stated they felt hurt, angry, and afraid (or some variation of these emotions). Because emotional response did not seem to be a component that differed among clients, it was dropped. The six components of an experiential hologram are the following:

The **Core Violation** is the essence of what is most dreaded or feared. It is defended against through avoidance and compensating strategies, yet it is repeatedly replicated in a person's life. This is not a particular event per se, but rather a theme that runs through a variety of events. It refers to a form of psychological or emotional maltreatment that may or may not be associated with physical or sexual abuse.

The **Personal Truths** are the resulting perceptions primarily about the self, including feelings, implicit beliefs and schemas, operating assumptions, and a felt sense about the self. These may also include limiting perceptions about others, and the world. These perceptions may have aspects of "truth" but are limited and overly restrictive.

The **Compensation Strategies** are the typical ways to counteract the personal truths and limiting perceptions. These strategies are generally ineffective and inadvertently recreate the core violation and residual negative emotions. Compensating strategies are typically in opposition to personal truths (e.g., a personal truth of "being inadequate" is countered with a compensating strategy of "being perfect").

The **Avoidance Coping Strategies** are used to minimize, avoid, or reduce discomfort brought on by personal truths and inadvertently recreate residual negative emotions.

The **Residual Negative Emotions** are the lingering feelings that occur between cycles of the experiential hologram. This is usually a negative feeling that may instigate strategies to relieve the discomfort of this state.

The **Acquired Motivation** is developed to counter negative outcomes in relationships. Clients may be motivated to seek something positive in a relationship such as love, attention, loyalty, or stability. Although the motive may be positive, it usually leads to behaviors that inadvertently lead to replicating the core violation (see examples).

Detailed Descriptions of the Six Components

The following are descriptions of each of the six components of the experiential hologram. Each component will be briefly discussed. Examples of each will be provided. The list of examples is not meant to be exhaustive, but is rather presented as examples of some of the more common experiential holograms of trauma survivors.

The Core Violation

The core violation refers to a theme of psychological or emotional maltreatment that may be present with or without physical or sexual abuse. The core violation is not an event such as an incident of abuse such as a rape but rather a theme that is consistent across several events (which may include the rape) and across several relationships. Also, an event such as a rape is too general, as people are distressed by a host of reasons (e.g., by feeling powerless, betrayed, humiliated, or endangered). The initial core violation typically originates in a relationship during childhood upon which one's perceptions about self and others are formed. This also creates a template for interpreting and responding to future events and relationships. As discussed earlier, how people respond to trauma can be explained in part to pre-trauma perceptions and sensitivities. Some common violations (not an exhaustive list) are clustered under the titles of: neglect, disapproval, betrayal, humiliation, and being endangered. Each will be discussed.

Neglect. This cluster of core violations refers to events that fundamentally neglect a person's psychological, emotional, or physical needs. People with this violation may describe feeling *ignored* such as not being noticed or asked their opinion. They may feel *invalidated* such as being told how they feel is not true, or what they want is unimportant. They may feel *deprived* of attention from acts of not allowing or withholding participation in activities, or basic food, medical attention, education, clothing, or shelter needs. Also, under this cluster is *abandonment*. This may come in the form of being abruptly left by a parent or caretaker such as through death, divorce, or because of chaos or pathology in a parent's life (e.g., leaving a child for several days while going on a drinking or drug binge). One client described how her alcoholic mother would leave for several days. She was the oldest of four and felt obligated to take care of her younger siblings. The only food in the house was a loaf of white bread and some sugar. She said they ate sugar sandwiches and waited by the window for their mother to return.

Disapproval. This cluster of violations refers to events where people feel denigrated and judged. People with this violation may feel that they are constantly being *criticized* and told that they are wrong or should be doing things differently or better. They may describe being *belittled, ridiculed,* and *accused* of being incompetent, having bad taste, poor judgment, or an inability to make the correct decision. For example, a disapproving violation may be an irritated authority figure saying, "Why did you do that?" or "You should have done this," in an accusatory tone implying that the person is stupid or incompetent. The violation may be delivered in obvious loud, harsh statements or may be delivered more subtly such as quiet passing comments or a disapproving gesture or facial expression. Clients who have experienced this violation report feeling anxious, on edge, insecure, and self-doubting. This violation is commonly seen in narcissistic parents toward their children, where a parent is constantly proving his or her superiority in a way that diminishes the child and or his or her partner.

Betrayal. This cluster of violations refers to experiences where people feel betrayed. This may come in the form of *broken promises, broken confidences, manipulations,* or *deception.* Often people who have experienced this violation feel duped, tricked, and lied to. They may also feel *trapped, mislead,* and "played a fool" especially if they agreed to the terms of their perpetrator and willing participated in their own betrayal. For example, Tanya loved her older stepbrother. She felt special when he gave her attention but did not realize that he used his position of power to manipulate her to do things for him. At first the manipulations were minor such as getting things for him or making prank phone calls to his friends. Eventually, they escalated into her doing sexual favors for him in exchange for a promise of attention and reward such as a trip to Disneyland. But these promises were never realized. He then further betrayed her by making fun of her to his friends for doing the sexual acts. Betrayal became a holographic theme in Tanya's life. She reported a series of incidents where she felt mislead and betrayed. Because of her motivation to seek loyal and faithful relationships, she was easily manipulated because she was overly trusting (naively trusting) of high-risk relationships such as someone she met in a bar and compensated by being overly mistrustful of low-risk people such as her therapist. She was unable to discern who was trustworthy which served to reinforce her personal truth that she was "stupid."

Humiliation. This cluster refers to events of being *humiliated, embarrassed, shamed,* or *treated with disgust.* People who experience this violation may feel like they are a failure, a disappointment, and a general embarrassment to themselves and others. For example, when Larry was a child, he liked to play with dolls with the neighborhood girls. His father was angry that his son was not interested in "macho" activities like sports and vehemently disapproved of his son's choices. As a punishment, he made Larry wear a dress and pushed him outside of the house so the neighborhood kids could ridicule him. This tactic of humiliating and shaming Larry made him feel worthless, insecure, and damaged his self-esteem. Years later, Larry attempted to seek his father's respect and enlisted in the U.S. Navy. While serving on a ship, he was ridiculed, and accused of being effeminate and gay. He reported that he was physically beaten, harassed, and humiliated in front of his peers. These incidents reinforced Larry's perceptions that he was worthless and shameful.

Endangerment. This cluster of violations includes *threats of danger, violence or death*. This may occur with actual events of being physically beaten or sexually abused with the ultimate threat that the perpetrator could kill the victim. The sense of threat or impending doom creates an environment of *intimidation, chaos, and unpredictability* based on the volatile moods of a perpetrator. People who live in this type of environment feel like they "walk on eggshells" or that at any unpredictable moment a perpetrator may explode and they would be seriously endangered. This pattern is typical in cases of domestic violence relationships. Perpetrators may use tactics similar to the other violations such as manipulation, betrayal, criticism, and humiliation to create a hostile, threatening environment. Also, certainly the needs of the victims are neglected. The difference between this violation and the others is that the endangered violation includes a threat of injury that could result in death. This can include an unstable perpetrator either from violent moods or from recklessness due to substance abuse, or an untreated psychiatric illness. For example, Russ's mother insisted that he get into a car with her. She was having a manic episode and was loud, impulsive, and reckless. She drove through red lights, was speeding, and swerving in and out of her lane. Luckily they did not get into an accident, but nonetheless, Russ was deeply shaken by the experience. This contributed to a history of being endangered by the unpredictable moods and behavior of his mother.

Four Clusters of Common Core Violations

Neglect	Disapproval	Betrayal	Endangerment
Invalidated	Criticized	Trapped	Threatened
Ignored	Belittled	Manipulated	Intimidated
Deprived	Judged	Deceived	Physical or sexual violence
Abandoned	Shamed	Broken promises	Chaotic environment

Personal Truth

There are several constructs that are similar to personal truth such as operating assumptions, implicit beliefs, appraisals, self-concept, and schemas. These terms may be broad or narrow and are, for the most part, considered to be cognitive. Whereas, personal truth incorporates aspects of the above terms, it is a narrow and specific term that is largely emotional as it is a felt sense or "gut feeling." Similar to implicit beliefs in CEST, personal truths are cognitive-affective networks. Typically, the personal truth is a conclusion or "knowing feeling" that, from the client's perspective, serves to explain why she experienced a violation. In other words, a violation occurred and the personal truth is the conclusion that it must have happened because of the personal qualities of the recipient. This is a narrow and limited conclusion, as objectively there may be more plausible explanations.

Some common personal truths are, "I am unlovable, incompetent, wrong, out of control, not good enough, disgusting/unacceptable, guilty, or flawed." The essence of each is an assumption of fault or responsibility. The personal truth is not a rational or logical statement and therefore, cannot be argued away with the presentation of disconfirming evidence to the rational mind. But rather, it resides in the experiential system and as Epstein (1991) states, information in the experiential mind is self-evidently valid, "experiencing is believing" and slow to change.

Personal Truths and Multiple Truths

The following is a hypothetical example to explain how personal truths are formed. A father is concentrating on preparing his taxes. He is upset and frustrated because he realizes that not only is he missing documentation, but that it appears that he will have to pay a substantial amount of additional money. He is in the middle of adding a long list of numbers when his 4-year-old son runs through the room, disrupting his father's concentration and blowing some of his papers on to the floor. Suddenly the father yells, "Get out of here, you lousy kid!" His son is jarred and frightened by his angry father. Since his father tends to have a sharp temper, the child experiences this event as a potential threat of losing love (of the parent), losing security (will the parent still provide?), and losing self-esteem ("I'm lousy"). The father's communication was angry, disapproving, and rejecting with a specific blame on the child.

The child experiences the words spoken by the parent as the truth and concludes that his father is angry with him because he is no good. After all, the father is yelling at the child and did call him a "lousy kid." Therefore, it is a perfectly logical conclusion for him to assume his father is angry with him. The child's conclusion is not faulty or wrong, it is merely too narrow and limited. In order to have a different perception of the event, the child would need to have the ability to see a bigger context for the parent's response. This is unlikely because (1) it may be beyond the developmental capacity of a young child to assume that there is a different context for his father's anger, (2) the child was not given any indication that his father's anger was a displacement from his own frustration with the taxes, and (3) even if the child was told his father was really upset about the taxes and not him, he still experienced his father's anger directed towards him and this would be difficult to refute.

An objective observer may perceive the interaction quite differently and be able to view the father's words as an indication of his own frustration and emotional problems. Both the child and observer made logical and accurate conclusions although they are contradictory. In other words, there are multiple, mutually exclusive "truths" to this event. From the child's perspective, there may be no doubt that what is perceived is the truth, while from the observer's perspective a different truth is obvious.

The personal truth is a perception of truth given a particular vantage point, usually formed from the perspective of a child but could also be formed as an adult. It is a limited perception as it does not take into account the perspectives of the other people involved in an interaction. This construct is called "personal" as it defines a narrow personal perception. Holographic reprocessing encourages people to see multiple explanations to events thus, broadening one's viewpoint.

Self-Blame and Personal Truths

John Briere (1992) proposes "abuse dichotomy" as an explanation for self-blame of victims of abuse, particularly child abuse. He explains that the victim goes through a series of logical steps where someone must be blamed in an either/or system. In other words, if a child is being hurt, and the parents are viewed as good, right, and benevolent, then, the child must be the one to blame. The dichotomy is, "If it is not you, then it must be me." However, this assumes that parental culpability is even a consideration. From the perspective of HR, it can also be argued, that in terms of forming a personal truth there is no dichotomy. From the vantage point of the child, the abuse couldn't be about anyone else except the child receiving it. The logic is, "If it is happening to me, then it must be about me." "If I am being hurt, then I must be bad and deserving of the hurt." To consider someone else in the equation, assumes having a broader perspective, of an adult or an objective observer. Although adults are capable of thinking in abstract ways to consider "other," they are also prone to limited personal thinking. After a traumatic event they may ask "why me?" Furthermore, as a society, there is often blame of the victim by asking the same question, "why her?" while the perpetrator may not even be considered! When society blames the victim, the logic is: "if it happened to her, then it must be her fault." As discussed in chapter 2, processing of the experiential system may override the rational system leading to logical "errors." As explained in the section on the global-evaluation heuristic (Epstein, 1994), recipients of abuse tend to evaluate themselves as being globally flawed as if this would account for why they experienced the violation.

Whether or not there is a dichotomy of "your fault versus my fault" or an assumption of blaming the victim, HR allows for a more honest and balanced consideration of what happened. Clients may learn that their responses make sense and are understandable even if they also contributed to the replication of their holograms. Clients may also learn to understand their perpetrators from the perspective of a larger context. (This does not pardon the abusive behavior but helps clients see a broader and possibly more compassionate view.)

Four Core Violations with Commonly Associated Personal Truths

Neglect	Disapproval	Betrayal	Endangered
I'm unworthy	I'm wrong	I'm stupid	I'm bad
I'm not important	I'm not good enough	I'm naive	I'm upsetting to others
I'm unwanted	I'm incompetent	I'm a "sucker"	I'm at fault
I don't matter	I'm inadequate	I'm confused	I'm to blame
I'm unloved	I'm unacceptable	I am a poor judge	I deserve it

Compensating Coping Strategy

The compensating coping strategy is the typical way a person counteracts or compensates for the negative self-perceptions and feelings produced by the personal truth. For example, if someone feels she is incompetent, then she may compensate by behaving in ways to prove that she is competent. If someone feels that he is unacceptable, he will tend to use a compensating strategy to prove that he is acceptable. However, as long as the personal truth is believed to be true, the compensating strategies are never convincing enough and never bring enough comfort to the painful underlying feelings. As the term suggests, it is a compensating strategy and does not heal or fix the personal truth. In fact, it is usually a rigid and ineffective strategy that inadvertently facilitates the replication of the dreaded violation. Referring to the examples in the beginning of the chapter, Lucy's compensating strategy of being "attentive and caring to others" not only was ineffective in securing the relationships she desired, but also contributed to further neglect since the people she was attending to already had a history of being inconsiderate and neglectful.

Similarly, in the example about Alex, her compensating strategies were equally ineffective. She was motivated to attract a man to rid herself of feelings of loneliness. However, the loneliness was created by her avoidance strategy of social isolation because of her personal truth that she cannot trust others. She compensated by being overly trusting and put herself into a situation where not only was she betrayed, but was physically harmed and endangered. To compensate for feeling "trampled upon" from experiences of betrayal, Alex's compensating strategy of "fighting for her rights" alienated her co-workers and boss from which she experienced another incident of betrayal.

Some Common Compensating Coping Strategies

Be Compliant	Be Defensive	Be Helpless	Be Competent	Be Sexy
Cooperative	Quick to fight	Dependent	Handle everything	Seductive
Submissive	Tough	Appear fragile	Stay in control	Flirtatious
Passive	Self-protective	Seek guidance	Independent	
Agreeable	Assertive	Need support	Get things done	

Be Sociable	Be Attentive/Helpful
Entertaining	Advise others
Funny	Attend to others
Outgoing	"Fix" others
Friendly	Do everything for everyone
	Assume responsibility for others
	Protect others

Avoidance Coping Strategies

Avoidance strategies are designed to deny, interfere with, numb, minimize, or otherwise avoid dealing with the feelings brought on by the personal truth. These can be deceiving in psychotherapy as people seem to be aware of the problematic nature of these behaviors and may choose to focus on these in therapy instead of on the underlying feelings. This, of course, is another avoidance strategy. However, some of these strategies are indeed problematic in and of themselves and need to be addressed before progressing with the therapy.

There are several common avoidance strategies such as: any form of addiction including substance abuse, smoking, gambling, over-spending, and over-eating; chaos or frequent crises; physical distancing such as frequent moves; mental lapses, dissociation, forgetfulness, and confusion; social withdrawal; and self-injury with the ultimate being suicide. Two additional avoidance strategies worth highlighting are symptoms of depression and anxiety. Although these may be problematic in their own right, they may also serve to avoid difficult feelings. When it is clinically appropriate, instead of focusing on these symptoms as the source of the problem, they can be reframed as the client's attempt to cope with overwhelming or unpleasant affect. This can be used as an opportunity to explore what the client may be avoiding such as feelings related to thoughts of trauma, a nightmare, a trigger, inter-personal conflict, or a pending test or evaluation.

If there seems to be an increase in avoidance strategies, it may be a com-munication that the therapy is close to feared emotional material. Clinical skill is required to judge when to slow down, set limits, and reinforce healthier coping strategies.

Some Common Avoidance Strategies

Addictions (or to a lesser degree, numbing distraction): substance abuse, smoking, gambling, over-spending, and over-eating, sleeping, watch-ing TV, video games, etc.

Chaos distraction: Frequent crises and emergencies in various realms such as finances, health, car trouble, relatives, and living situation

Physical distancing: quitting jobs, moving, not showing up for or cancel-ing appointments, running away from stress

Mental lapses: forgetfulness, memory lapses, confusion, dissociation

Social avoidance: ending relationships, isolation, social withdrawal, cheat-ing or creating reasons for someone to leave

Self-injury: non-compliance with medications, over or under eating, self-harm, risk-taking, suicide attempts or completion

Depression: feeling numb, "shut down," tired, unmotivated, indecisive

Anxiety: jittery, tense, can't sit still, being spacey, scattered, unfocused

Residual Negative Emotions

The residual negative emotions are the lingering feelings that occur between cycles of the experiential hologram. This is usually a negative feeling that may instigate strategies to relieve the discomfort of this state. Some typical residual emotional states are feelings such as being lonely, needy, insecure, or anxious.

Acquired Motivation

The acquired motivation is the desire to relieve negative feelings such as the residual negative emotions and those brought on by the personal truths. The motivation is typically to engage in a positive interpersonal interaction or relationship such as to find love, attention, affection, approval, or accep-tance. It may seem obvious, and yet necessary to say that people are not motivated nor do they seek abusive interactions, on the contrary, they are seeking to fulfill basic needs such as a favorable pleasure-pain balance, a coherent and stable conceptual system, relatedness, and self-esteem (Catlin & Epstein, 1992).

Chapter Summary

This chapter reviewed the six components of an experiential hologram: the core violation, personal truths, compensating and avoidance strategies, residual negative emotions, and the acquired motivation. The core violation is a repeating theme based on emotional or psychological maltreatment with or without physical or sexual abuse. Personal truths are limited, narrow perceptions based on the personal viewpoint in a situation without taking into account other people's agendas or motivation. Compensating and avoidance strategies are attempts to protect against re-experiencing a core-violation and the associated painful emotions. The acquired motivation is the attempt to fulfill unmet needs.

Yet, as discussed in chapter 3, the coping strategies and behaviors to fulfill the acquired motivation, inadvertently help recreate the core violation and reinforce the personal truth.

CHAPTER 5

Exposure Therapies and Reprocessing
Clarifying Concepts

Exposure-based therapies are commonly used to treat symptoms of trauma and anxiety. This chapter takes a critical view of clinical procedures using exposure. It covers topics such as extinction, habituation, and sensitization and discusses the therapies of Eye Movement Desensitization Reprocessing, Hypnosis and other imagery-based procedures, Traumatic Incident Reduction, Prolonged Exposure and a cognitive model for treating PTSD including Cognitive Processing Therapy. These therapies are compared and contrasted with Holographic Reprocessing.

A Case Example: Don't Tie My Fighting Hands

This example illustrates how two types of "exposure" to trauma can be utilized within the same therapy. The client first told his story from the "field" vantage point (as if reliving the event) to help repair his fragmented narrative. Then, he revisited the traumatic event from the observer vantage point (as if observing the event) to rescript it.

Edward, an Italian American male, was nearly seventy years old when he started therapy. He was referred by his primary care physician to address issues of depression secondary to his diagnosis of impotence. In his first session, he was tearful and embarrassed about his situation. He stated he had lost every relationship he had ever had because of his problem including two wives and four girlfriends. The women assumed he did not care for them and they were not sexually attractive to him. They felt hurt, isolated, and frustrated. He did not want to talk to them about his impotence which further pushed them away. He is currently in a "good relationship" and is sure that this woman, too, will leave. He was deeply saddened by his fate of doomed relationships.

The first task was to gather more information. Apparently, impotence was only part of the problem that drove the women away. He also would have abrupt sometimes violent reactions if he was touched from behind. This abrupt reaction sounded like a "trigger" and he was questioned about other symptoms. He admitted to having a short fuse, feeling irritable, and having fitful sleep. He denied emotional, physical, or sexual abuse in childhood and in adulthood other than his failed relationships. Then he was asked about his military career. He stated he was a light-weight boxing champion during high school and while he served in the military. He was particularly proud of this achievement and stated he probably would have "gone pro." Naturally, he was asked what happened.

His body froze and he became quiet. He did not want to talk about it but alluded to an incident that changed his life. He became tearful and very tense. The subject was changed and he was brought back to a feeling of safety. We discussed that avoiding this "incident" was having consequences on his life particularly on his relationships. He nodded as he knew he had never dealt with "it." We discussed that he has "stuffed his feelings" about this incident and Edward stated it felt like a heavy ball that resided in the pit of his stomach. He stated he never talks about it, yet hardly a day goes by where he is not reminded of it. Although afraid, he was ready to face his problems and he was highly motivated to engage in therapy.

Over the next few sessions, he revealed that as an 18-year-old, serving in the U.S. Navy, he was jumped by three men, blindfolded, gagged, and raped. After the incident he kept to himself for the rest of the day. He did not tell anyone nor did he seek medical treatment. That night he had nightmares and urinated in his sleep. His bunk-mates were upset about the smell in his bed and Edward was sent to the infirmary. He was given an immediate discharge from the military for the reason of having a diagnosis of "enuresis." Edward felt this action was almost worse than the rape. Within 72 hours, he lost his dream of a military career along with his pride and "manhood." He was raped, discharged, and given a humiliating and incorrect diagnosis. If he told his superiors that he was raped, he feared he would not be believed and would suffer further humiliation. He was most upset about the fact that he was unable to fight back not only at the rape but also at the military discharge. He felt he was prevented from seeking revenge and restoring his honor. His fighting hands were tied.

For the next 52 years, Edward lived a life enduring injustices coupled with thwarted attempts to fight along with inappropriate outbursts of rage.

He felt shameful to admit that when at work a man tapped him on the shoulder, Edward turned around and knocked him to the floor. Not surprisingly, he had difficulty sustaining employment because of his rage. There was one period in his life where he felt empowered. He was able to enlist in the National Guard Reserves during the Korean War. Finally, he was able to garner the respect that he so desired. He advanced quickly and achieved a level of Sergeant First Class. However, after the war, his unit was disbanded and he had to leave the service. Within 6 months of this loss, he made a serious suicide attempt.

Edward's Experiential Hologram: Disempowerment and Humiliation

Edward feels impotent and less than a man. → He seeks opportunities for respect and empowerment. → They end or fail. → He feels worthless, embarrassed, humiliated and "like a failure". → He tries to assert himself through anger and rage. → He feels depressed. → He feels impotent and less than a man.

Edward's Experiential Hologram

Core violation: Disempowerment, humiliation
Personal truth: I am worthless, an embarrassment and a failure.
Compensating strategy: Be tough, be assertive through fighting and anger
Avoidance strategy: Depression, suicide attempt, not talking about his feelings
Residual negative emotions: Impotence, feeling less than a man
Acquired motivation: Seek respect and empowerment

We identified that the goals of therapy were to help him regain his sense of power and self-respect as well as to help him maintain a healthy romantic relationship. The first set of interventions helped validate and normalize his experience.

1. He was educated about PTSD and was given an article about male sexual trauma in the military. He was shocked yet relieved to learn that this was more common than he realized.
2. He was validated for coming to therapy at this time in his life. This was reframed as "courageous" and "honorable." He was also validated for not reporting the rape while in the service as the social and political climate would not have been accepting of such a disclosure.
3. His belief was validated that he was misdiagnosed with enuresis upon discharge from the military. He petitioned for a change of diagnosis and I wrote him a letter of support. Not only was this removed from his current medical record, but he also received compensation for having PTSD as a result of his military service.

Next, we focused on his experience of the trauma. Until this therapy, he had never discussed the incident with anyone, including his past relationships. So far, his description of the event was brief, lacked details, and lacked a temporal narrative (i.e., a description of what happened in a linear sequence). He described his memory as "patchy" and "as if [he] only had pieces of a puzzle."

We agreed that he would tell me, to the best of his ability, the sequence of events as they occurred. He was nervous. I could see sweat accumulating on the underarm area of his shirt. We started with the breathing exercises that we had been practicing in sessions. In his first attempt, he told the story but it lacked significant details. He was tearful and it was clear that he was feeling overwhelmed. In his second attempt, he was able to tell the story in its entirety without being tearful or overwhelmed. Although it was challenging to do this exercise, he was able to complete the description from before the event to afterwards when he knew he was safe. He recounted the event in the first person. We agreed that this was "enough" for the day and ended with some relaxing deep breaths. During the next session, he stated he had a revelation. He remembered that he did fight during the event. He was not "just lying there" but struggled, fought, and yelled threats to the assailants. He remembered a knife was put to his throat and then he was pinned down by two of the men. He extended his neck and showed me the scar that remains. This recovered memory helped free him from one of his personal truths. He said, "Until I remembered that I did fight back, I thought I was a coward."

Next, our conversation moved toward broadening the context of the event. He stated he had a hunch about who did the attack. A week before the attack, Edward knocked-out the favorite "golden boy" in boxing. His victory angered many people as they had a significant amount of money riding on the fight. Edward thought he was "having to pay" for the fact they had to pay. Shortly after Edward's incident, the "golden boy" dropped out of boxing, but Edward never knew if it was related. We also discussed his perceptions of his 18-year-old self and how he thought life would or should have been.

We worked on reprocessing his perceptions of the incident, which included revisiting the event in a non-threatening manner from the vantage point of an observer. He stayed grounded as his current aged-self watching an incident that occurred to an 18-year-old in the Navy. He rescripted the scene by imagining yelling at the perpetrators and scaring them away. He then communicated to the boy that it was not his fault and that he was brave. This process helped him dislodge the limiting personal truth that he was "worthless and a failure." Afterward, he stated he felt less guilt and shame. He wanted to do two more rescripting sessions where he could imagine physically fighting the perpetrators and feeling empowered. He imagined that he at his current age along with the 18-year-old fought off the assailants. Afterward, he stated he felt much less shame and "very, very relaxed."

The last piece of the therapy addressed his current relationship. He and his fiancée came in for couple's therapy that helped them better understand each other and improve their empathy and communication.

Clarifying Concepts

The purpose of this chapter is to clarify concepts related to using exposure-based techniques when treating anxiety and trauma. There are many types of classical behavioral therapies that use exposure such as systematic desensitization (Wolpe, 1958), flooding (Rachman, 1966), implosive therapy (Stampfl & Levis, 1967), in vivo exposure, and graduated extinction and participant modeling (Bandura, 1969). The aforementioned therapies are designed to treat anxiety and stress disorders such as simple phobias, panic disorder, agoraphobia, and obsessive-compulsive disorders. There are also many types of therapies that use exposure-based techniques such as Eye Movement Desensitization Reprocessing (EMDR), Hypnosis and imagery-based procedures, Prolonged Exposure or Reliving (imaginal exposure and in vivo exposure), and Traumatic Incident Reduction (to name a few) which are designed to facilitate integration and decrease symptoms related to memories of trauma.

Exposure-based techniques are effective when they facilitate either the "extinction" of a conditioned stimulus or "habituation" to a noxious stimulus and ineffective if they lead to "sensitization." The concepts of extinction, habituation, and sensitization will each be discussed below. Clarifying how these concepts apply to treating trauma may help practitioners choose when it is most appropriate to use which technique within the course of treatment.

A Quick Review of Concepts

Extinction. Extinction refers to the process of reversing classical conditioning. In classical conditioning, a neutral or non-threatening stimulus such as a stuffed rabbit is paired with something that naturally produces fear such as a loud noise. Eventually, the neutral stimulus alone will produce the fear. The formerly neutral object has now become a conditioned stimulus. To extinguish the association of fear to the conditioned stimulus, a client is repeatedly exposed to the conditioned stimulus until it no longer produces fear.

Various techniques are used to achieve extinction such as systematic desensitization and flooding. In systematic desensitization, extinction is produced using a hierarchy of anxiety provoking stimuli. Clients are gradually exposed from weaker to stronger anxiety eliciting stimuli. The exposure is paired with relaxation to inhibit the response of anxiety. As clients are able to tolerate and relax at one level of the hierarchy, they can advance to the next level until even the most feared stimuli is tolerable and the associated conditioned responses are extinguished. In flooding, the exposure is focused on the most feared stimuli, in the context of a safe therapy, until the fear naturally diminishes. Both of these therapies extinguish the association of fear to an otherwise neutral or non-threatening stimulus.

Habituation. Habituation describes the phenomenon of a decreased sensitivity in response to either a repeated or prolonged exposure to an unpleasant or noxious stimulus. In other words, repeated exposure even to something that is inherently upsetting or stressful, over time, will produce a diminished response. For example, the noise of traffic outside an office window may be disturbing or loud when someone first enters the room; however, after prolonged exposure the sensitivity to the noise diminishes and it may even seems to disappear. This is because the person has habituated to the noise.

Sensitization. Sensitization is the increased response including an increased sensitivity, intensity, or reactivity to something unpleasant or noxious. For example, someone who is having difficulty falling asleep may find that with prolonged exposure to a ticking clock, the sound of the clock may seem to get louder rather than diminish. As the reader may note, sensitization is the exact opposite outcome of habituation to repeated exposure to noxious stimuli. One hypothesis is that sensitization occurs for more intense stimuli and habituation to less intense stimuli but this is not always the case. In fact, it is not clear how to predict which outcome is likely and for whom.

Exposure Therapy to Treat Associated Symptoms of Trauma

As stated earlier, exposure therapies are effective in reducing symptoms of panic disorder, agoraphobia, social anxiety, and simple phobias that are often present in clients who have experienced trauma. Exposure therapies can also be used to reduce the anxiety associated with "trigger" or cues of trauma such as certain places, objects, situations, smells, sensations, or emotions related to a trauma. A client may have fears that she would "die," "go crazy," "fall apart," "never stop crying," or generally be unable to cope if she was confronted with these cues. However, exposure in the safety of a therapeutic context facilitates the extinction of fear and the habituation to sensations. For example, a woman had an intense fear of Vaseline as it triggered memories of being raped by her father. Her phobia was treated with exposure coupled with positive self-talk. Eventually, her fear was extinguished and she was able to tolerate seeing a jar of Vaseline and saying the word, "Vaseline" without becoming overwhelmed, terrified, or injuring herself.

A Case Example: Utilizing Exposure to the Sensations of Anger

A 43-year old Asian American woman who was married and had three boys was seen for therapy to address issues of severe childhood abuse. She developed a coping strategy of being "compliant and helpful" so as not to agitate or upset anyone, *ever*. This worked to a degree, but she was exhausted trying to please everyone (she worked two jobs, did all of the housework without any help, and even cooked different meals for each child and her husband if they requested it).

One morning, her 14-year-old son demanded that she buy him expensive athletic shoes even though he already had a relatively new pair but of a different brand. We had been working on setting boundaries and she denied his request. He put his face inches from hers and threatened that "she better buy the shoes or else." She told him to get in the car and she drove him to school. Later that day, she came into session shaking from fear. I erroneously thought she was afraid that her son might hurt her. She shook her head "no" and had difficulty speaking. Finally, she managed to express that what she was most afraid of was that she was going to "get angry." Her fear was that if she got angry she would become like her abusive mother. For her, there was no such thing as healthy anger only out of control rage.

She was asked to list everything that made her angry about the situation. This was an easier place to start as she could tolerate talking about anger from the rational system rather than experiencing it in the experiential system. As she became more engaged in this exercise, her experience of anger intensified. Her avoidance strategy was no longer working and the anger feelings started breaking through. She was reassured that it was okay to feel her feelings. She struggled with not wanting to feel the sensations of angry. It was important to persist through the discomfort. She began to cry and repeat the phrase that she was "really, really angry!" She was being flooded by sensations of anger. This continued for several minutes. Eventually, she regained her composure and we discussed that she was able to feel anger without becoming "out of control" or "going crazy." With repeated exposure to feeling anger, she was able to habituate to the feared sensations and she was able to extinguish her fears associated with expressing appropriate anger.

We also distinguished between constructive and destructive anger. In other words, we reprocessed her conceptions of anger to include a broader and less rigid perspective. The initial breakthrough session was remembered as one of her most difficult yet gratifying sessions.

Exposure Used to Treat Memories of Trauma

Exposure to memories of trauma has a therapeutic intention that with repeated trials clients will integrate fragmented or partial memories, extinguish fear associated with cues, habituate to noxious stimuli, confront maladaptive cognitions and replace them with more positive cognitions. In the case of HR and Imagery Rescripting Reprocessing Therapy (IRRT), exposure is not for the purpose of integration but rather for the purpose of generating or rescripting new images. There are many therapies that use exposure to memories of trauma such as: (1) Eye Movement Desensitization Reprocessing (EMDR) (Shapiro, 1995), (2) Hypnosis and other imagery-based procedures, (3) Traumatic Incident Reduction (founded by Frank Gerbode, 1989, see Moore, 1993), and (4) Prolonged Exposure (PE) (Foa & Rothbaum, 1998). Each will be briefly discussed.

Eye Movement Desensitization Reprocessing

In this therapy, clients are asked to hold in mind a disturbing image, while experiencing the associated negative thoughts and bodily sensations. This is done while attending to bilateral stimulation either through watching a therapist's fingers moving from side to side, listening to tones alternating between each ear, or having the therapist lightly tap the backs of the hands in an alternating fashion. After about 20 back and forth movements, the therapist asks the client to let go of the memory and provide feedback about any changes to the image, thoughts, or sensations. This sequence is repeated until the anxiety diminishes as reported on a Subjective Units of Distress Scale (SUDS). Then the client is instructed to generate a positive thought and to associate it with the scene while continuing the bilateral stimulation. The client reports her level of belief in the positive thought on a Validity of Cognition (VoC) rating scale. Variations of the procedure are repeated until distress is reduced and maladaptive cognitions and behaviors have been replaced.

Chemtob et al. (2000) reviewed seven randomized, controlled studies and concluded that EMDR is an efficacious treatment for PTSD. However, two studies suggested that the bilateral stimulation may not be necessary to obtain results. There is little known about contraindications and who is more likely to respond favorably to this procedure. These authors' recommendation is that the choice to use this treatment modality is based on the skills and training of therapists as well as the desires of the clients (Chemtob et al., 2000).

Hypnosis and Other Imagery-Based Procedures

Hypnosis. Hypnosis is probably the oldest form of treatment for trauma dating back at least to the early 1900s. Hypnosis facilitates the recall of traumatic events that were encoded in a dissociative state that are otherwise not available in a conscious state. Many case reports attest to the usefulness of hypnosis to treat PTSD and trauma (Jiranek, 1993, Spiegal, 1992, 1989).

Clients are typically induced into a hypnotic trance. It begins by labeling the experience as "hypnotic." The therapist gives instructions to disregard everyday concerns and to focus only on the therapist's suggestions for relaxation, alertness, or a perceptual event such as a ticking metronome or a swinging pendulum. Once the client is relaxed, the therapist gives specific suggestions to alter sensations, behaviors, and cognitions. Clients are "hypnotized" when they have: (1) enhanced suggestibility, (2) a diminution in reflective awareness, and (3) a number of unusual experiences such as feeling detached from oneself or the environment (in Cardena et al., 2000). These authors explain that hypnotic-like phenomena may occur among highly hypnotizable clients without the intention of hypnosis. People with PTSD especially who have had multiple or repeated traumas are particularly prone to spontaneously becoming hypnotized, as earlier defined, even when the context is not explicitly for hypnosis. This population tends to easily dissociate especially in response to stress. Thus, even in "talking therapy" these clients may float in and out of a hypnotic state.

Hypnosis is useful to help clients relax, learn self-soothing, such as using imagery to go to a safe place, or to quell anxiety related to PTSD symptoms. Hypnosis may also be useful to help clients confront difficult issues such as phobias or feared memories of trauma without being overwhelmed. There are a number of hypnotic techniques to help maintain emotional distance to be able to review the event while feeling in control and safe (e.g., putting the image on a television screen, or changing the attributes of the memory by making it smaller, in the distance, quieter, or less focused). The goal of this use of hypnosis is to help clients integrate the traumatic memory including the images, thoughts, and sensations of the experience. The third use of hypnosis is to foster positive images of the self who is competent and able to modulate symptoms.

Visual/Kinesthetic Disassociation (VKD). VKD (Bandler & Grinder, 1979) is an exposure based procedure that helps clients view the event from a de-centered perspective with the purpose of integrating a traumatic memory from a safe distance.

Instead of a 2-point displacement of the observing ego watching the experiencing ego, Bandler and Grinder (1979) created a 3-point displacement where the client observes the ego watching the observing ego watching the experiencing ego. Clients are to imagine themselves (as if up in the projection booth) watching themselves (sitting in a theater) watching their traumatic experience as if it were a movie on the screen (Koziey & McLeod, 1987; Deitrich, 2000). The VKD procedure is the following: (1) clients establish a sense of safety and comfort with the therapist, (2) they form a picture of themselves prior to the trauma, and (3) they are to float outside of themselves to watch themselves, watching themselves re-live the traumatic experience. Affect can be modulated by changing attributes of the memory such as making is quieter or in black and white. After clients review the event as many times as necessary so that they no longer feel overwhelmed, they are to float back into the present day self. The present day self is encouraged to make new meanings and then provide these meanings to the younger self. The client then brings the younger self inside the body of the present day self.

The VKD procedure is designed to assist in the integration of traumatic material from a place of emotional distance. Bandler and Grinder (1979) caution against procedures that promote a "complete regression" where clients re-experience the sensations of a trauma as it can reinforce the associations between fear and the situation. If the experience is emotionally too intense, it could prevent the integration of the memory (van der Kolk, Burbridge & Suzuki, 1997) and could lead to biological sensitization (Yehuda, 1997). Therefore, revisiting memories may be counter productive if the level of arousal is too high (Cardena et al., 2000; Peebles, 1989).

Imagery Rescripting and Reprocessing Therapy. Smucker and Dancu (1999) have proposed an 18-session structured program to address adult survivors of childhood abuse. There are four phases to the program: (1) imaginal exposure, (2) mastery imagery, (3) adult-nurturing-child imagery, and (4) higher order cognitive/linguistic processing. In the first phase, clients recall the entire traumatic memory out loud. Clients are instructed to listen to a tape recording of the recall and continue with exposure sessions until there is a reduction in anxiety. In the mastery imagery phase, the client visualizes the memory and at a point of distress, the client imagines herself as an adult entering the imagery. She is asked what she would like to do in response to the perpetrator and is able to visually rescript the scene. In the adult-nurturing-child phase, clients imagine interacting with the traumatized child. The therapist asks, "What would you like to say to the child?" Imagery sessions are followed by a debriefing conversation such as asking how the experience was for the client. Clients are given homework assignments between each session and they complete rating scales throughout. In the final phase, (sessions 14–18) clients are asked to write about what victimization means to them including their beliefs, attributions, and core schemas. The therapist challenges maladaptive or negative beliefs via conversations such as confronting beliefs about blame, worthiness, and anger. The client is also asked to write about and discuss transforming suffering into a meaningful life experience using Viktor Frankl's book *Man's Search for Meaning* (1959) as a springboard for thinking about these issues.

The imagery rescripting aspect of IRRT is probably the closest procedure to the reprocessing done in HR. In both procedures, clients use imagery to have their current day self confront perpetrators and comfort the child self. The authors of IRRT do an excellent job of outlining specific questions to ask during the procedure. However, IRRT differs from HR in several ways. IRRT seems to be four distinct therapies practiced in a sequential order and they do not appear to be well integrated. In contrast, HR is designed to be holistic and integrative. For example, in IRRT, the imagery work is completed and not integrated with the reprocessing of core schemes, attributions, beliefs, and negative cognitions. These are confronted in sessions *after* the imagery work using rational discussions. In contrast in HR, schemas, attributions, and beliefs, are identified as an experiential holographic pattern *before* the imagery work, and are addressed during the imagery. IRRT follows a manualized protocol, which may or may not suit the needs of clients. Also, IRRT begins with imaginal exposure, which may lead to pre-mature termination for some clients. In HR, discussion of trauma occurs after client's coping skills are bolstered and a positive therapeutic alliance has been well established. Finally, IRRT is specifically a treatment for childhood trauma, although it probably could be applied to traumas incurred in adulthood as well. HR does not have this limitation and frames revisiting the younger version of the self as any time in the past.

Empirical Evidence for Hypnosis and Other Imagery-Based Procedures

There have been many published case reports using hypnosis (Spiegal, 1992, 1989; Peebles, 1989, See Cardena et al., 2000 for a review of over 20 reports and studies), VKD (Koziey & McLeod, 1987), and IRRT (Smucker & Dancu, 1999; Smucker & Niederee, 1995, Smucker et al., 1995). One randomized controlled study found benefits of desensitization, hypnotherapy, and psychodynamic therapy (in that order) compared to a wait-list control group to treat PTSD (Brom et al., 1989). There have been three published reports on VKD, two case studies and one uncontrolled study with a small number of participants. Also, Smucker and Dancu (1995) reported positive results of a pilot study using IRRT. Although there are a large number of published findings showing convergent clinical evidence, there is a lack of well-controlled studies. Lack of studies, does not diminish the value or effectiveness of these techniques; however, the relative effectiveness compared to a control group or to other exposure-based techniques remains unknown.

Hypnosis and HR

Hypnosis is similar and distinct from the reprocessing techniques used in HR. They are similar in that they both use procedures to induce relaxation and they both use techniques to distance clients from re-experiencing sensations of trauma to allow for processing from a safe therapeutic distance. However, they differ in that HR is not a context for hypnosis, the therapist does not say "You are going to be hypnotized" nor does the therapist encourage unusual perceptual experiences such as having one arm inexplicably raise up, or having clients feel that they can't move their feet or open their eyes which are commonly used in hypnotic inductions. HR is not a method to uncover, retrieve, or integrate dissociated traumatic memories. HR may use suggestions "to relax," but the therapist does not suggest changes in sensations, perceptions, or behaviors, (i.e., "you will now feel lighter"). The client is encouraged to remain anchored in the here-and-now, as their current-aged self. They are specifically *not* supposed to "float out of their body" as they are in VKD. Clients are expected to be able to interact with the therapist during the procedure as well as with the characters in the scene as themselves in the present time.

HR is not intended to be hypnosis although many clients are most likely "hypnotized" as defined as being in a relaxed and highly receptive state. Those with PTSD tend to be easily hypnotized. This can be advantageous as clients may be very receptive to their images of reprocessing but therapists also need to be aware of the potential disadvantages. Therapists are cautioned not to lead patients or give misinformation. Whether or not one believes their clients are hypnotized when using HR, the same precautions should be employed as if it were hypnosis for everyone.

Contraindications for Using Hypnosis and Other Imagery Based Procedures

Imagery-based procedures including AVK, IRRT, and HR should follow the same precautions as if they were inducing hypnosis. One concern is that under hypnosis, therapists can influence the client's thoughts. Although clients will not accept any suggestion that goes against their desires, therapists still need to be cautious about what is said during a procedure. A therapist should be a non-directive facilitator. In particular, if a client is describing a memory, therapists should not make any suggestions about what they might see or experience, and the therapist should not stating anything that is not true. Clients must be able to generate and report their own memories. A related concern is that under hypnosis, clients (with or without suggestions from a therapist) might create "false memories." Clients should be cautioned that memories retrieved by this method cannot be trusted. If involved in a legal proceeding where testimony could be an issue, clients should not use any form of hypnosis as their testimony may be called into question. A third concern is choosing appropriate clients for these procedures. Those with problems with reality testing (e.g., some client's with Borderline Personality Disorder), a history of psychosis, active substance abuse, or are highly dissociative (e.g., those with a Dissociative Identity Disorder) should *not* use these procedures.

Traumatic Incident Reduction (TIR)

In TIR therapy, a client is simply told to describe their traumatic incident. Usually the client begins by describing the situation in a way that produces low levels of arousal (i.e., vague and with few specific details). The initial description may be a brief presentation of just the facts. With repetition, she begins to bring in more detail and emotion. There may be a phase where the client feels intense emotions. However, with further repetition, the associated intense emotions are diminished and she is able to describe the incident, including her feelings, in a calm, coherent, and controlled manner.

The TIR procedure is consistent with the principles of graded stress inoculation whereby people have a natural healing process of the mind where exposure to weaker levels of stress enables them to gain mastery over stronger levels (Epstein, 1983). This is achieved by pacing the exposure to the increasing levels of intensity. Stressful incidents are mastered in small doses through repetition and graded exposure. TIR assumes that clients have an innate ability to pace themselves and integrate material according to their own timing. Because the client remains in control of the intensity of exposure, the risk of sensitization is reduced.

No randomized controlled studies have been conducted using this procedure (at least none to this author's awareness) and therefore, its effectiveness cannot be compare with other therapies.

Prolonged Exposure (PE)

Prolonged Exposure, as outlined by Foa and Rothbaum (1998), is practiced in a 12-session structured program that includes breathing retraining, in vivo exposure, and imaginal exposure. For the in vivo part of the therapy, clients are instructed to make a hierarchy of avoided situations and to confront these situations (either with or without a coach) until the associated anxiety diminishes. In imaginal exposure, clients are instructed to recount their trauma out loud, experience the event in the present and make the image as realistic as possible including their thoughts and feelings as well as what is happening. The technique starts just before the event and continues to the point after the event when the client is safe. If a client feels uncomfortable, she is encouraged to breathe and keep going. The intention is to get through the entire event. The exposure is repeated on multiple occasions until the recollection no longer produces anxiety. Clients are instructed to listen to the tape recording of their recall in between sessions. PE may lead to high states of arousal and discomfort but with repeated exposure the anxiety dissipates.

PE is widely acknowledged as an effective treatment for PTSD due to a rich base of supporting empirical evidence from well-designed studies (Foa & Rothbaum, 1998; Foa, Rothbaum, & Furr, 2003). Rothbaum et al. (2000) reviewed 12 randomized, controlled studies all of which showed positive results for treating PTSD. These studies compared PE to relaxation, a waitlist control group or to a cognitive treatment (CT or Stress Inoculation Therapy) with no exposure component.

Other positive results found that PE seems to contribute to the reduction of PTSD symptoms by repairing, organizing, and elaborating a client's trauma narrative. Foa and Riggs (1993) found that those who had poorly articulated narratives (more disorganized and more fragmented) of their rape two weeks after the assault were more likely to develop PTSD. In a follow up study, those who benefited from the procedure of PE (i.e., had reduced symptoms following the procedure) also had improved their trauma narratives, which became more coherent, longer, and better organized (Foa, Molnar, & Cashman, 1995).

However, not all studies on PE have been positive. For example, a randomized, multi-site, controlled study administered to 350 veterans of the Vietnam War found that PE was associated with a significantly higher drop out rate than a control group (Schnurr et al., 2003). Although no differences were found between the aggregate group's scores on outcome measures, it was noted that approximately one third of the treatment group benefited while approximately one third reported worsening symptoms. Ironson, Freud, Strauss, and Williams (2002) compared a randomly assigned sample to PE and EMDR to treat a mixed group of rape and crime victims. Although both groups reported a significant decreased in PTSD symptoms, those in the PE group had a significantly higher drop out rate and higher ratings of distress than those in the EMDR group.

Furthermore, PE seems to be under utilized in clinical settings (Becker & Zayfet, 2001; Feeny et al., 2003; Rothbaum & Schwartz, 2002). Although there may be a host of reasons why (e.g., lack of training of therapists or lack of readiness on the part of clients) some authors have cited evidence that clinicians are hesitant to use this treatment due to concerns that the heightened stress associated with this therapy has lead to symptom exacerbation, poor compliance, and premature termination of therapy for some patients (Tarrier et al., 1999; Scott & Stradling, 1997; Tarrier & Humphreys, 2000). Several authors acknowledge that PE is not broadly utilized, but argue that the concerns about its use are unfounded (Foa, et al., 2002; Feeny et al., 2003; Rothbaum & Schwartz, 2002).

Neurobiological research adds to the uncertainty. Yahuda (1997) reviewed several studies demonstrating a consistent finding that in contrast to a typical stress response, people with chronic PTSD have low cortisol levels and a sensitized negative feedback system. This is associated with a decreased ability to inhibit responses to stress (e.g., the startle response fails to habituate with repeated exposure). These people are not likely to habituate with exposure, thus, if they were treated with PE, they would run the risk of sensitization and reinforcing negative associations and cognitions.

In conclusion, PE has the strongest empirical support for being an effective treatment for PTSD compared to relaxation, waitlist control groups, and to other cognitive-behavioral therapies (Rothbaum et al., 2000). No studies have compared PE to a non-arousing exposure technique such as VKD. The aggregate results show that it is beneficial for some, but not for all clients, and can potentially lead to pre-mature termination, increased symptoms, and sensitization for others.

Making Sense of Contradictory Findings

How can contradictory findings about PE make sense? Some people benefit, some do not. Some seem to habituate to repeated exposure, while others may become sensitized. Some people with PTSD have fragmented and disorganized trauma narratives, while others may have completely intact narratives. The answer to this conundrum may lie in the fact that people have a wide range of responses to trauma. Friedman (1997) poses the question that there may be different subtypes or stages of PTSD that require different treatments at different times. This is supported by distinct neurobiological presentations as well as an acknowledgment that PTSD may be a dynamic process that changes over time. McFarlane and Yahuda (2000) caution against a simplistic view of PTSD as a singular response to trauma as this may lead to an underestimation of the complexity and disabling quality of the disorder. Also, only relatively few people develop the full-blown condition of PTSD and for those that do, there is a range from mild to severe.

Finally, those who do not meet criteria for any clinical diagnosis may still suffer from trauma with symptoms such as low self-esteem, difficulties in relationships, guilt, shame, and feeling unsafe or powerless. More research is needed to identify the nature and range of stress responses to trauma (McFarlane & Yahuda, 2000) and to identify who is most likely to benefit from which of a variety of procedures.

Risks of Various Procedures to Treat Trauma

Exposure in the form of in vivo exposure, imaginal exposure, and TIR runs the risk of sensitization for some (but not all) clients, while hypnosis and

VKD seems to minimize this risk but then runs the risk of creating false memories. EMDR appears to be a sort of hybrid procedure, combining the fear-activating portion of the former therapies and the calming portion of the imagery-based procedures. It is not clear what the risks are for this procedure. IRRT is also a therapy that combines techniques including imaginal exposure, which may increase the risk of sensitization but then this is minimized during the rescripting procedure.

HR Minimizes the Risk of Sensitization

In HR, the purpose of revisiting a scene of trauma is to facilitate perceptual shifts. HR is not concerned with activating a fear structure as it is in PE (Foa & Kozak, 1986). HR is also not concerned with issues of extinction and habituation, since it is not a treatment targeted to reduce anxiety. HR, minimizes the risk of sensitization and retraumatization through strategies that enhance emotional distance while keeping the client feeling safe, and anchored to the here-and-now: (1) The client remains her current-aged self and remains connected to her feelings in the present moment, (2) the approach is gradual, (3) relaxation is utilized before and during the procedure, (4) levels of distress are monitored, and (5) the client observes the scene rather than reexperiences it. If a client feels distressed, then the progression stops until she feels comfortable to proceed. In HR, revisiting an event is always done in conjunction with reprocessing and is always conducted within the context of a broader psychotherapy.

HR Minimizes the Risk of Creating False Memories

There are two reasons why HR poses a low risk of creating false memories. First, clients do not recall trauma for the purpose of remembering details or integrating fragmented narratives. However, clients may revisit a scene of trauma for the purpose of gaining insight and reprocessing their perceptions. The perceptions that they create are the ones that they have now as their current-aged self (e.g., "What do you think about it now as you look at the scene?") This is distinct from altering the perceptions and recall of what happened. Second, the imagery rescripting used in HR is a fantasy-based procedure. Since clients remain their current aged self while they interact with the characters in the scene, it would be very unlikely to confuse this with "reality."

The Vantage Point Advantage

One of the essential differences between EMDR, TIR, and PE versus the imagery-based procedures of hypnosis, VKD, IRRT, and HR is the perspective or vantage point used when revisiting the traumatic event. In the former therapies, clients revisit as if they were actually reliving the scene as vividly as possible. This is called a field vantage point. In the later therapies, clients observe the scene as a detached spectator. This is called the observer vantage point. How these vantage points impact memory was the topic of two studies by McIsaas and Eich (2002, 2004). In the first study, undergraduate students were randomly assigned to either the observer or field vantage point conditions for the recall of their experience of completing mundane tasks. In the second study, clients with the diagnosis of PTSD recalled a traumatic event from either of the two vantage points. Both studies found that those responding from a field vantage point made more statements describing their feelings, physical sensations, and thoughts, while those from the observer vantage point made more statements describing spatial relations, and self-observations.

The field vantage point produced a stronger emotional involvement while the observer vantage point produced more objective reactions and less emotional involvement. For EMDR, TIR, and PE the field vantage point would enhance the goal of activating a fear structure. Whereas for Hypnosis, VKD, IRRT, and HR, the observer vantage point enhances the goals of describing spatial relationships between characters and objects in the scene, and observing the younger version of the self in an objective manner, while maintaining therapeutic distance from the traumatic material to protect against the reexperiencing of trauma sensations.

Holographic Reprocessing and Cognitive Therapy

HR and cognitive models such as Cognitive Processing Therapy (Resick & Schnicke, 1992) or a Cognitive Model of PTSD (Elhers & Clark, 2000) share similar therapeutic goals for clients to shift perceptions about themselves, others, and assumptions they have about the world. These therapies both include building coping skills to help clients tolerate and manage affect as well as to promote positive behaviors. They both utilize an exposure aspect to the therapy with the primary goal to gather information about what remains "stuck," maladaptive, or promotes a limiting perception. Both therapies use specific techniques to help clients shift these stuck or limiting perceptions.

The cognitive model is mostly concerned with facilitating the integration of a memory and then confronting the negative appraisals that are associated with persistent PTSD. For HR, the intention is to help clients view the incident from a broader less personalized perspective enabling clients to shift their perceptions about the event in a holistic manner. The cognitive model and HR differ in two distinct ways: how clients are exposed to trauma, including the vantage point and level of arousal, and how they approach shifting unresolved issues.

A Cognitive Model

The cognitive model utilizes exposure similar to imaginal exposure used in PE either through verbal recollections or through writing. As discussed earlier, this form of exposure requires clients to describe the event from the field vantage point. The level of arousal is high, since the client is "reliving" the event. The points where there is the highest level of arousal usually indicates a "hot spot." Eventually, the PE focuses exclusively on hot spots or other problematic parts of the experience to garner information for cognitive restructuring. The content of these spots are then examined for negative appraisals. The therapist may use techniques such as reframing, cognitive restructuring, behavioral testing, and thought records (Greenberg & Pedesky, 1994) to engage the rational mind to confront the appraisal. Clients may be asked to gage the likelihood of such an appraisal by gathering evidence for and against it. Ultimately, the therapist will guide the client to discredit the negative appraisal and to adopt more likely and more positive appraisals. Common language used to discredit a negative appraisal is to label it as "faulty," "irrational," or "maladaptive."

A Cognitive Model and Holographic Reprocessing

Five distinctions between a cognitive model and HR are:

1. As discussed, a cognitive model uses imaginal exposure while HR uses a non-arousing revisiting of the event from the objective vantage point.
2. In a cognitive model, the event is viewed in its entirety and stuck points are identified and dislodged. In contrast, HR does not review the entire event, but rather confronts the parts that are relevant to the client. Some may view the scene after the abuse, and others go in to stop the abuse.
3. The cognitive model engages the rational system to confront negative appraisals where as HR engages both the rational and experiential systems. For example, a discussion about multiple truths engages the rational system where as imaginal rescripting engages the experiential system.
4. In the cognitive model, limiting perceptions are discredited as maladaptive, while in HR they are understood as making sense given the context. (However, both techniques ultimately focus on shifting these perceptions.)
5. A cognitive model focuses on one particular event. In contrast, HR takes a holistic approach where the goal is to reprocess a whole pattern of emotional and behavioral tendencies.

Comparison of a Cognitive Model and Holographic Reprocessing

Cognitive Model	Holographic Reprocessing
View scene as if reliving it	View scene as if observing it
Revisit whole event	Revisit only relevant part of the event
Endure anxiety	Stay relaxed
Identifies "hot spots"	Identifies client's needs to feel complete
Uses cognitive techniques such as restructuring, reframing	Uses cognitive techniques such as reframing, finding multiple truths
—	Uses experiential techniques such as imaginal rescripting
Focus on a particular event	Focus on shifting a broader pattern

A Word of Caution

Even with the techniques used in HR, any type of exposure to memories or images of trauma runs a risk of retraumatization or sensitization. Exposure is not appropriate for everyone. Some clients are not good candidates such as those with psychosis, active substance abuse or other addictive behaviors, suicidal ideation, self-injurious behaviors, or are highly dissociative. Some clients may be good candidates but they are not ready to engage in exposure. For some it may be too early in the therapy (e.g., a solid therapeutic alliance has not been established, or the client has not learned emotional coping skills), or they are dealing with too many other current stressors (e.g., medical, financial, relationship problems). Some clients with complex PTSD or Borderline personality may or may not be good candidates for exposure-based therapies depending on where they are in the course of their treatment. Basically, if a client is unstable or unable to tolerate or manage affect, then likely she is not a good candidate for something that could potentially be distressing.

Chapter Summary

In summary, this chapter discussed several exposure-based therapies to treat trauma, including classical exposure techniques, EMDR, Image-based therapies including Hypnosis, Visual/Kinesthetic Disassociation, and Imagery Rescripting and Reprocessing therapy, Traumatic Incident Reduction, Prolonged Exposure, Cognitive Therapy, and Holographic Reprocessing. There is strong empirical research supporting prolonged exposure. However, procedures that activate the fear structure may also run a risk of sensitization for some clients. In contrast, the imagery-based procedures seem to minimize the risk of sensitization by using low arousal techniques including the observer vantage point when recalling a traumatic event. Cognitive Therapy and Holographic Reprocessing were also discussed. They are both designed to shift maladaptive or limiting perceptions—the former uses the rational system to confront negative appraisals and the later uses the experiential system via imaginal rescripting to shift perceptions holistically.

CHAPTER **6**

The Therapeutic Alliance

This chapter addresses the therapeutic alliance as it is practiced in HR therapy. Although a therapeutic alliance is common to most if not all therapies, it is of particular importance when working with clients who have had trauma. Because there are potential difficulties and dangers when conducting therapy with this population, the therapeutic alliance is discussed in this text. This chapter is by no means comprehensive, but it does acknowledge and address some of the common issues. It is divided into three sections: (1) building and monitoring rapport, (2) the impact of breaking rules, policies and agreements, and (3) dealing with other challenges to the relationship such as resistance, transference and counter-transference, and vicarious traumatization.

Case Example

The following is a brief example illustrating the initial process of building rapport.

Mary was referred to treatment from her primary physician for the presenting problem of anxiety. She was on time to our first session and instead of having a seat in one of the chairs, she stood waiting in front of my door. She was a 23-year-old Caucasian woman. She entered my office and sat perched on the edge of the couch. She bounced her knees and fidgeted with her hands. She said she wanted help concentrating in school. She was enrolled in a physical therapy program and stated she could not retain "anything" that she read. She figured I could give her a few study techniques and our work would be complete in a couple of sessions. I validated that it would be difficult to do well in school if her anxiety was interfering with her ability to retain the material.

Showing concern for the extent to which the anxiety was impairing her life, I asked how else the anxiety was affecting her. She stated she had difficulty sleeping, did not feel safe in crowds, and did not trust people. Again, I acknowledge how these can affect her in general and specifically when she is going to school. From these few responses, I suspected she might have had a trauma history but I felt it was too soon to ask her about it. She was still perched on her seat and I knew she was not sure if she could trust me. My main goal at this point, was to help her feel safe and build rapport. I stopped asking questions and gave her time to "come to me." She looked around the room and her eyes rested on the metal cut-out of a Japanese letter I had on the wall. She asked, "What is that?" I told her it was a gift from my students and it meant "love." She nodded her head and said, "Cool." Then she asked about the three round rocks I had on the small table to the side of us. I told her sometimes people like to hold them when they are upset or scared. I picked up one of the rocks and showed her. The rock is solid yet smooth and soft. It feels good to hold. I offered her the rock but she refused it. As I put it down, I casually said, "They help people feel grounded and safe." Again, she said, "Cool" but this time she sat further back on the couch.

I asked her if she wanted to learn something "really cool." She was hesitant but interested. I said, "Do you see that black dot on the wall in front of you?" The dot was about the size of a half dollar and it was made from where an old doorstopper used to be. I instructed her to stare at the dot and then asked if she could see my hand waving while she continued staring at the dot. She said she could. Then I asked her to see 360 degrees around the dot while keeping her focus on the dot. Finally, she was asked if she could maintain her vision of the whole room while slowing moving her eyes to various places in the room. The exercise helped her to become aware of her peripheral vision which is naturally relaxing. I explained that this was a heightened state of awareness, and that if she listened to her lectures in this state she will retain more information. She said that she liked the exercise and proceeded to take off her shoes and sit cross-legged on the couch. The exercise served to distract her from her fearful thoughts, relax her, and it helped us build rapport. At this point, I discussed the specifics of our therapy including office policies, limits of confidentiality including state reporting laws, and assessed for issues of her safety.

In the above example, initial rapport was achieved in several ways. First, her complaint was validated. Second, she was given the space and time to become comfortable. Third, her language was mirrored, such as using the word "cool." The session evoked a positive experience. She felt comfortable, relaxed, and safe. By the end of the first session, I did not have a lot of data about her life, and she knew little about the therapeutic journey on which she was about to embark, but she said, "I have a good feeling about this. I can tell you are really going to help me."

The Therapeutic Alliance

As in most therapies, HR begins with establishing a secure and trusting relationship between client and therapist. Especially when dealing with issues of trauma, a trusting therapeutic relationship is crucial, yet not always easy to achieve. It is also not as simple as securing an initial bond, but rather it is a continuous factor to monitor and nurture throughout the therapy. Trauma work can be difficult and emotionally challenging to both clients and therapists. The reader is referred to other texts such as *Countertransference and the Treatment of Trauma* (Dalenberg, 2000) and *Trauma and the Therapist: Countertransference and Vicarious Traumatization in Psychotherapy with Incest Survivors* (Peralman & Saakvitne, 1995) for a more in depth discussion on countertransference, vicarious traumatization, and the therapeutic alliance. This chapter discusses a few common issues related to the therapeutic alliance and is not intended to be comprehensive. Issues specific to the practice of HR will be highlighted. For example, the text might read, "the HR therapist would do the following." This chapter addresses: (1) building and monitoring rapport, (2) the impact of breaking rules, policies, and agreements, and (3) other challenges to the relationship such as resistance, transference and counter-transference, and vicarious traumatization.

Building and Monitoring Rapport

Rapport encompasses safety, trust, and a general feeling of comfort between client and therapist. It is usually established through empathic listening, conveying genuine concern, and developing a sense of which metaphors, language, and socio-cultural experiences are relevant or significant to the client, while upholding boundaries, policies, and agreements. Nonetheless, developing and maintaining rapport can be very difficult for clients who might have been violated, betrayed, or emotionally wounded. This section on rapport discusses: (1) establishing "a good feeling," (2) issues of touch, (3) educating and normalizing, and (4) how to monitor rapport.

Establishing a Good Feeling

An important goal of a first session is to engender a feeling of safety, trust, and hope. The first few sessions are best used to observe and get to know clients, as they will inevitably reveal more when they feel safe and trust the therapist. Although some therapists may prefer to begin therapy by taking a detailed history, clients' responses should be interpreted with caution as the answers may or may not be reliable. Clients may be poor historians, may wish to create a positive impression upon the therapist, or simply do not yet trust the therapist. It is important for therapists to be sensitive to the fact that many clients have fears about engaging in therapy. Some common fears are:

- Fear of feeling emotions
- Fear of discovering something about themselves or their past
- Fear of being blamed for something that has happened
- Fear of being expected to change and then failing
- Fear they will be told to forgive someone that hurt them
- Fear of getting close to the therapist and then being abandoned or rejected
- Fear of not being believed, understood, or taken seriously
- Fear of being embarrassed, humiliated, violated, or retraumatized
- Fear they are crazy and being in therapy confirms it

Given these fears, clients' engagement in therapy is no minor task. There are many ways to reduce these fears such as addressing them as they surface during the course of the treatment, acknowledging them, offering reassurance, and normalizing clients' experience. A key factor in whether clients are willing to work through these fears is the quality of the therapeutic relationship. However, working with clients with trauma histories may be particularly challenging. Two such challenges are the therapist's level of emotional involvement and the therapist's authenticity.

Emotional Involvement

Therapists risk being either overly involved or not involved enough (i.e., showing empathy, concern, caring, and feeling emotions) with the client. Trauma clients seem to be acutely aware of this factor as they may be hypervigilantly monitoring if the therapist really cares or not. Beginning therapists (and seasoned ones as well) can get seduced into proving how much they care. They may inadvertently collude with avoidance of difficult material for fear that asking probing questions might upset or alienate the client.

Overinvolvement runs the risk of feeling trapped by client's dependency. Instead of internalizing and generalizing positive feelings from the therapist, the client becomes increasingly more focused on getting caring from the therapist. This is understandable, if the client has never had a consistent, caring, stable figure in her life, then the care from the therapist is highly enticing. Attempts of the therapist to pull back or modulate a clingy attachment may actually escalate destructive behaviors in the client. The client may consciously or unconsciously create crises or engage in risky behaviors or self-injury so that the therapist can prove she still cares. The therapist may feel trapped: If the therapist pulls away from the client, the client may escalate destructive behaviors, and if the therapist reassures and shows more caring, it may reinforce dependency.

If therapists are not involved enough, then they risk that the client will withhold information, remain on a superficial level, and prematurely terminate the therapy. If clients sense a decline in caring, it could induce rage and acts of self-destruction. For example, therapists may begin therapy being emotionally involved but then have difficulty maintaining involvement during clients' disclosure of disturbing material. They may consciously or unconsciously avoid or minimize the material. They may not believe it actually occurred, or they may appear distant or lacking compassion especially if they are repressing or minimizing their own feelings. If therapists are not involved enough, do not appear involved enough (whether or not they feel they are), or clients fear that their therapist is not involved enough, then there is a risk of clients feeling hurt, abandoned, and at the very least, less likely to disclose more material.

What is the solution if caught in a struggle regarding involvement? A complete answer to these issues is beyond the scope of this chapter. However, here is a brief answer. If a therapist is caught in a trap, or is feeling frustrated, afraid, ashamed, or wanting to avoid a client, then these are indicators that supervision or consultation may be warranted. Clients may benefit from the message that "I care about you *and* destructive behaviors are not acceptable." One technique is to offer a no-harm contract in writing and have the client and therapist sign the contract. If possible, it should also contain consequences if the contract is broken. This is comforting and containing for clients (and therapists). Insight for the client may be beneficial, if the client is capable and emotionally able to tolerate a discussion about her behavior. The therapist has to be careful that the client does not feel blamed, accused, or punished by the therapist. Insight for the therapist seems obviously beneficial, however, therapists may be in denial of their own emotional responses and may minimize the impact of their behaviors in therapy. To this end, self-reflection and consultation are helpful.

Authenticity

When clients idealize a therapist (e.g., "You're the most helpful, insightful, and wise therapist I have ever had"), it can be very appealing and can give the therapist a false sense of security in the therapeutic alliance. This positive transference can quickly shift to a negative one. Trauma clients can be hypervigilant or at least sensitive to interactions that are reminiscent of prior abuse. They may desire and yet defend against intimacy with the therapist, since intimacy has been associated with danger. How a therapist responds to distancing, criticism, challenges, rage attacks, acknowledging mistakes, attempts to push for more caring, attempts to bend rules, and accusations that the therapist is like a client's perpetrator are some of the challenges of authenticity.

Is the therapist willing to admit to being confused, frustrated, anxious, uncomfortable, or irritated? Is the therapist willing to admit to making mistakes, being emotionally over or under-involved, or distracted? And can the therapist do this without being defensive, negating the client's experience, or making the therapy about them? This is especially difficult when the therapist is being accused of not caring or understanding despite the therapist's efforts, or when a client overreacts to a true but minor slight from the therapist. Remaining nondefensive may be appropriate in some instances but it is not always possible nor is it always the best response. Confrontation between therapists and clients is a technique discussed by many authors (Perry, Herman, van der Kolk, & Hoke, 1990; Murry, 1993; Dalenberg, 2000). However, this is a skillful endeavor. The therapist may wish to defend or explain her good intentions and true innocence and in the process risks shaming or blaming the client.

These tensions points are to be expected during a course of therapy as clients' expectations and unconscious behaviors typically set up conditions to recapitulate their experiential holograms. Some reassurance may be offered in that (1) being able to "predict" client's sensitivities given an understanding of their hologram may give therapists some sense of control, and (2) a difficulty in the therapeutic relationship may be a useful and even a break-through opportunity to discuss issues related to the client's experiential hologram. However, these reassurances do not prevent these occurrences nor do they protect the therapist from experiencing disturbing feelings. Again, supervision or consultation may be helpful when therapists feel caught in the above-mentioned situations.

Issues Regarding Touch

Another important issue for therapists to address prior to working with trauma survivors is their stance regarding the issue of touch. Even a well-intentioned touch of reassurance can be misinterpreted or feel intrusive to some clients. For example, a male intern routinely shook hands with his clients at the beginning and end of his therapy sessions. For him, it was a gesture of respect. However, one of his female clients contacted me as his supervisor and stated she wanted to change therapists. She felt obligated to shake hands with her therapist and this made her feel trapped and violated. She felt embarrassed and guilty for not wanting to shake his hand and she did not want to offend him. Therefore, she started avoiding her sessions. However, she knew she still needed therapy, so she called me. This example shows that one cannot assume how a client will interpret any type of touch (both therapist and client initiated). For clients who feel comforted by touch, another option is for clients to hug themselves, a blanket, pillow, or stuffed animal. Although it may sound juvenile, some clients feel very comforted by this especially after deep emotional work.

Educating and Normalizing: Making Someone "Right"

A common therapeutic task is to validate, normalize, and educate clients about their experience. Clients may not be aware that their seemingly irrational behaviors are actually symptoms consistent with the criteria for a diagnosis. Clients may not realize that their symptoms may be connected to a trauma they experienced years ago. Some, but not all clients, prefer to read articles or descriptions about their symptoms and diagnoses as this gives them a concrete label and explanation for something that has otherwise been inexplicable.

When appropriate the HR therapist can reassure clients that they do indeed "make sense." A therapist might comment, "Of course you feel this way, it makes perfect sense to me . . ." and explain why. HR assumes that there is probably a good reason, or at least an experiential hologram that explains why a person presents in a particular manner. For example, a woman lamented that she got fired from 23 jobs. An HR therapist might say, "Well, given what we know about your history, it makes sense that you got fired from 23 jobs." The client has a history of getting into arguments with authority figures. Instead of letting minor issues go, she tended to escalate discussions into arguments and ultimately got herself fired. As a child, if she showed any signs of weakness she was teased and humiliated. By being on the offensive, she learned to protect herself. "Making her right" explains a negative behavior as a meaningful coping strategy from the vantage point of herself as a child. This facilitates compassion for the behavior rather than a negative judgment.

Monitoring Rapport

When a therapist and client have good rapport, they feel comfortable with each other and experience an easy flow of communication. This may sound vague and most noticeable when there is a lack of rapport. However, there are a few subtle cues to note. When therapist and client are in session particularly during an emotionally connected exchange, they will likely exhibit similar body posture, pace of breathing, and verbal tone. As one shifts position, the other will also likely do the same. If a therapist feels there is a need to deepen rapport with a client, one strategy is to match these nonspecific aspects of communication. Another way to deepen rapport is to move the conversation from the intellectual level to the experiential level.

Clients will communicate either verbally or more likely through non-verbal behaviors (e.g., withholding, attacking, missing or changing appointments) when there is a decrease in rapport. It is incumbent upon therapists to pay attention to the fluctuations of rapport and to honestly reflect on their own contributions to the relationship.

The Impact of Breaking Rules, Policies, and Agreements

In the first session, as in many therapies, the therapist reviews office policies (e.g., length of session, cancellation policy, issues of payment, phone calls, etc.), limits of confidentiality, informed consent, and whatever rules are pertinent to the client (i.e., some may have a no-harm rule). It is mentioned in this text because it is not uncommon for therapists to believe that an office policy is merely an issue of business and mistakenly believe it is separate from the therapy. All rules equate to containment and safety. Upholding these rules upholds boundaries. Although breaking a rule or agreement is sometimes inevitable, such as needing to reschedule an appointment, a therapist's vacation, or changing the therapist's office, it must be assumed that these changes come with consequences. Clients may feel anxious or insecure, uncared for or even abandoned, or may lose trust in the therapist or the therapy. If not addressed, these issues can result in a damaged therapeutic alliance.

Breaking an Office Policy

One client confessed that after three years of working with a therapist, she decided to quit shortly after her therapist raised her rates. The client could well afford the new rates and even stated that it was reasonable to have the increase, but felt that after the change, the therapist was less interested in her. The client expressed that she was hurt and angry with the therapist. The therapist was defensive and addressed the reasons why she needed to raise her rates. She did not realize that what the client needed was for the therapist to address her fear of not being cared for. The exchange left the client wondering if the therapist really cared for her or just cared for the money. Unfortunately, the therapist did not grasp how significant it was that she broke one of their rules.

As an HR therapist, the issues surrounding rules are opportunities, just like any numerous displays and experiences in the therapy, to observe (and resolve) experiential holograms. Whatever unresolved issue a client may have (i.e., abandonment, betrayal, violation of trust, etc.) is likely to be how he will feel when a rule is broken. This can be acknowledged and tied back to the client's experiential hologram.

Breaking Confidentiality for Legal Issues and Emergencies

As in most psychotherapy, safety always comes first. Therapists assess for issues concerning safety and continue to monitor potential risks throughout therapy (e.g., for risks of SI/HI, self-injury, substance use, psychosis, high risk behaviors, and abusive relationships).

Opening doors to treat trauma, means potentially opening doors to treat a number of life-threatening crises. Therapists need to be prepared not only for the safety of their clients but for the safety of themselves and their staff as well. I have had clients do the following *in my office:* gulp a bottle of pills in an attempted suicide; walk in with bleeding self-inflicted cuts; come to therapy strung out on heroine, cocaine, pills, or drunk; have a seizure; have a stroke; wave a knife; and bring a bag of illicit drugs. One client threw objects across the room, another client threatened to kill me because she loved me so much, and many others have threatened to kill themselves. Sometimes these threats are verbalized in session and other times they are expressed over the telephone or left on an answering machine. These things happen and therapists wanting to treat people with trauma histories should be prepared. It is important for the therapist to stay calm and remain confident. Most incidents are dramatic cries for help. Clients in extreme emotional states may want to express how much pain they are in, therefore, it is helpful to acknowledge their pain. In general, it behooves all therapists to think about several ways they might handle emergencies since dangerous events can happen very quickly.

A therapist may have to break a rule to ensure safety. Clients may feel violated such as when the therapist has to call the police, make a report of abuse, or initiate psychiatric hospitalization. Although necessary, these actions will have consequences to the therapeutic alliance. In most cases, the process of repairing the alliance deepens the work. In other cases, the alliance has been too damaged and clients may be best served with a referral to another therapist.

Undermining Communication

Another potential damage to the therapeutic alliance is a client's inappropriate involvement with other office staff, professionals, or other clients. If a client does not like a boundary or limit set by the therapist, she may go to multiple people until she gets a response that she desires (usually by omitting or elaborating certain features to sound more convincing). Clients may pit one person against the other, ask for help from multiple people, and make unfounded complaints. It is ideal for any staff to have a united front, which includes checking out allegations before assuming they are true, redirecting the client back to the therapist, and holding everyone including clients and staff, to standards of accountability for communications and behaviors. Nonetheless, an act of defiance could potentially break an agreement of mutual trust in the relationship. Although the therapist must maintain confidentiality, the therapist may develop negative feelings towards the client such as frustration, irritation, and resentment. If these feelings are not resolved (with or without the client) they could potentially negatively influence the therapy.

Other Relationship Challenges

Dealing with Resistance

Resistance is a client's unwillingness (either consciously or unconsciously) to confront, comply, discuss, or progress in therapy. The therapeutic relationship is important when dealing with resistances. If a client feels safe and trusts the therapist, the client will be more likely to remain in therapy and work through resistance. When resistances emerge during therapy, they are acknowledged, sometimes with humor, sometimes through exploration, and sometimes as a sign that clients are close to significant emotional content. If the resistance takes the form of self-sabotage, then this is discussed and, depending on the nature of the self-sabotage, may include behavioral contracting (i.e., a no self-injury contract) and monitoring for issues of safety.

Resistance may be occurring if a client is:

- Making unusual changes in the structure of the therapy (i.e., time/day of session, not showing for appointments)
- Veering the therapeutic conversation to mundane or unrelated issues
- Not connecting to emotional content
- Focusing on someone else's issues
- Creating unnecessary chaos or arguments with the therapist or others
- Engaging in increased distractions (i.e., taking on too many projects)
- Heightening addictive or avoidance behaviors

These, of course, should be acknowledged and discussed as part of the therapy.

One common source of resistance is client's avoidance of conversations that may evoke what is most highly feared: intense emotions. A cognitive reframe is used to foster the belief that emotions are beneficial because they communicate information. For example, anger may communicate that something is wrong, or blocked; fear may communicate that something is dangerous; and sadness may communicate that something is lost or disappointing. Helping clients to articulate their feelings is a step towards helping them to subside. It has been well documented that emotional expression reduces symptomology (Bootzin, 1997; Greenberg & Stone, 1992; Pennebaker, 1997; Pennebaker et al., 1988), although emotional expression in and of itself is not necessarily beneficial unless there is an associated learning of a new response (Littrell, 1998) or, in the case of HR, incorporating a perceptual shift.

Fear of talking about trauma and the fear or feeling the sensations associated with emotions is discussed as understandable and even reasonable, despite the rational knowledge that avoidance is only a temporary solution and ultimately prolongs the discomfort. Once this is acknowledged, the therapist might say, "Of course you want to avoid feeling your feelings. It makes perfect sense to me, especially if you are concerned that it will be too painful to handle." Then the specific fear is addressed. For example, if a client is concerned that she will start crying and may never stop, the therapist reassures her that many trauma survivors feel this way, but everyone eventually stops crying (i.e., "Usually people feel exhausted after a long cry but eventually feel some relief. The human body is wired to cry. Tears naturally flow as an expression of intense joy, sadness, or pain. It's the body's way to release these feelings and eventually regain its natural balance or homeostasis."). This may lead to working on building a foundation of coping skills to identify, express, and manage stress and emotions as discussed in chapter 7.

Transference and Counter-Transference

Transference and counter-transference are topics discussed in psychoanalytic models of therapy. These topics have been written about extensively in other texts (Greenson & Wexler, 1969; Wallerstein, 1984), especially in regard to treating trauma (Dalenberg, 2000; Pearlman & Saakvitne, 1995; Wilson & Lindy, 1994). The interplay of transference and counter-transference issues influences the course of therapy (or in some circles this *is* the course of therapy) from the moment of initial contact to the last moment of termination.

In simplistic terms, it is not uncommon for fears and assumptions about significant others to be projected on to or "transferred" to the therapist. When possible the therapist identifies the transference and links the client's reactions and assumptions to other relationships in the client's life thereby, illuminating her underlying experiential hologram. However, this is not always an easy task. As it may not be obvious what is transference especially when the client seems to be having a personal reaction to the therapist. The therapist's own responses may interfere with the process.

The therapist's response to clients including her feelings, attitudes, and conflicts is referred to as counter-transference. Counter-transference can be useful as it may provide vital information and insights as to how a client creates the holographic themes in her life. It is likely that the way the therapist feels is how others also respond to the client. However, counter-transference may also include the fears, biases, and other motives and feelings that therapists bring to the therapy, such as are they meeting their own needs through the therapeutic relationship (e.g., wanting to be liked, helpful, seen as competent, entertained, or tantalized)? Are they avoiding their own issues or feelings (e.g., feelings toward the client, their own experiential hologram, their own past relationships, other feelings such as fear of being inadequate)? Are they avoiding the client's issues (e.g., ones that are horrific, or trigger memories for the therapist)? These issues can potentially influence the therapy in unproductive ways. If undetected and unmanaged, this can seriously impede the treatment. Therefore, a thorough inquiry into the topic of counter-transference would benefit any therapist doing trauma work. In fact, Langs (1982) declares that unmanaged counter-transference is the primary cause of treatment failures.

The following is an example of a treatment failure due to unmanaged counter-transference: A trainee was feeling overwhelmed because one of his clients fell in love with him; however, he did not disclose this during supervision. He was a bright trainee, yet highly defensive and seemed invested in maintaining a posture of appearing competent, which is not uncommon for trainees (Katz, 2003). They had been working together for 8 months and most likely these feelings had been building for quite some time. Finally, he mentioned what was happening. The next day, while I was out of the office, the trainee had an opportunity to flee from the client and his uncomfortable feelings. The client had come in with a fresh cut on her arm (she had a history of cutting herself and she admitted in later sessions that she did this to elicit attention and caring). The trainee appropriately escorted her to the emergency room on station and notified the clinic director. Because he was highly distressed, it was easy to convince the director that this client was out of control and posed a risk of future dangerous behaviors. The director only seeing a potentially volatile situation concurred with the solution of immediately terminating with the client. The logic was that since the client was going to be hospitalized, she might as well deal with termination while in a safe environment. When I returned, the director asked me to take over the treatment of this client. Although I was able to contain the client, the effects of this abrupt termination given the client's history of abandonment, poor self-esteem, and dependency were dealt with for an entire year following the episode.

There is little doubt that working with this client was challenging; however, if the trainee was willing to confront his own fears and have honest, non-defensive dialogue it might have prevented his being overwhelmed and contained, if not prevented, her escalations.

Vicarious Traumatization

Hearing detailed accounts of client's stories risks traumatizing therapists through the vicarious experience. As Judith Herman (1992) says, this work "poses some risk to the therapist's own psychological health." It is not uncommon for therapists to have symptoms such as feeling anxious, vulnerable, and having nightmares and intrusive thoughts. If therapists have past traumas themselves, client's stories may bring up painful memories. Therapists may feel resentful, angry, irritated, frustrated, and afraid of their clients. Therapists can also become emotionally drained, exhausted, burned out, depressed, have decreased empathy, and heightened concerns about being ineffective.

A therapist's adverse reaction to client's material unless managed, could lead to a disruption in the therapeutic alliance, conflicts with other professionals, and increased symptoms for the therapist. Judith Herman (1992) discusses several defensive strategies typical of trauma therapists such as "withdrawal and impulsive, intrusive action." She states, "The most common forms of action are rescue attempts, boundary violations, or attempts to control the patient. The most common constrictive responses are doubting or denial of the patient's reality, dissociation or numbing, minimization, or avoidance of the traumatic material, professional distancing, or frank abandonment of the patient." Clearly, these responses are potentially problematic.

Therefore, therapists can best serve others if they figure out how they can handle the realities of their clients' stories, as well as manage the difficult counter-transference issues that may emerge over the course of treatment. Some may prefer a professional support system to be able to process intense feelings and reactions. Others may take a more private approach such as exercise or spiritual practices. It is also helpful for therapists to practice self-care and not to deny their own needs. Even when the therapist's needs seem so much less in comparison to those of the client who needs so much more. This may be incorporated into work habits such as taking breaks, varying the caseload of difficult and easier clients, and consulting with colleagues. As I frequently say in stress group,

> When you fly on a commercial airlines, they always say you must put your own oxygen mask on first before helping others.

Chapter Summary

This chapter reviewed issues related to the therapeutic alliance. It began by discussing how to build and monitor rapport. Rapport is an ongoing factor and is continuously monitored. Breaks in rules and agreements will most likely have consequences on the relationship. Clients are apt to respond in ways that mimic their experiential hologram, which provides an opportunity for the HR therapist to gather more information. The issues of transference and counter-transference were also discussed, including that it is important for therapists to acknowledge their counter-transference feelings so that they can be managed otherwise it could lead to disruptions in the alliance. Finally, vicarious traumatization was discussed and how therapists doing this work are advised to take care of themselves.

CHAPTER 7

Coping Skills I

Tolerating and Managing Affect

This chapter outlines eighteen techniques to help clients build coping skills to tolerate and manage distress. These techniques are optional in the practice of HR and are offered as adjunctive tools. Some clients may only require one or two of the techniques while others may benefit from several. The techniques cover skills for relaxation, identifying, tolerating and shifting feelings, and building emotional resilience. They may be taught during a course of individual therapy or they can be taught in a separate stress management group. Mastery of the skills provides a foundation for proceeding with the emotional work of HR therapy.

In HR, it is not only important for clients to trust their therapist, but also important for them to trust their own abilities to handle emotional experiences induced by therapy. If a client is not ready or is too uncomfortable to explore emotional content, then the conversation is redirected and the focus is on building safety and trust. Various techniques can be introduced in session to give clients tools to manage and tolerate affect. For example, traditional cognitive-behavioral techniques can be used to bolster self-soothing such as breathing exercises (e.g., Signal Breath, Cleansing Breath), relaxation techniques (e.g., Mindfulness, and Thought Stopping), and imagery exercises (e.g., imagining a Safe Place). HR encourages clients to choose their own set of soothing, comforting, and grounding strategies that are practical and effective for them.

The amount of time it takes to master these coping skills varies in length, depending on the need and level of functioning of the client. If a client needs a more intense structured program, then a course in Dialectical

Behavioral Therapy for Borderline patients (Linehan, 1995) may be appropriate. In this chapter, 18 abbreviated versions of coping skills are offered as tools to tolerate and manage affect. They have been adapted from *50 Ways to Deal with Feelings* (Katz, in press). Some of the techniques, such as those mentioned above, are well established while others such as "Feelings are Information," "Your own Biofeedback Machine," "Relaxation Sandwich," "5 Ways to Express your Feelings," "The Shrinking Machine," "How to Cope with Upsets," and "The Maypole of Support" are original by this author.

In general, it is suggested that coping skills are taught in the following manner: (1) the therapist gives the rationale for the skill. In other words, how will the skill be beneficial? (2) The skill is thoroughly explained so that clients are informed and have a framework for learning. (3) The skill is demonstrated to clients. (4) The skill is practiced with clients either by doing it with them or by guiding them through it. (5) Finally, clients are debriefed about the experience by discussing what it was like to do the exercise.

Eighteen Exercises to Manage and Tolerate Feelings

What Are Feelings?

1. Feelings are information. The task of learning how to manage and tolerate feelings begins with a reframe about emotions. Most clients assume that emotions (specifically, negative emotions) are painful and should be avoided. They fear that if they experience them, they will be overwhelmed and unable to stop or control them. Therefore, it makes sense that feelings are avoided sometimes to the extreme without regard to the cost to health, relationships, and general well-being. The reframe of "feelings are information" provides a new meaning to feelings. If feelings give information, then they are useful. A therapist may say, "Feelings are powerful tools of communication. They are the body's way of expressing vital information about a situation." For example, a therapist might ask, "What do the emotions of fear, anger, sadness, and joy communicate? How could each of these feelings be beneficial?"

Not only do feelings communicate something about a specific situation, they also provide information about underlying cognitive processes. According to the theory of CEST, feelings are the gateway to important schemas in the experiential system and therefore are helpful in uncovering information about experiential holograms. For example, a client's response of extreme sadness in a situation may reveal an underlying experiential hologram related to unresolved grief about being abandoned as a child.

2. Feelings are sensations: They come and they go. Clients may have a conditioned fearful response to any uncomfortable sensation in their bodies. These sensations trigger anxiety and a fear of being overwhelmed and out of control. One task in learning how to manage and tolerate feelings is to desensitize clients to the sensations associated with them. In this exercise, the therapist and client explore various sensations brought about by feelings. She may ask, "How does anger/fear/sadness feel in your body?" The feeling is labeled as a set of physical sensations that eventually dissipate. Feelings come and they go. Thus, clients begin to relate to their feelings as something that is a temporary—it will pass. They learn that they are merely having an experience. For example, anger may be experienced as tension in the jaw, forehead, neck, shoulders, arms and fists as well as increased temperature and heart rate, quickened, shallow breathing, and thoughts that something is not fair or is not right. These sensations will eventually dissipate.

Understanding feelings as information and as sensations sets the stage for using the following relaxation techniques.

Relaxation Techniques

3. **The Signal Breath.** This is the most popular coping skill taught in HR. It is easy to learn and clients can quickly gain a sense of mastery. The technique involves taking in a deep breath through the nose, holding it for the count of 10, and then releasing it through the mouth. Therapists might say the following:

> The Signal Breath literally takes 10 seconds to do and it will physiologically relax you. It is called a Signal Breath because like a traffic signal, it helps you slow down, stop, and then move forward in a more relaxed stated. It also gives you time to think in stressful situations. It is based on two principles: (1) You cannot be relaxed and tense at the same time, and (2) everything is connected . . . so, if you relax your mind, then you also relax your body, and if you relax your body, then . . . (let the client complete the sentence). That's right you also relax your mind. So, let's say you relax using your breath. What do you think will happen? (again, let the client answer that both mind and body will also relax).

The Signal Breath can be done either with the eyes closed or by softly gazing ahead at a slight downward angle, as some clients may not feel safe closing their eyes. The therapist first demonstrates the breath and then invites the client to do it with her. It is recommended that therapist and client practice the breath 2 to 3 times. After each breath, the therapist might direct the client to take a moment to tune in to how he feels.

4. **Clearing the Mind: Counting Exercise.** In this exercise, clients are taught how to concentrate and focus, thereby clearing intrusive thoughts and "idle chatter from the mind." The task used for this exercise is to simply count to

10. The simplicity is deceiving, as this exercise is much more difficult than it sounds. Clients are instructed to start with the number "1." They can picture the number and say it to themselves and then picture and say the number "2" and proceed through the number "10." However, if they have an intrusive thought, they are instructed to return to the number "1." It is not uncommon to have difficulties proceeding past the number "4."

5. **Personal Biofeedback Machine.** This technique helps clients learn how to breathe from their diaphragm, which is deep, relaxing breathing as compared to breathing from their thorax, which is shallow and tense. The therapist can demonstrate these two types of breathing in an exaggerated fashion. The Personal Biofeedback Machine is something that clients can take with them wherever they go. They simply use both of their hands. One is placed on the chest and the other is placed on the lower belly. Clients are instructed to watch their hands to get feedback about their breathing. If the upper hand is moving and the lower one is not, then clients are instructed to use the feedback to reverse this. By breathing slowly and deeply, the breath should move the lower hand more than the upper hand. This exercise helps clients become more aware of their breathing and the sensations associated with tense versus relaxed breathing.

6. **The Cleansing Breath.** The Cleansing Breath can be used on its own or after a series of other exercises. For example, when explaining the technique, a therapist might say:

> Take a deep breath in and a deep breath out. (When this is demonstrated, add a sound like a heavy sigh during the exhale. The breath is not held during this exercise). Oxygen in and carbon dioxide out. Practice this at least once every day.

7. **The Relaxation Sandwich.** The Relaxation Sandwich is beginning a set of relaxation exercises with a Signal Breath and ending with a Cleansing Breath. These two breaths are the "bread" of the sandwich, and any other exercise is the "filling." For example, a Relaxation Sandwich may be the following: Two Signal Breaths, three minute counting exercise, ten minute mindfulness observation (which is exercise eleven), and two Cleansing Breaths.

Identifying Feelings

8. **The Body Scan.** The Body Scan is a technique to help clients discover where they are feeling tension. Once these places are identified, the relaxation techniques can be used to release the tension.

The following are the steps to do the Body Scan:

Before doing the exercise, it is recommended to start with one to two Signal Breaths. Then the therapist instructs clients to bring the focus to the feet. She might say,

> Feel the soles of your feet touching your shoes and your shoes touching the floor. Notice how your feet may be feeling. Are they warm/cold, heavy/light, tingly? Do you sense that there is tension in your feet? Now move to your ankles.

The therapist mentions various parts of the body and asks clients to notice if there is any tension in each area. The therapist concludes with, "You have just completed a Body Scan." And then closes with two Cleansing Breaths.

The whole process should only take a few minutes as it is just a scan. If clients practice, they will be able to relax their entire body in the same amount of time. The more it is practiced, the easier it gets. Clients can release tension by doing one to two Cleansing Breaths or by giving themselves self-statements to "relax." However, if a client is upset, then the body will respond with tension. This is why an Emotional Scan is also implemented to detect any associated emotions that may be contributing to tension in the body.

9. The Emotional Scan. The Emotional Scan is a similar process as the Body Scan, but instead of simply identifying areas of tension, clients are instructed to explore what emotions may be associated with each particular area of tension. When the emotions are identified and labeled, then it is easier to release them. A therapist might say:

> Begin with the feet and go up through the body parts. Put an imaginary red "X" on the parts that are tense. Then stop at each red X and ask yourself, "What feeling is this tension communicating?" Take some time to tune in. You may not get an answer right away. Ask yourself again, "What am I feeling here?" If you can't get an answer ask yourself, "Is it anger?" Then wait and listen. Your body will tell you if the word is accurate. Look for a sensation that feels like "yes!" Go through the same procedure using the following words: hurt, fear, betrayal, jealousy, irritation, apprehension, and sadness. Do any of these ring true or feel right to you? When you get an emotion for your first red X then proceed to the next one.

After this exercise, clients may want to discuss what they discovered. As part of the discussion, therapists can help them verbalize specific feelings. For example, some clients may experience "hurt" for many emotions that they feel such as fear, jealousy, and betrayal. Therapists can guide clients to explore and label their emotions to help them distinguish the nuances of a variety of feelings.

10. Deciphering Messages Sent by Feelings. When clients have learned the Signal Breath, Cleansing Breath, the Body Scan, the Emotional Scan, and labeling their feelings they can "sandwich" them together with this exercise. The previously learned skills are practiced and reinforced with the following sequence:

1. Getting Centered and Relaxed: 1–2 Signal Breaths
2. Focusing on the Sensations in Your Body: Body Scan
3. Identifying the Feelings and Sensations: Emotional Scan
4. Decoding the Message
5. Releasing the Feeling and the Tension
6. Closing: Two Cleansing Breaths

The therapist may explain the rationale by saying, "What you feel is a communication about what you sense in a situation. The body responds to messages sent from the mind and expresses these messages as feelings. The task is to be able to detect and decipher the communication. As you might recall, feelings provide useful information."

Complete Steps 1 to 3 and then add Step 4: Decoding the Message. After completing the Emotional Scan, ask, "What is this feeling (or tension) communicating? Maybe an image or a thought will come to you. Maybe the feeling is related to something that happened earlier in the day or maybe it is related to something that was unresolved from long ago. Release the logical part of your mind and let yourself experience whatever comes up for you. Notice what associations, thoughts, images, conversations may surface."

The next step, Step 5, is to release the emotion and thereby release the tension. Therapists ask clients to focus on the area in the body that is tense and say, "Ask yourself, Am I ready to release this issue, transform it, or let it go?" If the answer is "no," then ask, "Is there something I need to express or is there an action I need to do to help me feel complete with this issue? Breathe into the tense area and notice what happens." The client is instructed to move to the next area of tension and repeat Steps 3, 4, and 5 until all of the messages are received. This exercise ends with two Cleansing Breaths.

Tolerating Distressing Feelings

11. Mindful Observation. In this exercise, clients are taught how to observe their feelings and the associated sensations in a nonjudgmental, detached manner. They are instructed to simply notice the experience without trying to change it, resist it, release it or doing anything about it. Just notice it. Some helpful metaphors are the following:

> Feelings are like waves; they come and they go.
> Feelings are like clouds; watch them pass.

With each of these phrases, instruct clients to imagine their feelings "like a wave" or "like a cloud" and to observe them. Noticing the experience often will naturally dissipate its intensity; however, if a client tries to dissipate the experience it will most likely intensify. Therefore, it is best to emphasize non-attachment and observation without expectation for anything to change.

12. Deliberate Distraction. Sometimes distraction is the most useful strategy to help someone manage overwhelming feelings. They may not have developed the concentration or skill to sit with or observe their feelings. Rather than have them escalate where a client is at risk for doing an impulsive or destructive behavior, they are instructed to use distraction in a deliberate and safe way. The goal of a distraction exercise is to shift the attention from an overwhelming negative feeling to something more pleasant. A common technique is using imagery to create a Safe Place or to use Thought Stopping.

Creating a Safe Place.
In this exercise, clients are instructed to use visualization to imagine a place that is safe, comforting, and pleasant. Some clients prefer to create a fantasy place while others prefer to recall a specific memory. The imagery may or may not include other people. If clients do not have a specific memory, then the therapist can suggest a nature scene such as on the beach, by a tropical waterfall, or in the mountains. Ask what the client prefers and then fill in the details of the scene including colors, sounds, smells, and textures. Anchor a positive feeling associated with the scene. For example, a therapist might say, "Imagine that you feel very relaxed and whenever you imagine this beautiful place you feel happy, safe, comfortable, and relaxed."

Thought Stopping.
This behavioral technique teaches clients that they have control over recurring negative thoughts. Before practicing thought stopping, the client should decide on a positive image to use for the exercise. The client is also instructed to imagine a large red stop sign when she hears the word "stop." The client is instructed to close her eyes and when she has a negative thought to nod or raise a finger. Then the therapist shouts "STOP!" It should momentarily jolt the client but then she is calmly instructed to go to the pleasant imagery. The client practices the exercise and learns to shout "stop" silently to herself.

13. Nurturing: Soothing and Self-Care. In this exercise, the therapist helps the client generate a list of activities that the client can do to soothe and care for herself.

For example, for a client with difficulty managing her time, she might work on creating a schedule which included self-care time to be alone, socialize with friends, or do a fun activity. Other examples of nurturing activities are: Taking a bubble bath, getting a manicure or pedicure, buying fresh flowers, and taking a walk in nature. Clients should have 2 to 3 items in each of the following categories: physical nurturing, emotional nurturing, spiritual or inspirational nurturing.

14. Five Ways to Express Feelings. This exercise outlines five ways to express feelings: Cry, Write, Talk, Sweat, and Pray. The following are some suggested dialogue that therapists can use to teach these strategies.

Cry them out.
"Sometimes a good cry can release pain and leaving you feeling exhausted but refreshed. However, if you cry, and cry, and feel that it is making matters worse, then splash some cold water on your face, look up to the sky, and switch strategies. (Cool water is soothing to the skin and sinuses that may become inflamed from excessive crying. Looking up is a technique used with stroke patients who have disinhibition and tend to cry. The action seems to interrupt the emotional outpour and stops the tears.)"

Write them out.
"Writing is a good way to express your feelings and leave it on a page. It is recommended that the writing you may use to process your feelings is kept private and to yourself. It is not a good idea to send a letter to someone when you write it in the heat of your upset. Cool off before you reread the letter. You may decide to edit your old letter, write a new one, speak to the person directly, or choose another action."

Talk them out.
"Talking with a friend or therapist can be very helpful to process through your feelings. However, what do you do when no body else is around? You can talk to yourself and coach yourself as if you were coaching a friend or you can imagine that you are talking to someone who is a sympathetic listener such as a specific person or to a saint, an angel, or God."

Sweat them out.
"Exercise is a great release for upsetting feelings. It takes your focus away from the event, it helps you release toxins that are generated by stress, and your body naturally produces endorphins (natural morphine-like chemicals in the brain) that make you feel good. Even after you exercise, the benefits can last for several hours."

Pray or meditate them out.
"Many people find deep comfort in spiritual practices such as prayer or meditation. If spiritual practices are consistent with your belief system, then you may want to go to a place of worship, read something spiritual or

inspirational, practice releasing your feelings (e.g., either through observation or handing over your upsetting feelings to God, Spirit, or a Higher Power), or using prayer to ask for assistance on a spiritual level."

For those who are interested in meditation, a therapist might say: "Meditation is a way to be at peace regardless of whatever thoughts or feelings you may have. There are many styles of meditation. One style is to sit quietly and focus on either the breath or an object. The practice is to clear the mind of any judgments. As thoughts and feelings arise, they are observed in a nonjudgmental manner and the focus is brought back to the breath or the object. Meditation helps people let go of the tendency to dwell on certain thoughts and feelings and recognize that they are simply fleeting mental reactions."

Shifting Feelings

15. The Shrinking Machine. In this exercise, clients are guided to use fantasy to "shrink" their fears. According to the theory of CEST, the experiential system responds to fantasy in a similar way as to reality. Therefore, shrinking a fear using imagery helps clients feel more empowered.

Clients are instructed to form an image of what is most fearful for them. The image could be represented by a specific person (such as a perpetrator), an object, animal, shape, mythical figure or whatever else the client generates. The image is then put into a "shrinking machine." Afterward, the client relates to the miniature version to realize that it is less scary and threatening than previously experienced. She also has more power, control, and choice over the matter.

The therapist can describe the machine such as a high-tech, sleek machine made of shiny chrome. It can have several flashing buttons and digital outputs. There may be a conveyor belt where the client is instructed to place the object or person that is the source of the upset. The client watches as it swiftly is moved along the conveyor belt and disappears into the machine. Then an automatic sliding door opens and out pops a tray with the miniature version of the original image.

Another version is a description of an old clunky machine with lots of pipes letting off steam. An old wood crate is lowered and the client is instructed to place the object, person, or image in the box. It is cranked up manually by a big metal wheel and placed into a big vat. The whole machine begins to shake and more steam comes out of the pipes. Then all of a sudden it stops. A small door near the bottom of the vat opens and a miniature version of the original image appears.

The client is instructed to take the miniature image and place it in the palm of his hand. If it is a person, have the client imagine the person waving her arms and yelling in a high-pitched squeaky voice. The tiny version is almost comical. Reinforce the client's perception of "I can handle this." Some clients may be able to stomp on it or dispose of it. Others may feel guilty or perceive such an action would be too violent. They can seal the miniature in a box, tie it to the end of a balloon and watch it disappear into the sky, or send it off on a leaf to float down a river.

For example, Valerie was raped in a parking lot by a stranger who asked her to help him put some packages in his van. She put the rapist into the machine and although she was deeply hurt by him, could not imagine doing anything to harm him. So she decided she would also put his van in the machine. Then she imagined placing the miniature perpetrator inside the miniature van and watched him scurry away. She stated practicing this imagery helped her decrease her fear as she gained emotional distance from the event.

16. How to Cope with Upsets. The following are six questions to guide clients through feelings of upset.

1. What are you feeling?
To help clients identify their feeling, suggest that they start with quieting the mind with one to two Signal Breaths followed by a Body Scan and an Emotional Scan to focus on their feelings. They can write them down and ask themselves if there are any more specific feelings they can identify.

2. What happened?
The next step is to have clients write down exactly what happened before, during, and after the upsetting event. The object of this step is to express the entire narrative of what happened, focusing mostly on the facts.

3. What did you expect to happen? Or what did you expect not to happen?
Have clients write down what they expected to happen. How "should" the scene have turned out?

4. Am I ready to accept life on life's terms?
This is a pivotal step in this process. Ask clients, "Can you let go of your expectation and accept that this is the way it is? Although you may not like or agree with the outcome, at this point, this is the outcome. Can you come to terms with this so you can move on to something more productive?" Note that acceptance does not mean that you agree or condone what happened. It just means letting go of the self-statements of I should have or could have or would have done something differently.

5. What actions can I take to make things better?
Coming from this new place of acceptance, what actions, solutions, or communications would be most effective? Sometimes there are not many choices

and the most productive action is to relax. Other times, it may be productive to take an action such as communicating with someone or making a change.

6. What positive learning did you receive?
A therapist might say, "For every experience, there is something positive to be learned. Such as did you have an opportunity to learn about patience, compassion, tolerance, or how to better assert yourself? Think if you can find one thing that you were able to learn now that you have gone through this experience." Help clients recontextualize the event by finding something positive.

Building Emotional Resiliency

17. Increasing Joy. Joy is very good for our physical, mental, and emotional health. It elevates mood, decreases stress, and improves relationships. The following is an exercise to help clients generate ideas to increase joy in their lives. The first part is answering a series of questions and the second part is analyzing the answers. Either the therapist or client can write down the answers.

- What things bring you joy (makes you smile, feel good, feel happy)?
- Name three things you used to do that you enjoyed.
- List three "other lives" you wish you could live.
- Name three ideal vacations or places you would like to see.
- If you had unlimited funds, time, and ability what would like to do?

The answers to these questions are reviewed with the client and any themes are noted. Then the therapist and client can brainstorm how aspects of the answers can be incorporated into the client's current life. For example, Susan enjoys water fountains and fantasizes about being an artist living in Italy. She could incorporate the "water fountain" aspect into her life by visiting or purchasing a fountain. The "artist" part can be incorporated by taking an art class or just make a commitment to do more art. She might carry a sketch pad with her in her car or in her purse so that she may find more opportunities to sketch. She may incorporate "living in Italy" by going on a trip to Italy, going to a "Little Italy" section in a nearby city, eating at an Italian restaurant, taking a class on Italian classical art, or learning to speak Italian. There are many ways Susan can incorporate aspects of her fantasy life into her current life.

A therapist might say, "Using the information that we just wrote, what can you do to experience more joy in your daily life? Name five concrete things you can do to incorporate more joy into your life."

18. Maypole of Support. This exercise gives a visual aid to the fact that a good support system helps buffer against the deleterious effects of stress. The image is a "maypole" where there is a center pole (representing the self) and several ribbons extending from the top of the pole to the ground forming a circle around the pole. The structure with many ribbons extended looks like a teepee-style tent or an inverted cone.

A therapist might say, "A maypole is a symbolic representation for the supports that are in your life. Let's say you are the pole in the middle and each support is a ribbon that is anchored down around you. If there is a big wind, the pole with one ribbon anchored down would topple over; however, a pole with many ribbons would stay sturdy through the storm. There are many types of ribbons that can keep someone feeling anchored. For example, sports, various activities, hobbies, friends, a certain routine, pets, a job, support groups, family, church, etc. are things that keep someone grounded, anchored, and feeling connected to others. Having good support also boosts self-esteem. What are your ribbons of support?" Help the client name at least three support ribbons on their maypole.

Chapter Summary

This chapter summarized 18 exercises to tolerate and manage affect. The exercises include a cognitive reframe about what feelings are, and provide a means of relaxation, identifying, tolerating, and shifting feelings, and building emotional resiliency. These are only a few out of many possible stress management tools. Clients and therapists can decide to what degree to focus on mastering these tools.

CHAPTER 8

Coping Skills II
*Managing PTSD, Barriers to Learning
and Implementing Skills,
and Creating a Feelings Plan*

This chapter offers more techniques for coping with emotional distress. Specifically, it addresses common symptoms people experience with PTSD, such as nightmares, intrusive thoughts, panic attacks, insomnia, and phobias. It also outlines several common barriers that interfere with the learning, practicing, or implementing of the coping skills. Finally, suggestions on what to include in a feelings plan are discussed.

---

*Case Example: If you simply know it, you will forget it.
But if you live it, you will remember it.*

> *This example illustrates how it is necessary to practice coping skills or they will be forgotten in a time of need.*

Serena had been in therapy for 8 months and was moving through the stages of HR. We had a solid therapeutic alliance, she had learned several coping skills, she had identified her experiential hologram, and was working through her feelings regarding the childhood abuse she experienced from her father. She was doing significantly better compared to when she started therapy (i.e., less depressed, no thoughts of suicide, fewer nightmares, less anxious, etc.). She started attending the women's stress management group and was a star participant. She would volunteer to demonstrate various coping skills. She received an "A" on a pop quiz on how to handle distressing feelings. She even made business card-sized cues cards for the other members in the group. She used her artistic talent and created a beautiful card with a drawing of a wave in the background ("feelings are like waves they come and they go") with the five ways to express feelings in the foreground. However, when her mother suddenly became terminally ill, Serena started reverting to her old patterns. Her nightmares returned; she cut on herself, she was abusing caffeine, she became anxious, impulsive, and easily overwhelmed. When asked if she had been using her coping skills, she replied that she had not. I asked her why not and her explanation was that she "forgot." Although we both knew that she knew the skills, it simply did not occur to her to use them. The answer to this puzzling phenomenon along with other common barriers will be addressed in this chapter.

This chapter is divided into three sections: (1) Skills to deal with common symptoms of PTSD, (2) barriers to learning, practicing and implementing coping skills, and (3) creating a feelings plan. Again, some of these techniques are well established such as basic sleep hygiene and the "lemon exercise" while other techniques are original to this author such as the "Invisible Negativity Shield" and the "COPE" strategy.

Skills to Deal with Common Symptoms of PTSD

One of the first interventions for clients with PTSD is to educate them about their symptoms and normalize their experiences. This in and of itself can offer great relief as many clients report they feared they were "going crazy." Therapists can explain the typical symptoms of PTSD including nightmares, intrusive thoughts and triggers, panic attacks, insomnia, agoraphobia and social phobias. The following section provides suggestions for coping with each of the above named symptoms.

Nightmares

Nightmares are one of the most common symptoms for clients who have survived trauma. The frequency can increase in periods of stress (either related or unrelated to the trauma) or when something triggers a memory of the trauma such as an anniversary or being exposed to a detail that is reminiscent of the trauma. Below are suggested ways to manage them. (Also, see the section on Insomnia for additional strategies for sleep.)

Back to Safety.
The immediate concern when someone has a nightmare is to help the client return to a feeling of safety. She may awaken feeling frightened, angry, disoriented, and breathless. If she tries to go to sleep without "returning to safety," she will likely resume the nightmare. Also, many people report having difficulty going back to sleep at all and usually spend the rest of the

night fighting off feelings of terror. It is suggested that the client get out of bed, feel her feet on the ground, and remind herself of being in the here and now. She may want to put a few comforting objects near her bed such as a stuffed animal, special rock or crystal, or religious object such as a rosary or picture of a saint or angel that she can hold and feel. Pets are also a good source of comfort. It is suggested that she take several deep cleansing breaths to help reduce tension and tell herself, "I'm ok," "I'm safe," "I release my fear," or any other phrase that is simple and comforting. Some people prefer to splash cold water on their face, listen to soothing music, watch television, read an inspirational passage, or do a "safety check" of the house before returning to bed. (These later strategies are also helpful when a client has a "flashback" or a vivid re-experiencing of trauma.)

Invisible Negativity Shield.

As CEST indicates, imagery and fantasy can induce experiences as if a client were responding to an actual situation. Thus, imagery can be a powerful tool to induce feelings of safety and protection.

For example, the image of having a force field of protection, or an invisible Negativity Shield, around the home can be very comforting. A therapist might use the analogous image from the *Star Trek* television show. In this show, the spaceship *Enterprise* generates a force field around the ship to protect it against attacks. The force field is so powerful that any incoming fire literally bounces off of the shield. A therapist might say:

> Imagine that your home is protected by an Invisible Negativity Shield. This shield is constructed from a golden light that resonates at such a high vibration that no one can see it. Now imagine this light is swirling around your home, surrounding it, and creating a force field that is so powerful that it wards off any and all negativity. Anyone or anything that would try to get near your home without your permission would be repelled and bounce off the light. You can put up this force field of light by intending that it is there. Imagine it, visualize it, and declare that it is so. This force field of light will protect you while you sleep.

Clients can use this imagery every night before they sleep, or they can set an intention that once the shield is up it will be there every night when they need it. The idea is to experientially invoke a feeling of safety so that clients can relax enough to go to sleep.

Understanding the Nightmare.

After the client has had a nightmare, it may be a topic to explore during therapy. Nightmares are framed as a natural way for the unconscious mind to express itself and attempt to resolve blocked or poorly processed emotional issues. One strategy is to explore the content and context of the nightmare. For example, a therapist and client might: (1) discuss the content of the dream; (2) identify the salient emotions; (3) identify memories, thoughts, or images that are associated with that emotion; (4) identify aspects of the client's current life that may be triggering the nightmare (e.g., an anniversary month, exposure to an image, sound, or smell, or a recent conflict). In other words, is there an unresolved issue that the nightmare is bringing up? The experience may provide material for discussion, a writing assignment, or future reprocessing. Some clients keep a dream journal and may wish to discuss their entries in therapy.

Intrusive Thoughts and Triggers

Other common symptoms for those who have experienced trauma are intrusive thoughts and triggers. An intrusive thought is a thought that seems to intrude or interfere with someone's current thinking. For example, a client may be doing a task and suddenly begin thinking about their trauma. A trigger is anything that serves as a reminder of the trauma—a sound, a smell, or an object. What is triggered is a sudden intense recollection of trauma. Both intrusive thoughts and triggers may be unsuspected and could catch people off guard. The surprise element is what makes them particularly distressing. Giving clients a strategy to cope with the sudden, sometimes overwhelming sense of anxiety evoked by these symptoms builds self-confidence and reduces the fear of having intrusive thoughts or being triggered. If clients have these symptoms, they can utilize the COPE strategy. Notice that COPE uses Cleansing Breaths and not Signal Breaths. The reason is that when people are anxious they already tend to hold their breath rendering the Signal Breath counter-productive. Instead, when anxious, clients are encouraged to exhale thereby releasing the tension and facilitating breathing.

> **C**leansing breath: Take several slow, deep breaths, exhaling completely.
> **O**bservation: Watch the sensations and thoughts come and go.
> **P**ositive self-talk: I'm Ok. I'm safe.
> **E**xplanation: This is only an intrusive thought. This is only a trigger.

COPE can be used several times until the anxiety passes. Further processing of the event may be useful during the client's next therapy session. Again, the goal would be to identify the associated unresolved issue that the intrusive thought or trigger is bringing forth.

Other techniques to deal with triggers may include avoidance, distraction, and confrontation. Some situations are obvious triggers such as going to a bar if someone was raped at a bar. Clients may choose to *avoid* these situations. Other triggers may not be avoidable. For example, for someone who endured combat, hearing a helicopter could be an unavoidable trigger. In this situation, it may be beneficial to engage in a *deliberate distraction* until the noxious stimuli passes. Other known triggers may be *confronted* to extinguish fearful associations such as the example in chapter 5 of the veteran whose job in the military was to uncover land mines and later developed a fear of passing over any dark spot on the ground.

Panic Attacks

Panic attacks are periods of overwhelming anxiety with several physical symptoms including shortness of breath, dizziness, and heart palpitations. Clients may fear that they are going to have an attack in public or that they are going to die. There are several strategies to address these attacks. For example, cognitive-behavioral therapy offers a well established effective treatment (Barlow & Craske, 1994). The first step is *identifying* the symptoms associated with the panic attack. The symptoms are *reframed* as "sensations" and clients are *educated* about the body's natural response to anxiety. Therapists may help clients with *behavioral testing* which includes inducing the sensations during a session and then assisting clients to relax and reduce the sensations. This procedure *reinforces* that they can handle the experience and the sensations will not harm them. Therapist may also explore the associated thoughts with the attack by identifying what thoughts clients have before, during and after an attack. The most distressing thought is labeled as the "hot thought." The hot thought is restructured by confronting its underlying logic.

The COPE strategy can also be used to manage panic attacks. Clients are instructed to use COPE for several rounds until the anxiety passes.

Cleansing breath: Take several slow, deep breaths, exhaling completely.
Observation: Watch the sensations and thoughts come and go.
Positive self-talk: I can get through this. I'm ok. This will pass.
Explanation: These are only sensations of anxiety.

Insomnia

For trauma survivors, insomnia is not only about not being able to sleep during the night, it is also often associated with several fears about going to sleep including the fear of nightmares and night terrors, the fear of being vulnerable or out of control, and the fear of being unsafe (e.g., attacked by an intruder). There are several strategies to address this. First of all, clients should be practicing good sleep hygiene (sleep enhancing habits) which includes: no caffeine or stimulants for several hours prior to sleep, not using the bed for activities other than sleep, not reading stimulating material or watching disturbing television, not taking naps during the day, engaging in relaxing activities prior to sleep such as a meditation, listening to soft music, or taking a warm bath, and engaging in exercise during the day but not right before bedtime.

Second, clients can set an intention for having a safe and restful sleep. They can use imagery such as the invisible negativity shield or imagery such as having an angel of protection watch over them and their home while they sleep. The intention can also include positive self-talk that they are safe and ready to have a peaceful sleep.

Third, clients can engage in pre-sleep positive thoughts, imagery, and sensations such as smelling pleasant aromas, using a soft comforting blanket or sleepwear, viewing a comedy or nature photos, listening to soothing or happy music, and reading an inspirational message before sleep.

Fourth, clients are encouraged to use whatever practical measures that make them feel safe such as sleeping with a phone, pet, or partner, installing an alarm system, and locking and checking all doors and windows before sleep.

Agoraphobia and Social Phobias

Often related to PTSD, clients may develop symptoms of agoraphobia and social phobias. As previously discussed, phobias are effectively treated with exposure therapy. During a therapy session, these symptoms can be addressed using the following: (1) The anxiety is discussed as a reaction to anticipating an unsafe, humiliating, or fearful event. (2) The client identifies and articulates the fear (to the best of his ability; it is often an unconscious irrational fear that is difficult to articulate). (3) An imaginary scene is constructed including a description of a positive outcome and the skills the client would have to handle the situation. (4) The imagery is practiced first in the therapy office and then as a homework assignment for the client. The therapist guides the client through the scene being sure to anchor positive, relaxed, and good feelings. The guided imagery can include imagining people responding to the client in a positive way.

Along with the imagery, clients are encouraged to practice positive self-talk and relaxation techniques. It is also helpful for clients to have "a way out." In other words, it may be more comfortable to attend a social function if he knows he can always leave. Finally, deliberate distractions (such as singing to oneself) can be used to ease feelings of discomfort.

It is suggested that clients begin with small do-able steps. Similar to systematic desensitization, she may start with something that produces a low level of anxiety such as just opening the front door. At each stage, she relaxes until she feels comfortable. Next, she might sit on the front step just outside of her door, then walk to the curb, etc. With each step, the client's sphere of safety increases. This strategy also applies to social situations. Clients are encouraged to start with non-threatening situations and to work-up to more challenging ones. If clients choose a situation that is too distressing, they set themselves up for failure and are less likely to make future attempts. For example, Cecilia had a fear of crowds, loud noises, and was easily overwhelmed by too much stimuli. She spent most of her time in her home and ran her errands at times when she could avoid as many people as possible. In therapy, she had been working on developing coping skills and wanted to increase her social activities. However, her decision to accept an invitation to attend a state fair as her first social outing was a poor choice and set her up for failure. She, not surprisingly, went to the fair and within 15 minutes had a panic attack. She left the fair feeling discouraged and generated a host of negative self-deprecating thoughts. She discounted the coping skills that she was learning without realizing that she was simply not yet ready to tackle that situation.

Another strategy is to encourage clients to go outside or to go to a social event with a friend to help them build self-confidence. When out, there may be opportunities to practice being alone such as when the friend goes to the restroom. These opportunities are similar to a stress inoculation where low doses of stress serve to strengthen the client's ability to tolerate higher doses of stress at a later time.

If a client becomes anxious, she can use the COPE strategy:

Cleansing breath: Take several slow, deep breaths, exhaling completely.
Observation: Watch the sensations and thoughts come and go.
Positive self-talk: I can get through this. I'm ok right now. I can always leave. Just go a little bit further.
Explanation: I am only responding to thoughts of fear. Nothing bad is really happening right now.

Barriers to Learning, Practicing, or Implementing Coping Skills

This section addresses several barriers and common types of resistances to the process of learning, practicing, or implementing coping skills. Suggestions on how to overcome these are presented.

Skills Not Integrated as a Life-Habit

The most common reason clients report not using their coping skills is simply, "I forgot." When I first heard this response, I was amazed. How could someone forget when, like a broken record, I repeat the phrase, "Use your coping skills!" almost every session? Did I say it too much causing my clients to ignore me? I know that my clients know these skills because they can easily recite them. However, I quickly realized that it was not just one, but many clients like Serena, who seemed to forget when it came time to actually applying them. The barrier is that the knowledge of the skill resides in the rational system and not in the experiential system. Clients intellectually know the skill but it is not practiced, experientially reinforced, or embodied. When an intense emotion arises, the experiential system is activated and only those skills that are encoded experientially will be remembered.

Solution: For skills to be remembered and used, they must be practiced. Telling clients about these skills is far less effective than their doing them. Therapists can start with one skill, such as the Signal Breath and incorporate it into the therapy sessions. Clients may also be encouraged to practice the skill between sessions. When therapists ask follow-up questions about using the skill it further encourages its application. Then, the therapist can introduce another skill, again by practicing it in session. One idea is to develop a routine of starting each session with a Signal Breath and ending with a Cleansing Breath. Some clients can only handle one to three skills while others can apply a complex array of skills. The former group may prefer a simple feelings plan and the later group may prefer to have a highly detailed one. Clients are also encouraged to use visual cues to remind them about their skills. They can post an index card on their mirror, refrigerator, at the office, and in their car. They can also enlist the help of friends and family members who may be able to remind them of using their skills in a time of emotional upheaval.

Feeling Stupid, Embarrassed, or Self-Conscious

Because many traumatized clients have been humiliated or embarrassed, they may feel self-conscious when learning new coping skills. They may not feel safe to close their eyes. This coupled with the fear that they will look foolish, may increase their feelings of vulnerability to the point of triggering a sense of being retraumatized.

Solution: First of all, it is important to acknowledge these feelings and to be sensitive to clients' perceptions of vulnerability. Therapists can normalize the feelings by letting them know that their feelings are perfectly understandable. This helps mitigate negative self-attributions such as "I am inadequate, inferior, messed up, a failure" and then feeling guilty and ashamed for those feelings on top of feeling vulnerable and afraid. The following are some suggestions: (1) Always start with a rationale and explanation of the exercise so the client is fully informed. (2) Demonstrate the exercise to reduce the client's worry about being tricked or inadvertently getting into a compromised situation. (3) Give clients the option to close their eyes or softly gaze forward but slightly downward. (4) Do the exercise with them. (5)

Look away or turn your chair away so you are not directly facing your client if this is an issue. (6) If clients refuse to practice the exercise in the office, write it down for them and let them practice it at home. Sometimes clients may forget to follow-through with the practice at home. If clients agree to practice the exercise at home, then the therapist should ask about their experience in the next session. Even if the client did not do the exercise, knowing that he will be asked about it during session will increase the likelihood for future compliance. The therapist could demonstrate the exercise again for the client to observe. As clients become more comfortable with seeing the exercises or doing them at home, they may be more likely to do it in the office with the therapist. Then the therapist will be able to correct or modify their practice as needed.

Lack of Support

Some clients may report that their immediate family including romantic partners, children, and other family members are not supportive of their new skills. They may feel criticized or devalued by certain comments or may be interrupted when attempting to practice the skills. Lack of support may also include making extra demands on the client's time or not creating or respecting privacy for the client to practice the skills. Family members may have a host of motivations to explain why they might not support a client's therapy (e.g., they may fear being blamed, fear that the client will leave them, or feel threatened by unknown change).

In a more extreme version of this barrier, some clients may be conditioned to believe that an act of independence is an act of defiance which could lead to a beating. If a client is currently in an abusive relationship, it can be expected that the perpetrator will attempt to sabotage the therapy or any positive changes that the client makes. If the client is in danger, then getting the client to safety becomes the priority of the therapy. However, sabotage is still an issue even when the client is out of the abusive situation. Based on Boal's work (1995), Marc Rich, PhD, and I have coined the term "residual antagonists" to refer to the lingering construct of "oppressor" that resides in a victim's head. Even though there is no longer an actual abuser, the victim continues to act according to the same rules once enforced by the abuser. An act of independence, even in a place of safety, could evoke similar physiological and emotional responses of fear.

Solution: Therapists can encourage clients to assert boundaries, find places of privacy (e.g., the bathroom or car), and continue to practice the skills. Family members or a significant partner may need education such as: (1) understanding the client's symptoms, (2) understanding the rationale behind doing exercises (and therapy for that matter!), (3) how they can be involved in the client's healing process, and (4) how they can support the client. Family members or a significant partner could be invited to attend a therapy session. If therapist and client agree to extend an invitation (after discussing potential ramifications), then it is important to ask the invited member in a way that is non-threatening. One strategy is to frame their participation as a way to help the client.

Others' lack of support may alert clients to examine these relationships. This could be framed as useful information, and may be a means of bringing underlying problems in these relationships to the surface so that they can be addressed. It is possible that the client's attempt to change could unleash a cascade of relationship issues that would need to be addressed before the client would be ready to continue with HR therapy.

Fear of Responsibility

Some clients fear taking responsibility for their lives. They report feeling an overwhelming pressure and assume that they will fail. They report feeling inadequate and uncomfortable to take on this new, foreign role. They tend to give up easily and may even unconsciously set themselves up to be overwhelmed and fail (like the client who chose to go to the state fair to practice being in a social situation).

Being more self-reliant may evoke feelings of being alone, isolated, or abandoned. Some clients may be overly dependent on others and would readily sabotage their progress to remain close to someone or something else. They may fear losing secondary gains from being in the "sick role."

Solution: The first intervention would be to start with small do-able steps to test to what extent clients will sabotage efforts of responsibility. Second, therapists can discuss their observation of their behavior and their underlying fears. They can point out specific ways clients sabotage their progress to help them become more accountable for the way they wiggle out of their responsibilities. Clients will eventually be able to identify and admit to their self-sabotaging behaviors. This is a first step toward change. Therapists can help clients have small successes and then gradually they will be able to tolerate being more responsible.

Fear of Diminishing the Trauma or Discounting the Pain

Some clients assume that if they feel better, particularly less angry, then their trauma was "not that bad," or their perpetrators are no longer held accountable for their acts of abuse. They fear that if they are okay or even happy, then it diminishes, minimizes, or discounts what they went through. They may fear that nobody would believe them, including their therapist, if they are "too happy."

Solution: First, these clients need validation. They need to feel they are believed, heard, and understood. Second, they also need to have some type of resolution to the injustices that they experienced. Holding their perpetrator accountable by remaining angry may make sense at an experiential level, but in actuality, does nothing to the perpetrator and only harms the client. Many perpetrators never get caught, punished, or even show remorse. Therapists can help clients resolve this fact. Does the client believe in spiritual justice (i.e., everyone will be judged when they die), or in karma and reincarnation (i.e., the perpetrator will pay the consequences in the next life)? Regardless of these beliefs, how much more of the client's own life is she willing to sacrifice for the sake of the perpetrator? Being angry or happy has no bearing and no impact at all on the perpetrator. Third, many clients get stuck on the idea that they are supposed to forgive their perpetrator. They feel pressure to forgive before they have worked through their own feelings. In my experience, this only leads to resentment and negative self-attributions for not being able to forgive. Instead of using the word "forgiveness," therapists can use the word "acceptance" as it is more palatable and less laden with religious overtones.

For example a therapist could say, "You don't need to forgive someone for unforgivable acts. But it is important to come to terms with the fact that this happened to you. By accepting that this was your reality and your experience, you can work on releasing the hurt and pain so you can move forward with your life. Forgiveness may or may not be part of your healing process but if it is, it is much further down the road. For now, let's focus on coming to terms with and accepting that this happened."

Fear It Won't Work

"Oh, I've tried breathing exercises before and they do nothing for me," and "I can't focus on an exercise when I become upset," are common statements indicating a belief that the skills are useless and that they do not work. These clients have given up before they even got started! They may half-heartedly attempt to learn a skill in the therapist's office (to appease the therapist) and not follow through on the practice.

Solution: First, the therapist could reiterate the rationale for doing the exercise. It is important to get the client onboard and to be in agreement with the purpose of the skill otherwise, they will not participate. Second, it is helpful to make the skills personally relevant to increase motivation. For example, the therapist could link the act of doing and mastering the skills with something that the client feels is important such as being a good role-model for a new grandchild, or to help realize the dream of being a teacher.

The more integrated the skill is to the larger goal of why they are in therapy, the better the motivation. Third, the therapist can induce an undeniable experience in the office. Two exercises that easily lend themselves to this are the lemon exercise, and the heightened state of awareness exercise (see the case example from the beginning of chapter 6). These experiences engage the clients and increase the likelihood of further participation. Fourth, it is helpful for the therapist to convey confidence. The therapist can tell the client that she knows the skills work because she's seen hundreds of clients make amazing transformations and she knows that this client has what it takes to also make an amazing transformation.

The Lemon Exercise

The therapist says, "Close your eyes and imagine going into your kitchen. You open the refrigerator door and inside you see a bright yellow lemon. Reach inside and pull it out. You can feel the cool rippled skin of the lemon in your hand and you can smell the fresh citrus scent in the air. Put the lemon on the counter and take a knife and slice it in half. A spray of juice squirts onto the counter. As you separate the halves, you can see the light glistening on the pulp. Now take one of the lemon halves and slice it again so that you have two quarter wedges. Lift one of the wedges to your mouth and bite into the lemon . . . " (Wait for a few moments while clients open their eyes.)

"Notice the saliva pooling in your mouth? (Give people time to notice.) Your body had a physiological reaction, but to what? Was there really a lemon? No. But your body responded as if there were a real lemon because of the images and thoughts you generated."

The lemon exercise can be a springboard for a discussion about the mind-body connection. For example, a therapist might say, "Your body is like a robot and an instrument of the mind. It responds to your thoughts. For example, how do you feel when you have defeating or sad thoughts (e.g., tired, achy)? How do you feel when you have angry thoughts (e.g., tense, agitated)? Now imagine how you might feel with thoughts of hope, challenge, and joy? Just as your body responded to the image of the lemon, your body will respond to the images that you create about your life."

The therapist continues. "The point is this, if you generate positive images for yourself, you will feel better, and will be more likely to follow-through on health-enhancing and health-sustaining practices."

Creating a Feelings Plan

Therapists can help their clients come up with a written plan that can be posted in a visible place, such as on the refrigerator, to help remind them of their skills. The feelings plan should be individualized for each client. Some may prefer to have many options (e.g., an extensive feelings plan) while others may be best served by a more simple plan. Either way, the plan can incorporate coping skills that they have learned along with personalized and specific actions they can do to manage and tolerate feelings. The following are some suggestions on what to include in a feelings plan.

1. Social network: A Social Network is a Safety Network
List of contacts in case of an emergency or emotional crisis. Clients may want to generate at least three resources to call in case of an emergency such as a local ER, 24-hour crisis line, suicide hotline, battered women's shelter, their therapist, AA sponsor, 911, police, clergy member, family member, or friend. List each resource with their corresponding phone number. For example:

People I call for help:
24-hour crisis number _____
Emergency room _____
My sister _____
My AA Sponsor _____
My therapist _____

List of contacts or activities available when clients need to talk, to be understood, or to express feelings.

When I want to express feelings I can:
(for example, call my sister, talk to my therapist at our next session, or write in my journal)

List of contacts or activities available when clients want to laugh or have fun. This list of social contacts is helpful to motivate clients to engage in social activities. For example:

People I call for fun:
Call my friend Amy
Go to the dog park with Max (dog) and say "hi" to at least one other dog owner

2. Safety Strategies: These strategies help remind clients of things they have or can do to foster a sense of security. For example:
My blue cozy fleece blanket
Setting my alarm system
Using positive self-talk to remind myself "I am ok"

Reciting the 21 Psalm from the Bible
Sleeping with my cell phone
Knowing my dog, Max, and my cat, Buttons, are with me

3. Feel Good Strategies: These strategies are designed to elevate the client's mood to help her feel good. Therapists can help clients name specific items or activities. Some suggestions are: looking at pictures and special items, listening to music, taking a bubble bath, walking in nature, using scented candles/incense, watching a video or DVD. Clients can list these specific items. For example:

Pictures from my trip to Yosemite
James Taylor CD
Cinnamon incense
Popcorn and a comedy with Whoopie Goldberg or Steve Martin

It may also be useful to run through a list of questions to help clients name several feel good strategies and to have them name one to three items under each category:

Music that makes me feel good:
Movies that make me feel good:
Activities that make me feel good:
Things I enjoy thinking about:
Images or pictures that make me feel good:
Prayers or inspirational passages that remind me I am ok:

4. Taking Care of Basic Physical Needs: These are reminders to keep a balanced healthy life. If a client has a tendency toward a particular unhealthy activity, this should be addressed on the feelings plan (i.e., if she tends to binge on sugar, then this item would remind her to do something healthy such as taking a walk, dancing, or deep breathing). Basic physical needs such as healthy eating, sleeping, taking daily showers, and getting fresh air may need to be mentioned.

5. List of Coping Skills: Based on the coping skills clients have learned during therapy, this list can be extensive or brief. It serves as a reminder for clients to use their skills. Included in the categories are:

Breathing
Observation
Labeling
Distraction
Nurturing
Expression

6. **Recipes for Success:** A feelings plan can also include specific "recipes" or if–then statements for typical types of problems a client may face. For example:

When I feel anxious, tense, antsy, jittery, nervous, spacey, or unfocused I will:
> Do three signal breaths; Do the Deciphering message technique; Do mindful observation, walk outside, remind myself that I am safe, and call my sister.
> My goals are to soothe and ground myself.

When I feel sad, depressed, lonely, self-hatred, or inadequate I will:
> Hug my pets; Do the Thought stopping technique to stop negative thoughts; call my sister or Amy; look at the prize-winning model I built; read my grateful list of the good things that I have in life.
> My goal is to nurture and remind myself that I am connected to others.

When I feel angry, jealous, betrayed, resentful, bitter, or furious I will:
> Do three signal breaths, do the How to cope with upsets technique, go jogging at the park with Max, read my grateful list.
> My goal is to validate and acknowledge my hurt and to work on releasing, accepting, and knowing that I will be ok.

When I have a nightmare I will:
> Get out of bed, look at my pictures, pet my animals, put up an invisible negativity shield.
> My goal is to comfort and ground myself in the safety of the here and now.

When I have an intrusive thought or am reminded about my trauma I will:
> Use COPE and think of something positive like my trip to Yosemite.
> My goal is to acknowledge the reminder and then shift my thinking to something positive and affirming.

CHAPTER 9

Experiential Discovery

This chapter reviews how to gather information to identify the six components of a client's experiential holograms. Experiential and cognitive techniques are used to facilitate associations through physical sensations, emotions, and imagery.

Case Example: Mission Impossible

> *This example illustrates the process whereby a recent event may trigger past events with similar emotions.*

Carissa completed therapy about a year ago. She called and asked to come back for a few sessions because she felt something was wrong ever since the September 11th, 2001 attack on the World Trade Center in New York. Although she lived in California, she felt the attack was at the root of a vague feeling of "not being ok." Specifically, she reported having careless accidents such as loosing her footing and falling on the sidewalk, dropping a bowl of salad, cutting herself while she was cooking, and making mistakes at work. She denied feeling depressed but did state that she was tired, spacey, and unfocused. When asked about her sleep, she said it was "fitful" and she was having disturbing nightmares.

She described what she could remember about the nightmares. She was looking for people and was afraid they were trapped. She thought maybe she was looking for dead bodies from the World Trade Center. She stated, "There were a lot of people wandering around but I was very focused and determined. I had a job to do." She was asked to "tune into her body" to feel what feelings came to her. She listed: "tense, frustrated, scared, confused, stressed . . . guilty." She continued, "It is my responsibility, I have to figure out how to get the people to safety. If I don't find them, it's my fault." I asked, "What else do you feel?" Carissa responded, "I feel tricked, set up, angry . . . helpless . . . sad, grief. I feel a lot of grief. . . . " She became tearful.

Her feelings were acknowledged. When she felt more composed, she was asked if there were other images, thoughts, or events where she might have felt similar feelings. She stated she had not thought about it before but there was a time when she served in the U.S. Coast Guard and she was assigned to be in charge of a rescue mission. This was the first mission where she was actually in charge and she felt it was "dumped" on her at the last minute with only a skeleton crew. She was put in a position of responsibility and, being the only woman in her unit, she felt pressure to prove herself. It was a foggy night and she had to rely almost completely on the instruments to navigate through the tricky waters off the coast of Maine. They were looking for the occupants of a small fishing boat that was found abandoned. She remembers scanning the waters with a large headlight. She returned after several hours with nothing to report. Apparently, the bodies of two men in their 20's were never found.

In her dream, she had merged the September 11, 2001 attack with the event from the Coast Guard. She had not realized that she still had unresolved feelings about the rescue mission. We further discussed how this fit within the larger pattern of her life. When she was 10 years old, her parents divorced after years of arguing. She described dreading to go home after school because she never knew what kind of mood her mother would be in. Carissa remembered being tense and anxious. She felt personally responsible for soothing and pleasing her parents to "keep the peace" in the household. Her experiential hologram included the core violation of living in an unpredictable, unstable home, a personal truth that she and the world is out of control, a compensating strategy of being overly responsible (to the point of being overwhelmed), and an avoidance strategy of becoming confused, unable to concentrate, and likely to make mistakes. Because she reported similar symptoms related to the September 11, 2001 attack, it was likely that her experiential hologram was being triggered. The three emotional events and her coping strategies were written on a dry erase board so that she could see how the September 11, 2001 attack was related to the rescue mission, which was also related to her childhood.

Emotional Event and	Compensating strategy of being responsible
September 11, 2001 attack	"find bodies or it's my fault"
↓	↓
In charge of rescue mission	"find bodies, run the ship"
↓	↓
Parents arguing	"keep the peace or else"

We discussed these associations and the related feelings. She understood why it made sense that the September 11, 2001 attack and the rescue mission triggered similar emotional responses. We worked on accepting the reality of the incidents and appropriately grieving the losses. After discussing her feelings and the associated events of the Coast Guard and her childhood, she stated she felt some relief. She acknowledged that she no longer had to fix or change the events. She could release: (1) the fear of the world being unstable, (2) the strategies of being responsible, and (3) avoiding her feelings by being spacey, confused, and unfocused. We scheduled a two-week follow-up appointment and she reported that the nightmares had ceased.

Carissa's example illustrates the process of experiential discovery to elicit information about unresolved emotional experiences and experiential holograms. After rapport, trust, and safety are established, a deepening of the therapy begins. Clients are engaged in a process of discovery where feelings, associations, memories, and images are related to the client's current issues. Information in the experiential system may be accessed through focusing on internal cues, such as feelings and bodily sensations and by asking a series of feeling-oriented questions, as in Gendlin's (1981) focusing procedure (e.g., "What does the problem feel like? What word describes the feelings that seem to move the body forward?"). Correctly identifying the feeling associated with a problem leads to a "physical easing" and a "felt release."

Clients may be asked to list feelings, describe a feeling, or focus on where they might feel a feeling in their bodies. Clients may be taught how to scan their bodies for physical tension (i.e., the Body Scan) and are also taught the author's technique of the Emotional Scan, where clients scan the areas of tension in the body and identify associated emotions in each area of tension. After the tension and related emotions are identified, the client is asked to associate to images, events, and memories.

For example, Melinda, a hearing daughter of two deaf parents, came for treatment because she felt disconnected from people. She described being "raised by television" since that was her main source for learning about social skills with hearing people. She also had an unusual skin rash on her arms that baffled her medical doctors.

When asked to focus on her body, she stated that she felt tension in her stomach. She had mentioned this symptom during other conversations where we touched on emotional issues. When asked what she was feeling when she "connected" to her stomach, she replied, "It was too scary to know." She did not want to pursue the issue any further. (This is not uncommon, as many clients fear exploring their feelings and fear physical sensations especially if they experienced physical trauma. Clinical judgment is necessary to know when to gently encourage further work and when to step back.) In this case, acknowledging the fact that she knew connecting to her stomach was a source of information and that she was afraid to find out what it was, was a sufficient breakthrough for one session. The acknowledgement in and of itself could prompt further processing of the issue in between sessions. At the next session, she brought in a poem describing her feelings. (Printed anonymously with her verbal permission):

Stomach!

If I connected to my stomach what would I see?

I'd see a little girl screaming at her knees.

If I connected to my stomach, what would I see?

I'd see old men staring down at me.

If I connected to my stomach what would I see?

I'd see a bunch of doctors trying to figure out me.

If I connected to my stomach what would I see?

I would see a black hole and no one looking at me.

If I connected to my stomach what would I see?

Why doesn't anybody just listen to me?!

This poem facilitated a discussion that revealed her experiential hologram related to a theme of being ignored (not listened to) and a personal truth that she was invisible and unimportant.

Recounting difficulties in present-day events and the emotions they elicit produce associations with earlier events. The earlier events may include memories of the trauma. However, in many cases, how the trauma is incorporated into the experiential system appears to be related to a "pre-trauma" hologram. Thus, HR continues to inquire about associations until formative events are revealed.

For example, one client came to therapy because she felt overwhelmed with anxiety, depression, anger, and guilt since her experiences as the sole nurse working on the night shift of a burn unit during the Vietnam War. She stated that she was tormented by nightmares about her patients who experienced tremendous pain, many of whom died during her shift. Instead of assuming what disturbed her about the experience, HR encourages further discovery. She identified feeling responsible ("I should have saved them," "It was up to me to help them") and angry with herself for not being able to do more and particularly angry with herself for currently having symptoms ("I'm such a wimp for being here").

By focusing on the feelings and associating to past events, we discovered that an event that occurred when she was five years old set a holographic stage for how she handled the events in the war. When she was five, she had to walk to school by herself. She had to pass by a house that had two large barking dogs in their front yard. This terrified her. She asked her parents to walk with her, but they told her that she was a "big girl" and could do it herself. This revealed her hologram of being left to fend for herself in the face of feeling overwhelmed. Her compensating strategy was that she "had to be tough." Everyday this hologram was reinforced as she ran by the house with the dogs. Later, during the war, she again was left to fend for herself. She recounted an event where a soldier was having cardiac problems and she paged the physician. He was annoyed by her page, told her some basic treatment and that he would not come in until the morning. The soldier died that night while she stayed by his bedside. She stopped asking for help. She felt alone, abandoned, helpless and yet responsible. She told herself to "be tough." She never allowed herself to grieve for losses, nor to have compassion for herself for what she endured. There were several other examples in her adult life that recapitulated this holographic theme. Her compensating strategy could not protect her from her feelings of helplessness, loneliness, and depression. She attempted suicide on two occasions and suffered from severe PTSD.

Words of Caution

The discovery process is an important and delicate phase in this therapy. It requires clients to open up parts of themselves that may feel particularly uncomfortable and vulnerable. The HR therapist needs to be sensitive to clients' experiences and to reinforce that they can rely on their foundation of coping skills and can use their feelings plan. As mentioned earlier, sometimes the process itself triggers an unfolding of associations in between sessions. Clients may revert to old self-destructive coping strategies or may complain of increased symptoms. Therefore, this process should not be rushed.

Also, the therapist can not assume what associations or what parts of an event are the source of the core violation. For example, even in a clear cut traumatic event such as a rape, it may seem that the source of violation or the source of an unresolved emotional blockage is the physical act that occurred. Usually, this is *not* the case and it would be an incorrect assumption. The goal is to find out specifically what about the event was emotionally traumatic and what remains emotionally unresolved, conflicted, or distressed? What aspects are incongruent with a client's assumptions about the self, others, and the world? There are a variety of issues that may need to be addressed such as loss of power, self-blame, betrayal, and loss of self-esteem. The discovery process finds out the specific associations and meanings for each person. Then the reprocessing or transformational part of the therapy is easily tailored for the client. In other words, this process is called "experiential discovery" with the emphasis on the word "discovery." The HR therapist is encouraged to stay true to the spirit of the word.

Finally, clients may associate to events that they have never spoken about before. If this is the case, then the therapist and client may need to discuss how they want to address this. Voicing what happened is often scary for clients. A supportive therapeutic alliance, reassurance (e.g., "You can do it!"), and encouragement to use coping skills (e.g., "Let's take a couple of Signal Breaths") helps clients to overcome their fears. Some clients may prefer to write about the incident before talking about it in therapy.

Summary of Techniques for Experiential Discovery

Connect with the Experience

The first step is for the client to identify feelings by connecting with his current experience. It is not sufficient to intellectualize the feelings but rather important to feel them because it opens the channels for association. Therapists can ask clients where in the body they feel the feeling. This helps bring focus to the sensations of the feeling thereby strengthening them.

Discover the Feeling

To help clients articulate exactly what they are feeling, therapists can ask them to list everything they are feeling. If a client is having difficulty generating words, the therapist can help by listing several feelings and then asking if any of them resonate for him. When a particularly strong or accurate feeling is articulated, the client will have a felt sense or experiential confirmation as Gendlin (1981) describes.

Free Association Following the Feeling

Finally, therapists can ask the client when she has felt this feeling before and wait for memories, images, or other associations to arise. Discuss the association and listen to the aspects that connect to a broader theme in the client's life.

What If Clients Have Difficulty Accessing Feelings?

Not all clients are able to access feelings and even if they can, not all are able to articulate them. Also, some clients have difficulty connecting with feelings in session. Nonetheless, the discovery process is still an important part of the therapy. One alternate technique is to create a time line of events. Therapists can ask clients to list all of the significant events that have happened to them. If a client has difficulty beginning at childhood (which could be for any number of reasons such as having memory loss for significant periods of childhood) then start with a time line of significant relationships. Because the goal is to find holographic themes, the same issues should be present from one relationship to the next. Sometimes people play out both extremes of an issue in various relationships such as being submissive and abused in one relationship and then being dominating and abusive in another relationship. The dynamics of each relationship should be noted and then therapists and clients look for repeating patterns or themes among the noted events. These themes become the working hypotheses for identifying the specific components of the experiential hologram. The therapist can also ask if the theme has been present in any other situation such as on a job, with friends, or with family members not already mentioned.

Seven Questions to Help Gather Information About Experiential Holograms

While working in the discovery phase with clients, the questions in Table 9.1 may help the therapist gather information and become aware of what is missing in their conceptualization. The therapist may ask these questions or clients may answer them by themselves. But the discovery process, in general, is designed to be collaborative between therapists and clients. The HR therapist can introduce the idea of "the pot on the stove" (see chapter 10) to the client and together they figure out the various components. Therapists are encouraged to stay with the "spirit of discovery" until both therapist and client agree that the description of the experiential hologram resonates on an experiential level, or in other words, feels right.

Additionally, a therapist may just want to write a description of a client's life including formative events from childhood, and significant events and relationships throughout adulthood, paying particular attention to features that seem to repeat themselves across time. What are the significant emotional events that occurred in the client's life? This can be written in a paragraph or on a time line.

Common Mistakes When Engaging in Experiential Discovery

There are several common mistakes that therapists might make when they are first learning experiential discovery. First, they may not engage the client's experiential system which activates the system of associations. Second, they may have difficulty identifying the client's feelings. Third, they may fail to do an adequate discovery about other feelings to find the one that "moves the body forward." Fourth, they may fail to fully explore the associations to uncover the client's core violation and associated emotional and behavioral responses. The following is an example of some mistakes that can be made when learning experiential discovery:

Table 9.1 Seven Questions to Elicit Experiential Holograms

Instructions:
Think of a past romantic or significant relationship and answer the following questions with brief descriptions. Then repeat the exercise for as many relationships as you can. Look at all of your answers and circle any answer that you wrote more than once. What patterns do you notice? (You may want to make columns on a piece of paper with each column representing a relationship. Then it is easy to see all of the answers on one page.)

Example:
1. What did you find initially attractive in that person?
Answer: "Self-assured, successful, competent"

1. What did you find initially attractive in that person?
2. What roles did you both play in the relationship (e.g., controlling, submissive, caretaker)?
3. What disappointed you with that person? You probably thought your partner was one way but turned out to be another—what way did he or she turn out to be?
4. How did you feel after the relationship was over?
5. What did you do to cope with those feelings?
6. What did you think about yourself after the relationship was over?
7. How do you feel in between relationships?

Trainee: My client stated that she feels her friend is being selfish. I asked what other feelings she was having and she said she felt hatred. I asked her where she felt the feeling and she said in her heart but she could not articulate the physical sensations. I asked her what the feeling could be conveying to her and she replied that her friend was a jerk. Then I explained that feelings convey that something important is going on and that understanding the message they're trying to express can reduce the intensity of the emotion. She stated she understood this idea and then we started working on a feelings plan.

What Is Wrong with the Above Example?

Although this therapist seemed to grasp many of the concepts of HR, it is apparent from this description that there is still a need for clarification. There are several mistakes. First of all the statement, "I feel my friend is selfish" is not a feeling. It is a thought, a judgment, and a perception about her friend. Just because someone uses the words "I feel" does not mean they are describing a feeling. Often people use the phrase "I feel" before declaring a statement as way to soften the statement. There is an implication of a feeling such as hurt, disappointment, or anger but the statement "my friend is being selfish" in and of itself is not a feeling.

Next, the therapist asked about "other" feelings and the client articulated the feeling of hatred. Hatred is a feeling and could have potentially been an opening for further discovery. The therapist should have explored what other feelings the client was having that fueled the hatred such as anger and hurt. It is likely she felt a host of other feelings such as jealousy, betrayal, or neglect. This would have given a richer glimpse into the client's experience and could have opened up a discussion about relationships where she felt similar feelings.

Then, the therapist asked what information the feeling could be conveying. This question was an attempt to find an association. Nonetheless, the client's response that "her friend was a jerk," did not further the exploration into the client's experiential system, but rather she maintained her focus on her friend. The exploration process was prematurely halted.

Finally, the therapist's closing comments were on an intellectual level revealing his disconnection from his client. He stated she understood this idea, which also revealed the collusion between client and therapist to stay on an intellectual level and avoid exploring the client's experiential hologram. The therapist basically confirmed the client's notion that her friend was "a jerk" and stated that articulating it would reduce the intensity of her hatred. Unfortunately, neither the client nor the therapist gained insight about the client's experiential hologram from this interchange.

A Case Example

As the previous example demonstrates, experiential discovery takes practice to master. The following case example is offered as a good example of a session with a client. It highlights some techniques used in experiential discovery and is followed through with a reprocessing procedure. However, in general practice, the discovery may take several sessions interspersed with learning new foundational coping skills to uncover the core issues. This session is written in the first person to give insight into the therapist's thinking during the therapy process. It is an excerpt from a previous publication (Katz, 2001).

> A middle-aged, well-dressed woman sat across from me and described feeling a vague sense of depression and malaise. She also mentioned feeling constipated and uncomfortable. She stated this has been occurring since last week and she did not know why.
>
> I asked her to close her eyes, focus on her feelings, and ask herself, "What am I feeling?" She thought for a moment and then said, "I'm feeling nothing really, kind of numb." I hypothesized that her

"depression" and "numbing" resulted from an attempt to avoid a different feeling. I also wondered if the avoided feeling is anger because of her symptom of constipation. I let these thoughts cross my mind and asked her to ask herself the same question again. She said, "I don't know, I feel kind of bad, kind of hurt." I asked her where she felt bad and hurt and to put her hand there. She indicated that she felt it in her stomach and intestine/bowel area. I said, "The body is a very sensitive instrument and knows exactly how you are feeling. It communicates directly with the unconscious mind. So ask your body if it feels anything else." By asking about her physical sensations, I bypass an intellectual discussion or lengthy explanation about her feelings. Instead, I pursue the associations from her experiential system.

She said, "I'm scared." "Take your time and do what is comfortable for you," I responded. This response did not deny her experience (i.e., don't be scared), but rather offered an empathic statement that could counter the subtle transference that she may be projecting onto me (i.e., "that she was scared to reveal herself to both of us"). She took in a deep breath and then started to rattle off a number of emotions, "hurt, upset, betrayed, lonely. . . ." "Anything else?" I waited.

Finally, she said, "I feel angry." I knew we had hit upon the core feeling by the way her whole body responded with relief to this acknowledgment. Her posture was more relaxed and her attention was more focused. I acknowledged, "Yes, you feel angry." She repeated, "Yes, I do! I feel really angry!" I could sense she really wanted to let this out, so I encouraged her to express what she was feeling. I repeated, "Yes, you do!" She burst into a sobbing release of tears. Through her gasps, she kept saying, "I'm so angry!!" After she hit the peak of her release and her crying subsided, I asked, "What are you angry at?"

She said, "My dentist!" She continued to sob. "I am angry at everyone! I am angry at my mother, and my neighbor, and the guy I met yesterday! I am just so angry!" I encouraged this release for another minute or so and then asked, "Who did you get particularly angry with last week?" I hypothesized in my mind that her sense of anger toward everyone may be a generalization from one particularly triggering event. I wanted to hear the specifics of the most upsetting event to gather clues about what was going on in her experiential system.

She then proceeded to tell me the story about her dentist. She had been working with this dentist for several weeks, and they had come to a point where she agreed to have a complicated bone graft and reconstructive surgery. She accumulated her finances and had $11,000 to pay for this. However, the dentist told her it would cost $14,000 and he refused her request to make payments for the additional $3,000. She was angry. She said, "I want to write him a nasty letter or write to his licensing board about his behavior!" I asked her how it feels to acknowledge her anger. She said, "Good, but I am still angry."

She said, "You know, it is scary for me to feel so angry." This implied to me that she had difficulty with anger in the past. As emotions of fear and anger were activated, I expected them to facilitate the retrieval of situations that evoked similar emotions in the past. I asked her, "Do you remember a time when it was particularly scary to feel anger?" She said, "Yes, when I was a child. I was abused by my alcoholic father. If I ever talked back to him or expressed my anger, my mother would take me down to the cellar. I was left alone in the cellar." I thought about the words she used to describe her feelings earlier in the session (hurt, upset, betrayed, lonely). I considered that several of these might be associated with this earlier event. As I was least sure about the word "betrayed," I wondered if this word might be related to both the dentist and to her early feelings of unexpressed anger. When asked about betrayal, she revealed that she harbors a deep sense of betrayal from her mother. Sometimes her mother was kind to her, and at other times she would physically abuse her.

I asked her if these were similar feelings to how she felt with the dentist. She thought about it for a moment and said that they were. She stated that she could not express her feelings to the dentist, and this was exactly like being locked up in the cellar. She also felt that he was kind to her during the diagnostics but then ended up betraying her. At this point, it becomes clear that her experiential hologram is exposed. The incident with the dentist is the perfect overlay for her experiential hologram. The core violation of someone betraying, intimidating, and controlling her was reminiscent of the feeling of "being locked in the cellar." Her personal truth of "I'm helpless," "It's not safe to express anger" lead to a coping strategy of suppressing her anger and developing somatic symptoms.

Based on the associative principle of the experiential system, I pointed out the connections between her current feelings and those of the emotional experiences of her past. The associations were made through similar feelings, use of words, and relevant images (being locked in the cellar). Also, I was able to point out her coping response as revealed through her behavioral demonstration in the office, including her fear of expressing her anger and her somatic symptoms. She acknowledged that these observations resonated with her as true.

Chapter Summary

This chapter reviewed the processes for experiential discovery including: (1) connecting with the experience, (2) identifying the feeling, and (3) associating to memories that evoke similar feelings. Also, answering a list of seven questions could help identify the components of an experiential hologram. Examples of poor and good descriptions of this process were provided.

CHAPTER **10**

Mapping Experiential Holograms

This chapter reviews a client-friendly method of how to map the six components of an experiential hologram. The model of a pot on the stove is used as a template to map each component. Several examples are provided to help therapists learn the skills of mapping holograms.

The Pot on the Stove

Identifying a client's experiential hologram is not always an easy task. Some therapists confuse the various components and some clients become overwhelmed with all of the new terms. Thus, a simple image of a pot on a stove is offered to help organize and explain the components of the experiential hologram. Each component is matched with an aspect of the image (e.g., the acquired motivation is matched with turning on the stove, and the core violation is matched with the hot burner). These will be outlined in the following paragraph. The image also helps describe a sequence of events that corresponds to a holographic cycle. Clients seem to be able to quickly grasp the components of their experiential hologram with the use of this image. They may be able to label the components themselves and thereby, increase their awareness of their own experiential hologram.

Review of the six components:

1. Acquired motivation
2. Core violation
3. Personal truth
4. Compensating coping strategies
5. Avoidance coping strategies
6. Residual negative emotions

The pot on the stove metaphor:

1. Turning on the stove corresponds to the acquired motivation and associated actions that initiate a cycle of the hologram.
2. The hot burner corresponds to the core violation that causes pain.
3. The boiling contents inside the pot correspond to the personal truth including the associated feelings, assumptions, and beliefs that boil to the surface.

4. and 5. The lid on the pot attempts to contain the boiling contents. The lid represents coping strategies. Keeping the lid on tight to avoid the steam is the "avoidance strategy," and keeping the lid on loosely to release the pressure of the steam is the "compensating strategy."

6. The steam that escapes from the pot corresponds to the residual negative emotions that linger in between cycles of the hologram.

For example, Sheila feels lonely and anxious. She grew up with a father who has a history of ignoring her while spending his time dating many

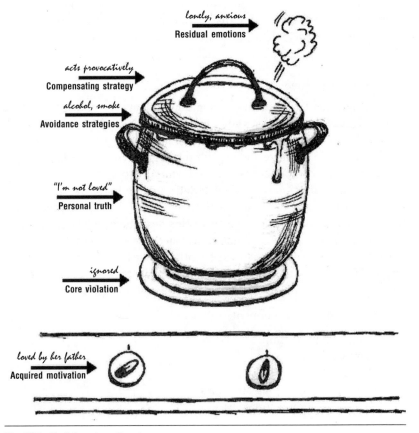

Fig. 10.1 Sheila's pot on the stove.

women. She longs to be loved by her father and unconsciously chooses to date men like him (turns on the stove). Soon, they ignore her while sexualizing other women (hot burner). Sheila feels that she is neither loved, nor desired (boiling contents) so compensates by acting provocatively (compensating lid). She also avoids her feelings by drinking alcohol and smoking cigarettes (avoiding lid).

Learning Exercises

To help therapists become familiar with mapping the components of experiential holograms, several descriptions of clients are offered as examples to develop skills for mapping holograms.

Exercise 1: Stephen/Stephanie

Stephen experienced criticism and rejection as a child from his father. His father was an angry man. He tended to get annoyed with people, held grudges against them and then expressed his frustration on Stephen. If Stephen performed poorly, his father would use it as evidence to put him down. If he did well, his father would still put him down. He stated, "My father would pick apart everything good that I did." For example, when he got good grades or was given an award for his scholastic achievement, his father would put him down for being "too full of himself." Stephen also reported that his father never listened to him. Everything was a one-way discussion with his father telling him how things should be. As a result, Stephen developed the belief that he was "wrong" and unworthy of attention and love. In order to avoid associated negative feelings about himself, he used the defense of blame and anger. This anger made him feel good at first, but then it became destructive and he couldn't control it. He saw himself becoming like his father.

Stephen also felt conflicted about his gender. Although he never told his father, he always felt he was supposed to be a female. As an adult, he went through counseling and decided to have a gender reassignment operation. He became Stephanie, but continues to feel the distress he felt before the operation. She has been depressed for the past 3 years. In order to compensate for her feelings of being inadequate, she continues to use anger and, as a result, threatens and rejects others. In general, she is very defensive and argumentative. She criticizes others before they have a chance to criticize her. She also talks incessantly so that others won't have a chance to say anything to her. Unfortunately, by these strategies she is setting up the repeating pattern of being criticized and rejected because people do not want to be in relationship with such an angry, pushy person. It is easy to find reasons to reject and criticize her. And her hologram stays in place.

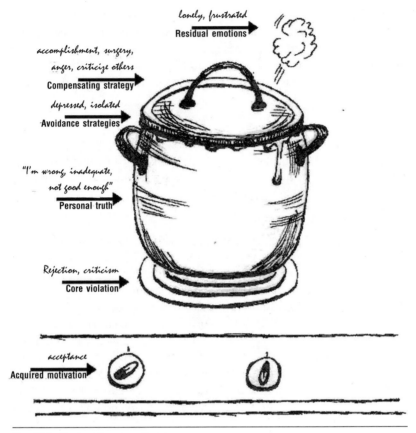

Fig. 10.2 Stephanie's pot on the stove.

Acquired motivation: Seeking to be accepted and okay with herself.
Core violation: Rejection and criticism
Personal truth: I'm wrong, inadequate, flawed, not good enough, unlovable.
Compensating strategies: Try to accomplish scholastically and financially, use anger to feel powerful instead of inadequate, criticize others, reject others.
Avoidance strategies: Depression, isolation from others, or dominates the conversation
Residual negative emotions: Lonely, frustrated

Exercise 2: Lorna

Lorna is a 62-year-old single Hispanic American female. She presented to therapy because of stress and depression. The precipitating event was being fired from her job as a waitress in a coffee shop after 16 years. She believes she was fired because of her age and the rasing costs of health care insurance. She loved her job. She looked forward to seeing her regular customers who always asked for her. The job gave her a routine, friends, self-esteem, and, of course, income. She stated that the job was her life. Other than her job, her life revolved around taking care of her elderly mother and attending church on Sundays.

Lorna and her younger sister agreed to move into their mother's home so they could share the responsibility of caring for her. However, Lorna does most of the work while her sister socializes with her friends. Lorna feels taken advantage of by her sister and her mother. Neither has acknowledged her losses from her job and neither shows concern for her depression. Lorna does not have any personal friendships and feels obligated to stay at home (except for running errands and making doctor's appointments) to take care of her mother. She stated she feels drained, tired, and disappointed. She feels she gives all that she can to others, but that they do not give to her in return.

Lorna's hologram is replicated in her dating history. When she was much younger, she used to throw herself into her relationships and was willing to do anything to please her boyfriends. She ended these relationships after feeling mistreated and used. (One relationship ended after she found out that her fiancée was cheating on her, another ended after she was fed up with her boyfriend who did not work but expected Lorna to pay for everything, do all of the housework, and demanded that she serve him.)

Lorna's childhood history included being sexually abused by her maternal grandfather starting at age 6. She feels deeply guilty and ashamed about this because although she knew it was wrong, she allowed it to continue. She thought that because he wanted it, she was supposed to please him. She harbors "resentment and hurt" because she was not protected from the abuse by her mother. She is also resentful because she was expected to take care of her younger sister while her mother went out and socialized.

Acquired motivation: Seeks to secure love, affection, and attention

Core violation: Neglect

Personal truth: I'm not important. I won't be noticed or loved unless I please others.

Compensating strategies: Please others, be "good" to earn love, choose relationships where others are dependent on her.

Avoidance strategies: Depression, neglects own needs, isolates from others

Residual negative emotions: Lonely, drained, and tired

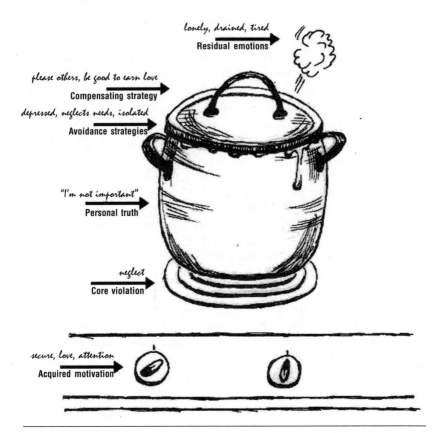

Fig. 10.3 Lorna's pot on the stove.

Example 3: Michelle

Michelle was an African American woman in her mid-fifties. She discussed a situation in which she had plans to go out for the evening with a friend. This was particularly important for her since she had been isolated from social contacts for several months. Her friend was driving and they ended up going to the motel where her friend's new boyfriend was staying. They went to his room and agreed to stay for a while. They decided to watch a movie. Her friend was on the bed next to her boyfriend and Michelle sat in a side chair. Her friend and boyfriend started kissing. Michelle felt helpless and trapped. She tried to ignore them but became increasingly agitated. She thought she was going to have a panic attack. Without warning, she flew into a rage. She started yelling at them and demanded that she and her friend leave at once or she would do something drastic. They tried to calm her down which escalated into more yelling. Eventually, they left. She has not spoken with her friend since.

Michelle has a history of being raped in her early twenties while she was serving in the U.S. military. She went to an officer's party and met a handsome officer. When he invited her to go on a walk, he pushed her to the ground and pinned her down so she could not move. Afterward, she attempted to file charges against him but she was never given any support. In fact, she was told to "just deal with it." He was never prosecuted.

Acquired motivation: Seeks healthy trusting relationships
Core violation: Being trapped, betrayed, controlled, dominated
Personal truth: I'm helpless, I'm powerless. I was duped and tricked; therefore I am stupid and naïve.
Compensating strategies: "Be powerful" uses rage to assert control, demand for justice
Avoidance strategies: Panic attack, anxiety, isolation and depression
Residual negative emotions: Lonely

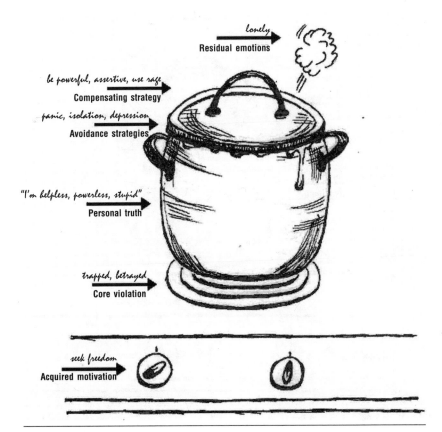

Fig. 10.4 Michelle's pot on the stove.

Example 4: A client

A client says to her therapist, "If you let me down, I will leave you." Although, no life details are presented in this example, what hypothesis can be generated about this person's experiential hologram based on this one sentence?

> *Acquired motivation:* Seeks trust
> *Core violation:* She was "let down or left" either disappointed, betrayed, or abandoned.
> *Personal truth*: I'm helpless, I'm powerless."
> *Compensating strategies:* I'll leave you. Assert control.
> *Avoidance strategies:* Probably isolation, avoids working through relationships
> *Residual negative emotions:* Probably lonely

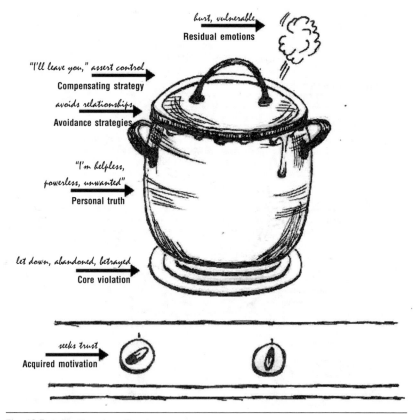

Fig. 10.5 A client's pot on the stove.

Identifying Components

Personal Truths and Compensating Strategies

Personal truths and compensating strategies may be components that are opposites of each other. For example, if the personal truth is "I'm powerless" then the compensating strategy would be "be powerful." Similarly, "I'm unworthy, unimportant, and unwanted" goes with "Be worthy, important, and wanted." "I'm wrong, not good enough, incompetent" goes with "Be right, be extra good, or perfect," and "Be competent." "I'm stupid, naïve, and a sucker" goes with "Be smart, cleaver, and shrewd." "I'm bad and upsetting to others" goes with "Be good and appeasing to others." And "I'm an embarrassment, unacceptable and disgusting to others" goes with "Be acceptable and non-offensive to others."

Also, compensating strategies may be the opposite of the core violation such as if someone feels criticized and rejected, it is common to find that she criticizes or rejects others. Doing the very behavior to others that is experienced as violating, is a strategy to rid the self of the disempowering feelings caused by the behavior. This is close to the phenomena that is referred to as "identifying with the perpetrator." Victims feel that the perpetrator is the strong one with power, therefore, to be like the perpetrator means having the power. This, of course, is not true since perpetrators do not have authentic power and in fact, are only playing out a piece of the same continuum of powerlessness. Compensating by "doing to others what was done to you" most likely leads to the recapitulation of the hologram. For example, Kelly who was sexually abused and dominated by men, also has a history of seducing and then "dumping" men. Although, she feels more "powerful" being the one who ends the relationship, she avoids developing intimate fulfilling relationships. Either way, she has the residual emotions associated with feeling empty and lonely.

Incorrectly Identifying the Core Violation

A traumatic event such as rape, even if it occurred several times through out a person's life, would not be considered the core violation. Although it is clearly a physical violation, there is no information about what made the event *emotionally* violating. It may sound strange to ask, but what about the rape was violating? Was it a betrayal, loss of power, loss of self-esteem, humiliation, or threat of loss of life? In other words, the core violation is not a specific external event (i.e., natural disaster, accident, combat), but rather it is the emotional pain that is associated with the event (i.e., neglect, rejection, betrayal, threat of loss of life).

A specific event such as "baby brother was born" may have been emotionally traumatic for a client but it is also not the core violation. The core violation should be a theme that is present across several events in a person's life. It may be helpful to list specific traumatic events and then as part of the discovery process, ponder with the client about what emotional themes are present across the events. For example, the client might have felt ignored when her baby brother was born. This may be one of many events where the client felt ignored. Therefore, the core violation would be feeling ignored.

It is recommended that therapists spend sufficient time to correctly and precisely identify the components of their client's experiential hologram. It may be something that is refined and revised throughout the therapy. However, the clearer the hologram the better it is for setting the stage for reprocessing.

Chapter Summary

This chapter gave several examples of client descriptions to practice mapping the six components of experiential holograms. The template of a pot on the stove was used as a metaphor to explain and organize the six components.

CHAPTER 11

Reprocessing I

Overview and Non-Arousing Revisiting Techniques

> This chapter provides on overview and general guidelines for the prac-
> tice of reprocessing. Nine steps will be outlined. Each step is illustrated
> by excerpts of a session between a therapist and a client. Information
> on how to ensure minimal arousal during reprocessing is covered.
> Suggestions for how to manage a client who is unable to do the tech-
> niques or becomes overwhelmed are also included.

What Is Reprocessing?

As discussed in earlier chapters, reprocessing is a method to alter or recon-
struct a client's perception of a past event that has been poorly or partially
processed and remains the source of lingering emotional strife. The emotional strife has been referred to as "a blockage" because the poor processing
renders people stuck in a pattern of relationships and events that replicates
an aspect of the original trauma. These are the experiential holograms that
have been previously discussed. The source of the experiential hologram
may include a limiting or negative perception about the self, an unresolved
conflict, an undelivered communication, or constricted affect such as guilt
and self-blame.

Reprocessing allows clients to revisit and revise the source of their hologram through imagery, emotional activation, association, and fantasy. These
are ways of reaching the experiential system according to the theory of CEST
(Epstein, 1998). Clients imagine that they re-visit the younger version of
themselves who lived through the traumatic event. The younger version of
the self is the person who experienced any event of the past. In other words,

reprocessing is not limited for events that occurred in childhood. Clients imagine that they remain their current age and look back on a scene from the vantage point of an observer. Not only are they able to view the scene from a new perspective but, they are also able to imagine interacting with the characters in the scene for the purpose of bringing closure to the client. This approach is distinct from a rational, verbal, intellectual reprocessing of the event as it is accomplished in the experiential system where the emotional blockage resides.

Reprocessing is not a procedure for reviewing an entire event of trauma for the purpose of integration. In fact, if clients are not able to talk about an event, have fragmented or disorganized memories, or are not certain about what has happened to them, then they are *not* candidates for reprocessing.

Guidelines for Practicing Reprocessing

There are nine steps for reprocessing:

1. Asking for permission
2. Contextualizing the scene
3. Inducing relaxation
4. Approaching the scene
5. Setting the stage
6. Assessing the client's level of distress
7. Rescripting the scene
8. Completing the scene and ending the exercise
9. Debriefing with the client

The following are guidelines for practicing the nine steps of reprocessing. Interspersed is dialogue between a therapist and client to illustrate each step.

Step 1. Asking for permission. The first step is to ask the client if she is ready to go back and "re-work" the traumatic scene. The therapist explains the rationale for the exercise, describes the procedure, and obtains permission to proceed. In other words, this is an informed consent. It is recommended to keep the discussion brief and immediately preceding the exercise. For some clients, thinking about doing an exercise where they revisit their trauma is anxiety provoking (regardless of a rational explanation that they will be observing the event not re-experiencing it). Therefore, it is recommended to discuss the procedure on the day of the exercise to minimize the client's level of anxiety.

Step 2. Contextualizing the scene. Before doing a reprocessing exercise, the therapist and client discuss the facts of the scene (e.g., what lead up to the event? Who was there? And what happened?). The therapist may use one or more appropriate preparation techniques such as "age comparison" and "finding multiple truths." These techniques, which are discussed in detail in chapter 12, initiate a cognitive shift for understanding the trauma in new ways.

Therapist: . . . You have been describing how you feel unable to take care of yourself and make decisions since your husband has gotten ill. We've discussed how this was also the feeling you had in other situations when you faced a big change. We've also discussed that one of the events in your life that was particularly distressing was when your first husband became ill and passed away. I'm wondering if you would like to do an exercise today where we look back at that time and work through it a bit. You would stay your current age and interact with the younger version of yourself.

Client: Okay. How do we do it?

Therapist: Well, first we have to decide on the scene.

Client: Like right after my husband died?

Therapist: Yes, that would be perfect. Can you describe the scene that you are thinking about such as who was there and what happened?

Client: We were alone in the apartment and the paramedics came and took him away.

Step 3: Relaxation. A variety of relaxation techniques can be used to help clients relax (e.g., Signal Breath, Body Scan, Guided Imagery, Mindfulness Meditation). The purpose for relaxation is to help clients feel safe and comfortable during the procedure as anxiety could interfere with their ability to maintain imagery. The therapist can assess the client's level of relaxation on a 10-point scale with 1 being completely relaxed and 10 being completely tense. The relaxation techniques should continue until both the client and therapist feel that the client is relaxed and ready to proceed.

Therapist: Okay . . . The first thing we're going to do is some relaxation. So, if you are ready, go ahead and close your eyes and take a couple of deep breaths . . . good. Now let's do a Signal Breath . . . take a deep breath in through your nose . . . hold it . . . and now release it through your mouth. (*Repeat three times.*) Now on a scale of 1 to 10 where 1 is completely relaxed and 10 is very tense, where are you?

Client: Oh, I'm about a 5.

Therapist: Great. Continue to breath with nice, slow, deep breaths . . . very easy, very relaxing. Feel your feet on the ground and imagine they are warm and heavy. Feel your ankles, calves, and thighs. Imagine each part getting more and more relaxed. Feel your back as it sinks further into the chair. Now imagine relaxing your shoulders and arms . . feeling very, very relaxed. With each breath, imagine you are breathing in relaxation and exhaling any tension that's left in your body. On the scale of 1 to 10, where are you now?

Client: About a 3.

Therapist: Very good. Now imagine that you are walking into a magical forest. It's a beautiful sunny day and you can feel the warmth of the sun on your skin. You look up and can see the clear blue sky between the branches of the tall pines. And you can smell the hint of pine in the fresh air. You can hear some birds chirping in the distance as you continue to walk along a dirt path. You take a deep breath to breathe in all of the beauty of the day.

Step 4: Approaching the scene. As the therapist continues to encourage the client to relax, the client can be guided to approach the scene (e.g., the house where the client grew up). The therapist mentions the scene but states that it is far away and in the distance. Maybe it is hazy and difficult to see. Then, the client slowly approaches the scene while it becomes more clear. During this process the therapist assesses the client's level of relaxation. If the client appears very tense or states a number that is much higher than previous assessments, then the therapist refocuses on relaxation. (Note: It is not uncommon for clients to have a slight increase in their level of tension as they approach the house.) The therapist can use the pace and tone of her voice to induce a safe, relaxing feeling or may prefer to focus on using slow, deep breathing until a relaxed state is re-established.

Therapist: Imagine you are still walking in the forest. Notice how relaxed you are feeling as you are enjoying the beautiful scenery. As you look ahead, in the far distance, through a foggy haze, you can see the house that you and your first husband lived in. You notice a path that leads to the house, and as you continue to walk down the path, you are nearing the house. As you observe the house what level of relaxation are you at now?

Client: (*softly*) I'm still about a 3.

Therapist: As you walk closer to the house, the haze begins to lift and you can see the house more clearly. As you approach the front of the house, what level of relaxation are you at?

Client: 4.

Therapist: Okay, keep breathing, nice and slowly. Releasing the breath . . . When you begin to feel a bit more relaxed, and only when you are ready, approach the front door of that house remaining the 71-year-old woman that you are today.

Step 5: Setting the stage. Based on the information the client has shared in previous sessions, the therapist can ask questions to help the client set up the characters in the scene. The therapist might ask the client to describe the scene. (Note: The scene should not be an image of trauma but rather just before or after.)

Therapist: As you walk into the house, what do you see?
Client: I see the kitchen to the left, and the living room directly in front of me. There is a couch in the living room. . . . (*the client continues to describe the house*).
Therapist: As you continue to look around the house can you see a woman who is 22? What is she is doing?
Client: (*beginning to cry*) She is standing in the door way, watching the paramedics take her husband out on a gurney. (*She stops talking and continues to cry*). Now she is sitting on the couch.

Step 6: Assessing the client's level of distress. The therapist observes the client and assesses if she appears to be overwhelmed or highly emotional. The client is encouraged to maintain the observer vantage point and to remain her current age. If necessary, the therapist may need to intervene to help the client manage these feelings. There are several techniques to reduce emotional upset (see later in this chapter). The idea is for the therapist to reinforce the fact that the client is not actually in the scene but is observing it from a safe distance and he is in control of the image. This will help to reduce strong negative emotions.

Step 7: Rescripting the scene. Next, the therapist asks the client what she would like to do and/or say to 1) the perpetrator or 2) the injured or hurt younger version of the self. The client is instructed to imaginally do and/or say these things. The therapist may take on the voice of one of the characters to facilitate role-playing.

Therapist: What is the 22-year-old woman experiencing?
Client: She is in shock. She cannot say anything. She wants to know that he's okay.
Therapist: Do you want to speak with her husband and find out if he is okay?
Client: (*still crying*) I don't know . . . Yea, I do.
Therapist: How would you like to do that?

Client: I can speak to his spirit.

Therapist: Okay, then imagine his spirit is in the room with you and the 22–year-old. Ask him what you want to know.

Client: Are you okay? I mean . . . I know you're not in pain, it's just that . . . (*client is crying*)

Therapist: It's just that . . . ?

Client: It's just that it's unfair that you had to go! It's so unfair! We were supposed to have our whole lives together!

Therapist: (*As the voice of her husband*) I know, I thought we were too. But I have had other things I had to do. I've watched you grow up to be a wonderful woman.

Client: "I will always love you."

Therapist: (*As the voice of her husband*) I will always love you too. (*As therapist*) Is there anything else you want to say?

Client: Good-bye. . . . (*client is tearful. There is a long pause.*)

Therapist: How are you doing?

Client: I'm okay.

Therapist: As the woman you are today, is there anything that you would like to say to the woman who is 22 who is sitting on the couch?

Client: I'm so sorry this happened.

Therapist: (*As the voice of the 22-year-old*) Yea, me too."

Client: We have to take care of ourselves from now on. We can't let our family make decisions for us anymore. (*Pause . . .*)

Therapist: Is there anything else you want to say?

Client: I am sitting close to her (the 22-year-old) and I put my arm around her. Everything is going to be all right. I know, I've already been there. You're going to be fine. We're going to be fine.

Step 8: Completing the scene and end the exercise. If the client is complete with the scene she can imagine leaving the younger self in the original context or move her to another place. Some clients prefer to imagine holding the younger version of the self in their hearts, some prefer to keep them in the house, and others prefer to remove them from the house and take them to a safe place in the forest. The therapist asks what the client wants and guides them through the imagery. Afterward, the client is instructed to walk back through the forest while the therapist facilitates the client's awareness of the here and now.

Therapist: Are you ready to complete your visit?

Client: (*Nods yes*) But I want to take her to a special place that is just for her.

Therapist: Okay, where do you want to take her?

Client: How about a beautiful garden . . .

Therapist: Okay. Imagine walking with the 22-year-old, out of the house, and into the most beautiful garden. Imagine it exactly how you want it to be.

Client: We're sitting on a bench. (*Silence*) I told her I will always know where to find her and she'll be safe here with the birds and flowers. . . . I'm ready to go.

Therapist: Now, take a deep breath in and release it. Imagine walking back through the forest. Remembering where you are, in this room, sitting on this couch. (*Deep breath*). When you are ready you, slowly open your eyes.

Step 9: Debriefing with the client. After the procedure, clients may want to discuss what their experience was like, how they are feeling, or may just want a few moments of silence. The therapist can answer questions and help clients stay connected to their experience or in therapy terms, "sit with their feelings." Some clients go through a period of time where they work on incorporating the experience. It is helpful if therapists encourage their clients to take care of themselves in the weeks following reprocessing. Clients may recall certain memories, or may have unusual dreams, or insights. They may want to discuss their experience over several sessions. Other clients report that the exercise itself brought them closure and seem to have immediate acceptance of the new reprocessed perception.

Debrief: The client discussed her feelings about the exercise. She stated that she felt more at peace with the death of her first husband. During the next few sessions, the client reported many instances in which she had the strength to make decisions that best suited her needs regardless of what others encouraged her to do. She reported that she "definitely felt stronger" even though her current husband continued to be ill and she feared his death would be soon.

Ensuring Minimal Arousal During Exposure

Several techniques are used to ensure therapeutic emotional distance, a sense of safety, and relaxation throughout the exercise. The following are descriptions of some of these techniques.

Maintaining an observer vantage point. As discussed in chapter 5, the observer vantage point helps clients focus on what happened in a situation rather than on their affective experience. It may be helpful to use a model such as "observe the situation as if you are a reporter (scientist, or detective) gathering facts (data, or evidence)." It is important to encourage clients to describe the scene in the third person (i.e., "The girl did this" instead of "I did this.")

Remaining the current age. Therapists reinforce that clients remain their current age looking back at a younger version of themselves. (The person who experienced any event of the past is by definition a younger version of the self.) This creates emotional distance and helps maintain the observer vantage point. The current age also helps anchor clients in the "here and now."

Hindsight advantage. The outcome of the situation is already known. The fact that the client is sitting in the therapist's office means that she is "okay" and she has survived. This is particularly helpful when reprocessing events where there was a threat of danger. For example, a client who survived a near fatal accident was able to tell the younger version of herself that she was going to be "okay." First of all, this helped her to be able to revisit the event since she was terrified of reliving the pain. Secondly, the hindsight advantage helped her release her fear and integrate the feelings she had about going through the accident.

Communicating with clients. During the reprocessing, it is important for therapists to communicate with their clients. Some therapists may feel that talking will bring the client out of the relaxed state. The goal is not to have full conversations per se because that would interfere with the procedure. Rather, the therapist can ask questions requiring short responses to keep in communication. For example, a therapist might ask how clients are feeling, how relaxed are they on the 1 to 10 scale, and if they are ready to proceed. The therapist reassures clients that they can slow down, shift images, or stop at any time during the exercise.

Observing and monitoring clients. It is up to the therapist to keenly observe the body language of their clients. The therapist should notice if the client appears tense or uncomfortably shifts positions. One clue is to pay attention to clients' faces. If their eyebrows furor or they look worried or in distress, a therapist can ask what is going on and possibly redirect the scene. Not all intense emotions are signs to intervene. Many clients cry during this procedure and this could be a sign that they are fully engaged in the imagery.

Redirecting the imagery. Despite efforts to maintain emotional distance, it is possible for clients to have an abreaction (an emotional or physical reexperiencing of the trauma). Usually this occurs if the client cannot maintain the observer vantage point. It is recommended that the therapist remains calm and conveys confidence that the client can "breathe through" the sensations. The therapist helps the client redirect the imagery to a "safe place," or shifts the client's focus to the here and now, by bringing her attention to the breath, to feeling her feet on the ground, or to an object in the room. The therapist can reassure her that she is "okay."

For example, Dee Dee was doing a reprocessing exercise where she revisited a scene when she was four years old. Her father was playing "Russian roulette" with his gun. He pulled the trigger while holding the gun to her temple and she wet her pants. Then he laughed. In the reprocessing exercise, we visited the little girl after the scene to comfort her. However, even though we made clear attempts to visit her after the trauma had already occurred, Dee Dee became very upset and afraid. The first line of intervention was to remind her of her current age and that she is okay. Dee Dee identified with the little girl and could not keep her emotional distance. At that point, she was quickly redirected to a safe place—a garden. We remained in the garden until Dee Dee felt calm again.

Changing attributes. One way to increase emotional distance during reprocessing is to change the attributes of size, distance, clarity, color, and sound of the imagery. In general, when clients describe a traumatic image, it is big (life size), close (right in their face), clear, bright, and loud. In other words, a traumatic image is big and bold. Changing these attributes to smaller, further away, fuzzy, black and white, and silent allows clients to maintain emotional distance from the event. The image is easier to tolerate. Changing one attribute may be sufficient, or some clients may need several or all of the attributes to be muted.

Chapter Summary

This chapter presented an overview of the techniques for reprocessing. It demonstrated how HR facilitates a constructive reorganization of the perception of trauma which in turn modifies the associated emotional and behavioral tendencies that render people stuck in the repetitive cycling of experiential holograms. The nine steps of reprocessing were illustrated by a dialogue between a client and therapist. It also presented seven techniques to ensure minimal arousal during reprocessing.

CHAPTER 12

Reprocessing II
Preparation

This chapter focuses on the first three of the nine steps of reprocessing, namely: "Asking for permission," "Contextualizing the scene," and "Inducing relaxation." These steps prepare clients for reprocessing. Strategies such as "Age comparison," and "Finding multiple truths" are presented. This chapter also includes a detailed description of a relaxation script.

Case Example: From Idol to Idiot

This example illustrates a course of therapy whereby several months were spent on stabilization including addressing issues of medications, addictions, and pseudo-seizures. Next, there was a phase of deepening the therapy and identifying her experiential hologram. This example also illustrates in a naturalistic manner the technique of "age comparison."

Barbara was a 27-year-old Hispanic American woman who presented with a complex mixture of problems. These included abusing multiple medications used for multiple medical problems prescribed by multiple doctors including a neurologist, urologist, gynecologist, internist, gastro-intestinal specialist and two psychiatrists, all of whom did not have contact with each other. She also was having 12 to 16 seizures per day. Although she was married, she was living with her parents while her husband was stationed in a different state serving in the military. She moved to her parents' home because her medication abuse had become so extreme that she did not get out of bed. Her husband had enabled her addiction, as it freed him to go out with his friends and to have affairs with other women. Barbara's parents insisted that she came home. Barbara's mother accompanied her to every appointment since Barbara could not drive.

Barbara had a history of sexual trauma, which was why she was referred to me. I assured her that her history was something to address but that she first needed to get chemically and medically stable. Her primary care physician was identified and Barbara requested that her mother provide him with a list of all of her medications and all of her pending doctor's appointments. She also agreed to have one psychiatrist and he too was given a list of all of her medications. Her primary care physician referred her for a diagnostic work-up for seizures and the tests showed negative results. She was given a diagnosis of pseudo-seizures. Slowly, her medications were decreased. All medications were stored in a locked cabinet. Her mother was in charge of dispensing the medications. Barbara was encouraged to attend Narcotics Anonymous which she did on a sporadic basis. I remained in contact with both her psychiatrist and primary care physician who seemed particularly pleased that she was in therapy. We agreed that she was more alert and significantly better since decreasing her medications.

The next issue was decreasing her pseudo-seizures. We discussed the situations leading up to the seizures and identified that they seemed to occur at times of stress and, in particular, when Barbara felt angry. In response to the seizures, her mother was very attentive and Barbara's emergency seemed to stop the immediate chaos in her environment.

During one session, Barbara was describing how her alcoholic father became belligerent when he drank. She rolled her eyes back and started to shake. I calmly talked to her in a soothing voice and let her know that she was okay. She came out of it and we both took some deep breaths together. She stated she was able to hear me, which seemed to be helpful. She asked to go to the bathroom. When she returned, her mother came into the office and sat down next to Barbara. She started having a second pseudo-seizure. Her mother demonstrated her response of being anxious and attentive. I modeled how to remain calm and to "talk her down." Her mother seemed appreciative because she had been feeling helpless and overwhelmed. Both Barbara and her mother felt contained and safe. In subsequent sessions, we continued to frame the seizures as a strategy to avoid or minimize intense feelings of anger and stress. Eventually, she stopped this behavior. She learned how to tolerate her feelings and appropriately express herself.

Next, we began discussing patterns of abuse in her family and in her relationships. She saw how the men in her family were verbally and emotionally abusive and how the women in her family were submissive and enabling. Barbara discussed her own history of relationships including: (1) her current husband who "at least doesn't hit me" but constantly lies, cheats with multiple women, and steals her money; (2) the countless number of men Barbara had previously seduced, used, and dumped and her continuing to do so by meeting men on the Internet, fabricating stories about herself, and then abruptly ending the relationship, and finally, (3) the torturous relationship she had with a gang member.

We identified her experiential hologram including a core violation of "endangerment" (which encompasses multiple core violations), a *personal truth* of being a worthless, powerless objectified sex object or "being a piece of meat" as she described it, a *compensating strategy* of making others feel worthless and powerless, *avoidance strategies* of using medications and a history of drugs and alcohol, excessive sleep, avoiding responsibilities, and pseudo-seizures, *residual negative emotions* of feeling lonely, bored, empty, and an *acquired motivation* to "get attention."

This pattern was evident in almost every action and relationship that she discussed. We explored her childhood and the origins of this pattern. She stated when she was 5 years old she was sodomized by her 17-year-old cousin. He was in charge of babysitting her and her neighbor's two children. Barbara described how she felt "special" because he always wanted to play with her in the house while the other kids were sent outside to play. One day the play escalated into sodomy, which caused her "unbearable pain." Because she wanted to be with him and she liked the special attention, she concluded that the sexual activity was her fault. She also developed a personal truth that she was a "sex object" and the way to get attention was to be sexually provocative. Reprocessing would address this scene by (1) putting Barbara in an empowering role to respond to her cousin, (2) help her release feelings of guilt, and (3) shift perceptions that she was a sex object rather than an innocent girl who just wanted attention and love.

Barbara was ready to engage in reprocessing on the bases of the following: we had a good rapport, she was medically and chemically stable, she was able to use coping skills to tolerate and manage affect, we identified her experiential hologram, and we identified the target event to be rescripted. We worked on the preparation for reprocessing. We discussed how she always thought her cousin was the "greatest man on earth." She was asked, "Now that you are 27 years old, what do you think about a 17–year-old forcing sodomy on a five-year-old?" She said, "It's sick!" "What is?" I asked. "He is." "Why do you say that?" "Because he just is! A 17-year-old guy shouldn't be messing around with a child. It's just wrong!" "Do you know anything else about your cousin, like whatever happened to him?" "Yea, he's a real idiot. I don't know what happened to him. I know he went to jail for auto theft . . . I think he's like a recluse or something. I think he lives in Nebraska or maybe Iowa, I'm not sure."

"And how about the 5-year-old? How old is your nephew, isn't he around 5?" "He's a little over four and a half . . ." "Ah huh, and do you think he would know if he was being manipulated?" "Tommy? He's so gullible! I tease him all the time. He believes everything I say and then I have to tell him Auntie Barbara is only teasing and then he goes around repeating it over and over again. . . . He's always following me. He's cute but he can get really annoying." "Little kids like a lot of attention." Yea, that's for sure!" "And it's perfectly normal for a little kid to idolize his aunt . . . or her cousin." "Yea, I guess so . . ."

Next we discussed the reprocessing procedure. "Are you ready to do an exercise where we go back in time and revisit the 5-year-old who was being babysat?" Barbara seemed hesitant, "What do I have to do?" "Well, first we'll do some relaxation and then, staying your current age, we'll look back on the scene with the 5-year-old. You can imagine talking with her and letting her know how you feel about things. How does that sound?" "Okay."

During the reprocessing, she removed the perpetrator by calling the police. With the police present, she envisioned herself literally kicking him out of the house. She told him to "Get a life!" She saw that the abuse was not the 5-year-old's fault and that she innocently just wanted attention. She held and comforted her younger self. Afterward, she reported feeling much better.

The next phase of therapy discussed her "addiction to attention" and avoidance of building mature, sustainable relationships. This included a distinction between doing what is right (which she is usually aware of) versus doing what feels good in the moment. We discussed that she needed to work on herself so that she values herself more. She increased her ability to hold her boundaries, increased her responsibilities starting with doing home chores, increased positive recreational activities such as joining a gym, and enrolled to take one class in junior college. Throughout the remainder of this therapy, she referred to the positive efforts she made in her life as things she did to "nurture her little girl."

Barbara came back to visit about a year after she completed therapy. She wanted me to know that she was doing "great." She was enrolled in school full time and stated she was sober from her addictions to men. When asked if she had anymore "seizures" since therapy and she stated "not one single one!" She stated she was taking good care of herself and was very grateful for the therapy.

Preparing for Reprocessing: The First Three Steps

Before attempting to reprocess, it is necessary to understand the nature of the client's experiential hologram. As illustrated by the trainee's example in chapter 9, without a thorough understanding, the rescripting could miss the problem. The work of mapping experiential holograms and discussing formative experiences through experiential discovery should give both the therapist and client a clear sense of the issue that is in need of addressing. When the timing is appropriate, reprocessing begins with the first three steps: (1) asking for permission, (2) contextualizing the scene, and (3) inducing relaxation.

Step 1: Asking for Permission

This step includes several tasks such as presenting the rationale for the procedure, describing the procedure itself, offering reassurances and answering questions, and finally obtaining permission to proceed.

1. Present rationale for the procedure. This is usually a brief statement explaining that going back to revisit the event will help view it in a new way. It is an opportunity to rework the scene and possibly dialogue with the younger version of the self. As noted earlier, it is recommended that this is done immediately prior to beginning the process as anticipation of revisiting an event may induce anxiety.

2. Explaining the steps of the procedure. Before doing any procedure, it is important to explain exactly what will happen and what the client can expect to experience in the exercise. The therapist can briefly explain the processes of relaxation, guided imagery, slowly approaching the scene, using the observer vantage point, and rescripting the scene. Therapists can ask if clients have questions about the procedure.

3. Reassuring clients. It is important for clients to be reassured that they will not be re-experiencing their trauma as this is very frightening to many clients. Therapists can let their clients know that they will remain their current age as they are observing the scene.

4. Getting client's permission to proceed. Before proceeding, therapists should make sure to get clients' permission to continue. If clients are hesitant or nervous about doing the exercise, they might opt to just do the relaxation and guided imagery parts of the procedure. A pre-reprocessing relaxation script is presented later in this chapter. The therapist can reassure clients that they always have control—they can communicate how they are feeling, they can change the imagery, or stop the procedure at any time.

Step 2: Contextualizing the Scene

1. Choose the scene for reprocessing. Deciding on which scene to use for reprocessing depends on several factors: what is most relevant for the client, what seems to embody the core issue preferably targeting the original source of the core violation, or what is accessible or tolerable to the client.

Reprocessing can occur without revisiting the point of trauma (e.g., the physical act of rape) and in fact, it is strongly recommended that images of physical violence are avoided. Even if a client desires to rescript the physical aspect of an event, the current-aged self immediately stops the violence. As stated earlier, reprocessing is careful to protect against retraumatization and sensitization.

Because experiential holograms replay the same core violation, it is possible that reprocessing a current situation may be effective to break the holographic cycle if the client is able to link the current situation to her pattern of similar experiences. However, for most clients, revisiting a formative event or an early childhood event seems to be the most effective or at least seems to yield the most dramatic results. Some clients reprocess several events including specific traumas from adulthood as well as from childhood.

2. Discuss the event. In preparation of reprocessing, it is important to discuss the specific event that will be reprocessed. This should not be the first time discussing the event. As mentioned previously, if a client has difficulty articulating the event or has questions about her memory of the event, then it is not appropriate to proceed with this procedure. Again, the details of the actual violence need not be discussed as this will not be reprocessed. Rather, it is an opportunity for the therapist to hear about what lead up to the event and what happened afterward. The therapist can inquire about who was there, what were they doing, and what was their motivation or the context of their behavior? The goal is to set the stage for the reprocessing imagery.

3. Find multiple truths. This technique gives clients a framework so that they can adopt a new perception of the trauma without discounting their current perceptions or memories of the event (see chapter 4 for a discussion of personal truths and multiple truths). The therapist explains that it is possible to have multiple and contradictory ways of perceiving an event that are all valid and true. For example, if a therapist picks up a tissue box (assuming that many therapists have one and that the typical shape is a long rectangle with square ends) and shows a viewer the short side of the box, if this view was all that was seen, it would be accurate to say that the object was perceived as a square. If the square side was blue, it would be accurate to say the object perceived was a blue square. Now if the long side of the box was shown and this was red, then from that viewpoint, the viewer would accurately perceive the shape as a red rectangle. Both perceptions are accurate given the data available to the viewer. It is not until the viewer can see multiple viewpoints (by rotating the object) that what is perceived is a multi-colored rectangular-shaped box with square ends. Reprocessing is a

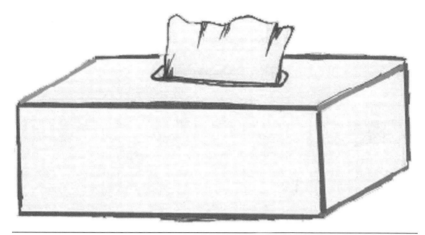

Fig. 12.1 Tissue box showing the concept of multiple truths. From one vantage point, this object appears to be a flat rectangle. From another vantage point, it appears to be a flat square. And yet, from another vantage point, one can see that it is a three-dimensional object.

way to see a broader more comprehensive perception of an event that incorporates multiple viewpoints or "truths" to the situation.

In terms of reprocessing, multiple truths opens clients to the possibility that they may understand the same event differently if viewed from the perspective of the younger self who actually experienced it versus from the perspective of the current-aged self who can objectively view it.

4. Age comparison. A technique that may be appropriate in some cases is age comparison. It is usually helpful when reprocessing a childhood event or an event that occurred when the client was much younger as it allows the current-aged self to gain a new perspective on the younger-aged participants in the scene.

To gain perspective on perpetrators, a client is asked how old the perpetrator was in the scene. This age is then compared to the client's current age. For example, Leslie was going to reprocess a scene where she was 3 years old. Her parents were arguing and shortly thereafter, her father moved out of the house and filed for divorce. Leslie remembers hearing that her father did not want her and she has been devastated by this ever since. She also has a history of failed relationships with men who tend to leave her. Leslie was asked how old her parents were at the time of this event. She stated her mother was 22 and her father was 23. Her parents were only 19 and 20 years old when they had her. Apparently, her father who was neither ready to be married nor ready to be a father, felt trapped when her mother got pregnant.

Since Leslie was 30 years old at the current time, she was able to have a new understanding about her father's feelings as a 20-year-old. Age comparison helps clients see their parents from the perspective of a peer rather than that of authority figures.

To broaden the clients' view of their younger-self, they are asked to identify the age they were at the time of the trauma. Then, they are asked to find someone of that age to remind them of what it was like to be that age. This technique was used in the opening example about Barbara. Another example of using age comparison is Karen who is now 53. She served as a nurse in the Vietnam War. She harbors "survivor guilt" and blames herself for not doing more, saving more lives, knowing more, being more competent etc. When she looked back at the situation and realized that she served in the war when she was only 19 years old, fresh out of a two-year nursing school, she was able to have more compassion for her young self.

Step 3: Relaxation

The following is an example of a detailed description of a relaxation script. This can be used before doing a reprocessing procedure or on its own to desensitize clients to the procedure.

> Let's start with two Signal Breaths. Take a deep breath in through the nose, hold it (for five counts) and . . . release. Breathe normally letting yourself release all the tension in your body. And again, deep breath in through the nose, hold it . . . and release. Good.

The Signal Breaths help clients prepare for relaxation.

> Keeping your eyes closed, feel how you are already more relaxed. Now, tune into your feet. Feel your feet on the ground, connected to the floor and to the earth—anchoring you, grounding you, feeling safe, connected, and solid. Now feel your ankles and legs also connected to your feet and to the ground. Relax even deeper as you feel each part of your body. Feel yourself sitting on the couch, sinking into the couch, supporting your back and legs. Feel your back relaxing as you allow the couch to hold you and support you. Feel your arms and hands also supported—feeling heavier and relaxed. Now tune into you shoulders and neck. Feel your shoulders release a little more as you exhale and become more relaxed. Feel your forehead soften as you relax your eyes and all of the tiny muscles in your face. Relax your jaw and around your mouth. Now feel a warm relaxation flow over you as if warm syrup is flowing on the top of your head down your arms, down your torso and back and down your legs. Feel this warmth . . . it is so soothing and comfortable. *The goal for this section is basic relaxation. It can be extended, shortened, modified or even skipped depending on the need of the client.*

OPTIONAL:

Some clients might benefit from reassuring words from the therapist. Some therapists and clients may view this as beneficial and others may view it as intrusive. This is entirely optional and not necessary for the practice of reprocessing. The goal for this section is for the client to hear positive, encouraging words. It further relaxes clients and helps them maintain the vantage point of their current age.

Now you are relaxed and ready for deep healing . . . know that your life experiences have led you to this point and have prepared you for this exercise. Now you are ready to complete the past, make things right, so you can live a satisfying and happy life. You are ready to get help and heal from the deepest part of your being. You have the wisdom and perspective of your current age to help you understand and appreciate life in new and meaningful ways.

The goal for the next section is to introduce imagery. All the senses are mentioned which helps deepen client's engagement. The imagery is typically walking down a path either on a country road or into a forest. If the client was traumatized in the forest, then of-course the imagery would be changed so that the client would feel safe and relaxed. Again, this can be extended or shortened depending on the need of the client.

Imagine you are walking down a dirt path into a forest. It's a beautiful sunny day with bright blue skies. You can feel the warmth of the sun on your skin. You look around and see tiny pink and yellow wild flowers against a backdrop of majestic pine trees. You can smell the distinct scent of pine in the air. A little bird flies by and you can hear other birds chirping in the distance. You take in a deep breath of the fresh air, so nice and clean and refreshing. You continue walking on the path and can feel some dried leaves crunching underneath your shoes. It's a beautiful day and you are taking in all the beauty of nature. On a scale from 1 to 10, where 10 is tense and 1 is very relaxed, where would you be on this scale? (After whatever answer is given, say, "Good.") If clients are still tense or if they report a number higher than 6, then it is recommended to continue with relaxation. The goal of this section is to check the level of relaxation for your client.

If the client is *not ready* to do a reprocessing procedure then continue with a guided imagery such as:

Up ahead you see a grass clearing. There is a big boulder resting on the bank of a stream. You walk up to the boulder and see that it is smooth and shaped in such a way that it would be very comfortable to lean against it. Imagine sitting by the stream with your back resting on the rock. You look into the stream and it appears so clean and refreshing. This is a magic stream where you can make wishes come true. You pick up a leaf and think of a wish. Now blow your wish into the leaf so that it is infused into its fibers. When you are ready, toss the leaf with your wish into the stream. Watch as the stream carries the leaf away. Know that your wish has been made. Take in a deep breath. Are you complete with this scene

If the client *is ready* to do a reprocessing procedure then continue with the following:

Up ahead you see a grass clearing and far in the distance you can see a house. It is foggy but you can see that it is a house that looks familiar. Are you ready to move forward? (Client nods assent.) Good. Now, imagine we are approaching the house (or place of the scene). It is the house (or place) were you grew up in as a child (or where the event took place). The image is still a little hazy. Remain yourself as you are right now at your current age. Where are you on the 1 to 10 scale?"

Check to see if the client is ready to approach the scene. The approach is slow keeping the image distant, hazy, and small. If the client is able to maintain relaxation, then guide the client closer to the image and proceed with reprocessing.

After completing either the imagery or the reprocessing, the therapist closes the procedure with the following:

Imagine walking back through the forest. Everything appears to be a bit brighter, crisper, and clearer. . . . You look around and see the beautiful trees and flowers. Breathing in the fresh air. Coming up (*tone of voice goes up*) through the forest. Now bring your awareness to where you are in this room, sitting on this chair. Feeling your toes. When you are ready, slowly open your eyes.

Allow clients time to adjust by sitting with a few moments of silence.

Chapter Summary

This chapter reviewed the first three steps of reprocessing. A detailed description of relaxation procedures and a guided imagery exercise were included.

CHAPTER 13

Reprocessing III
Techniques

This chapter presents various objectives or goals of reprocessing including: completing communications, releasing perceptions of personalization, increasing a sense of power, returning to safety, and releasing negative affect. It also discusses a variety of techniques to achieve these objectives. Techniques such as imaginal rescripting (similar to Smucker & Niederee, 1995; and Smucker et al., 1995) are used; however, they are expanded to include the use of fantasy, role playing between the client and therapist, "story board," emotionally connected conversation, and guided imagery. Two examples of reprocessing sessions are included.

Objectives of Reprocessing

There are several objectives that can be addressed through reprocessing. Each will be discussed:

Completing communications. This objective helps clients literally say things to perpetrators, parents, their younger version of their self, or others that they wish they could have said. These communications may be angry or distressed (i.e., "This is what you did to me!"), or tender (i.e., saying goodbye to someone who died or left suddenly, or giving and receiving an apology). The idea is to facilitate closure by reenacting a scene where the communications can be delivered. Using various techniques discussed in the next section (such as role-play and fantasy) the client can imagine the recipient of the communication responding in an appropriate manner.

Gaining a new perspective. This goal includes releasing perceptions of personalization by broadening the context of the event. From the vantage point of their current-aged self, clients are able to construct a more comprehensive and less limiting understanding of the event.

Increasing a sense of power. If the traumatic event and core violation result in feelings of powerlessness, then a goal for reprocessing is to increase a sense of power. This is achieved by putting the client in an empowering role. The client can rescue the younger version of the self and reclaim power by communicating to, removing, or fighting the perpetrator. Sometimes clients find it easier to fight for someone else (in this case younger version of self) than for themselves. This helps them experience a sense of power and reinforces that they do have the ability to be powerful in difficult situations.

Returning to safety. If a traumatic event rendered a client feeling unsafe, then a goal for reprocessing would be to increase a sense of safety. This is achieved by having the client reassure and comfort himself. Clients may visit their younger versions and reassure them that they did survive and are okay. Using the hindsight advantage, clients learn to reconnect with feeling safe and to trust that they can make it through difficult situations and still be okay.

Releasing affect and self-forgiveness. If clients harbor negative affects such as guilt, shame, and blame, then an objective for reprocessing would be to release these affects. Reprocessing helps clients understand the event in new ways, which facilitates self-acceptance and self-forgiveness.

Forgiving Perpetrators

Sometimes clients feel obligated (or even feel pressured by family or their religion) to forgive their perpetrator. It is recommended that this waits until the client thoroughly processes her own feelings first (e.g., focus the reprocessing on the needs of the younger self in the scene). Premature forgiveness of a perpetrator can lead to resentment and further incomplete feelings. For example, Rachel had an extensive history of sexual trauma (including incest from multiple family members). She sought help from various sources such as Alcoholics Anonymous, a sexual trauma support group, church, and individual counseling. It became evident that she had been focusing on releasing her anger and blame toward her perpetrators. She stated, "I know I need to forgive them!"—as if this would solve her problems. This may have had the appearance of a good goal, but the reality was that Rachel blamed herself for not being forgiving enough and therefore, it was "her fault" for being symptomatic and it was "her fault" for bringing disharmony to her family. The strategy of pursuing forgiveness of her perpetrators was clearly not effective and she remained highly agitated about what had happened to her. She described a recent incident where one of her perpetrators was invited to a family function and everyone treated him well. He smiled at her and "accidentally" brushed up against her. This infuriated her and then she felt angry at herself and guilty for not being able to forgive him. She never considered focusing on her own feelings that she had as the victim. She realized that by focusing on the perpetrators, she continued the pattern where she was attending to their needs (in this case, giving forgiveness and complying with the family denial) while her own needs were still being ignored.

Forgiveness of a perpetrator may or may not ever occur for some clients. As one client stated, "some things are just not forgivable." Effective reprocessing does not require or even suggest that clients need to forgive the perpetrator. A more reasonable goal is for clients to feel empowered as well as safe, distant, and protected from the perpetrator. Then the client may consider forgiveness or at least releasing their negative feelings toward the perpetrator. The purpose is not to help the perpetrator per se, but rather to release the feelings because it helps the client. As in the "Catcher's Mitt" visualization discussed later in this chapter, the client can become free from the burdensome role of having to hold negative feelings and can metaphorically "toss the negativity back to the person who generated it."

Reprocessing Techniques

The following are some reprocessing techniques. The list is by no means comprehensive, but rather gives a therapist several possible tools.

Imaginal rescripting. The main technique discussed in previous chapters is that of imaginal rescripting. In this technique, the client is guided to imagine a scene before or usually after a traumatic incident. The client remains her current age and interacts with the characters in the scene such as confronting the perpetrator and comforting the younger version of the self.

Fantasy. Fantasy is a technique that is done in conjunction with imaginal rescripting. Similar to what De Rios (1997) contends in her work on "magical realism," reprocessing is facilitated by the use of culturally relevant symbols. In HR, clients generate their own symbols that are personally relevant. For example, Kira presented with chronic symptoms of depression, an inability to complete projects, and difficulty moving forward in her career. Over several sessions, she pinpointed that the beginning of this pattern occurred when she was 10 years old. Her parents had been arguing and threatening each other for several months before they divorced. She realized that a part of her felt that she had to stay and referee her parents for fear that someone would get hurt. She felt that part of her is still stuck "holding the peace." During a reprocessing procedure she realized that, in order to free the 10-year-old, someone else had to watch over her parents. She came up with the idea of having Archangel Michael come in her place so she could go play with the other children. This image was personally significant, and therefore, effective in transforming her experiential hologram. After this session, she noted a significant improvement in her mood, increased motivation, and an inexplicable remittance of a chronic pain/sensitivity in her ears. These shifts, including the improved physical condition, were sustained throughout the period of contact in our therapy.

Role Playing. Role playing is also a technique usually done in conjunction with imaginal rescripting. Clients imagine they are communicating with the characters in the scene. The therapist might take on the voice of one of the characters to facilitate the conversation. For example, if a therapist takes on the voice of a child version of the client, she might say, "I'm so glad you came here today to see me." "I've waited so long for you to help me." "Was it my fault?" These statements may help faciliate the conversation between the client and the younger self. The therapist should let the client take the lead in the conversation and focus on responding according to the client's comments.

It is possible for the therapist to take on confrontational or challenging roles if this is agreed upon and seems necessary. For example, if a client has undelivered communications to a perpetrator but is having difficulty expressing them, then the therapist may be able to assist in this conversation. It is incumbent upon the therapist to closely monitor the client's ability to handle this. The therapist does not want to put the client-therapist rapport at risk. If the client, identifies the therapist as a perpetrator, it can damage the alliance. So, if this is done, it should be discussed with the client, and the therapist should proceed with caution and, of course, good clinical judgment. As others have suggested, an empty chair or an object could also be used to represent the perpetrator in order to facilitate a conversation.

Story Board. Omar Alhassoon, PhD, originated the technique of Story Board, and it was modified through discussions with this author. It provides a visual tool to help clients discuss and reprocess their hologram. This is particularly helpful for clients who have difficulty with imagery (either because they do not feel safe or are unable to concentrate or visualize). The tool consists of a felt board and an array of pictures (people and objects). The pictures may include people of various ages (e.g., infant, child, teenage/twenties, middle-aged adult, and elderly adult), both male and female, and depicting a variety of emotions (e.g., excitement, distress, and neutral). Clients can also bring in any pictures or small objects that have an emotional significance for them. This technique can be particularly powerful, if a client can bring a picture of himself as a child and as an adult. The process is to let clients choose items that are emotionally relevant with which to construct their story. The therapist observes the ways the client places people and objects on the board to understand the client's relationship with other people. The client tells the story and the therapist helps direct reprocessing through the use of the chosen items. Some of the other techniques discussed in this chapter can also be used such as rescripting, fantasy, and role-play.

Guided Imagery

The following are examples of guided imagery exercises developed by the author to help reprocess aspects of abuse. These exercises use images and metaphors as effective ways of communicating with the experiential system according to the theory of CEST (Epstein, 1989).

Catcher's mitt. This is a guided imagery designed to help clients depersonalize emotional abuse. The imagery helps them see that someone with an abusive character is that way regardless of whether or not the client is present. Clients are guided to imagine the place where they would usually interact with the perpetrator (e.g., the home or office). They are instructed to calmly approach this place. When inside, they see the perpetrator but she is turned away and the client only sees her back. The client can see that she is upset and talking or yelling about something, but can't hear anything because the image is silent (keeping the image silent helps maintain emotional distance). The perpetrator slowly turns toward the client, and the client can see that black smoke has been coming out of her mouth. This represents the negativity that she is spewing forth. The client observes that she is upset (angry, judgemental, abusive, etc.) and that she was this way before the client walked into the room. The black smoke then comes toward the client. The client raises a large catcher's mitt to catch the smoke. The client imagines gathering the smoke in the mitt, rolling it into a ball, and tossing it back to the sender. The therapist can guide the client to say, "This is yours, not mine." Then the perpetrator slowly turns back to the orignial position, still upset and talking or yelling in the same way as she was when the client walked into the room. The client experiences that the perpetrator is the one generating the negativity and the client no longer has to accept it. The therapist then guides the client out of the imagery.

In another version, the client imagines holding up a plexiglass shield so that the smoke bounces off of the shield and protects the client. Some clients feel uncomfortable tossing the smoke back because they do not want to harm the perpetrator, so this version allows them to simply not accept the negativity.

Ghost buster machine. This technique (similar to the incredible shrinking machine described as a coping skill) is designed to deminish the overwhelming fear that clients may have of their perpetrators. The image of a dangerous perpetrator is usually large, close, and bold. The idea is to "shrink" the image and thereby shrink the fear associated with it. If a client is open to it, humor can also be used to diffuse the fear. Clients are instructed to imagine that they are equipped with a special backpack with a connected spray hose that can shrink, freeze, wrap, melt, evaporate, explode, launch into outerspace, or vacuum the perpetrator (use whatever is most preferable). They are instructed to imagine spraying the perpetrator until he is no longer considered a threat.

Two Examples of Individual Reprocessing Sessions

The following examples are descriptions written by psychology interns about their reprocessing sessions. These are included as examples to show slight variations in personal style when doing these procedures.

Client 1

Therapist: Tom, when I listen to the issues you discuss in therapy with me, frequently it seems as if you feel your family does not like or love you.

Client: Yes, I do feel that way; I have felt that way ever since I was a little boy. Sometimes I still feel that my dad moved away to Canada because he did not love me.

Therapist: Tom, the fact that your father moved away when you were younger seems to have had a pretty strong impact on you. I'm wondering if you would be comfortable doing an exercise in which we looked back at that time.

Client: Sure.

Therapist: Okay, great. Why don't you close your eyes, and begin to relax. Take some deep breaths. Breathe in through your nose and out through your mouth. Good. Let's do it again. Breathe in through your nose and out through your mouth. Relax your shoulders, your neck, and your arms. Feel the chair beneath you, and relax your stomach muscles. Feel the floor underneath your feet, and relax your legs. Good. Now take another deep breath, in through your nose and out through your mouth. Okay Tom, now on a scale of 1 to 10 if 1 is very relaxed and 10 is tensed. Where are you right now?

Client: One.

Therapist: Okay, imagine that you are taking a relaxing walk through the forest. You are walking along a path, really enjoying nature. You are enjoying the fresh air. Surrounded by trees and the silence of the forest creates a very peaceful feeling within you. You continue to walk down the path, and in the far distance you see a house. As you get closer, you realize that the house is the one that you lived in as a kid. The house is still a ways a way so you cannot see it clearly. As you continue to walk toward the house, you can see the house much clearer. Approach the house. Now on a scale of 1 to 10 with 1 being very relaxed and 10 being extremely tensed, where are you?

Client: I am at a 3.

Therapist: Okay, why don't you take another deep breath and when you are ready, open the door to the house?

Client: (*Takes a deep breath*) Okay.

Therapist: When you are ready step inside the house.

Client: Okay.

Therapist: Tell me what you see.

Client: I see a little boy sitting on the floor playing with some toys. His mother is in the kitchen cooking, and his grandmother is sitting on the couch. The little boy's older brother is outside playing.

Therapist: Tell me what the little boy is feeling.

Client: He's about seven, and he feels sad and lonely. He wonders why his dad has moved away.

Therapist: As a man in his mid 20s, what would you tell the father who has moved?

Client: I would explain to him how the child feels about him moving. I would tell him that he needs to talk with the child about why he is moving and help the little boy deal with it.

Therapist: Go ahead. As a man in his mid 20s, tell the father, who is in his late 20s, these things.

Client: (*Becomes teary*) Why are you leaving your family? Why are you living with another woman and her daughter? Your son is so sad that you have left. He feels like you don't love him. He does not understand why you have left. Talk to him. Explain to him why.

Therapist: Now, approach the little boy. As a man in his mid 20s, what would you say to the little 7-year-old boy?"

Client: (*In an extremely soft voice*) You are a great kid and everything will be all right.

Therapist: Let him know that there is nothing about him that made his father leave (*based on discussions in previous session*). Explain to him that his father and mother were having problems.

Client: (*Continuing in a very soft voice*) Your father did not move because he did not love you. He and your mother were having problems and he knew he could make a better life for himself in Canada.
Therapist: Is there anything else you would like to say to the little boy?
Client: I'm always going to be here for you. I'm going to take care of you and make sure you are alright.

The therapist slowly led the client out of the house, back through the forest, and into the here and now. After the exercise client stated, "That was amazing. I feel really good. It was weird to see myself as a little boy. Wow." We discussed the fact that it is important to understand that his father's decision to move was not based on the fact that he did not love his son. However, if the situation was not explained to the 7-year-old, it is understandable how the young child might interpret it as such.

At the next session, the client reported that his father had called him in the middle of the night after he did the reprocessing that day. His father said he had a dream about him and he wanted to talk to him. The client became teary and stated that his father told him he loved him over the phone that night.

Client 2

When Cara began therapy, she had a lot of anger at her father. Even though her father has been dead almost 35 years, she used to talk to him daily in angry words. She had said that she would *never* be able to forgive her father for some of the things he has done. However, lately she has wanted to work on forgiveness. Cara had been reading a book called *Letting Go of Shame* (Potter-Efron & Potter-Efron, 1989), which had given her some perspective on people like her father. The book explained that people who criticize, belittle, and abuse their children are often very wounded themselves. The book went on to explain about their "woundedness." Cara had found this very interesting and saw that it was probably accurate. She even said that she knew his wounds came from three things: (1) being born premature and probably brain damaged, (2) dealing with a learning disability, and (3) knowing his own father was put in jail for molesting him. She talked about how these things had probably affected her father growing up.

I asked Cara if she would like to go back into her childhood and talk to the 7- or 8-year-old Cara about these new discoveries. Cara had identified that it was at age 7 that her sister was born and that this was when her father had started hitting and spanking her.

Cara was hesitant about the exercise because she was not sure how to do it. I assured her that I would guide her.

I asked Cara to close her eyes and explained that I wanted to assure her safety with some kind of image. I said that people sometimes like to envision a white light around them. Cara said "no" that she did not want a white light. She envisioned herself as a "dark hole." Okay, a dark hole was the image we used. I had her imagine the safety and protection that she received from the dark hole and imagined her starting a journey to her childhood. She walked through the forest on a path, imagining the scene with all of the senses. Eventually, she came to a clearing in the forest and in it was her childhood home. She walked to the front door and paused. Before going in, the image of protection and safety was strengthened. She walked into the home and found her 8-year-old self in the bedroom hiding in a closet because she was afraid of her father. Cara talked to the 8-year-old and told her that she was there to protect her and to keep her safe. I had Cara tell the 8-year-old about the perspective she now had on their father. Cara told the 8-year-old about her father's wounds. She told her that she no longer needed to be afraid of her father. And, she assured the 8-year-old that her father's behavior had nothing to do with her being "unworthy" or "wrong"—beliefs that the Cara had carried for all these years.

After this discussion, the image of the father was brought into the room and I took on the voice of the father saying, "I am so sorry that I hurt you. I am so sorry that I abused you and made you feel the way you did. I know it is asking a lot and you might not be able to, but can you ever forgive me?" To this Cara actually responded a small, and quiet, but definite "yes." She said that her father had asked for forgiveness before he died but that she had not been willing to give it to him then. And, she was sure he probably was sorry. In the imagery, the father came and hugged both her and the eight year old. Cara was then ready to come back into the present. She said good-bye to both her father and to the 8-year-old and headed back up the forest path to the present.

After the imagery, Cara said that it felt good to do the imagery (although she did not like getting sad at one point). She said that she was tired of being so angry. She also said that, when she was walking back up the path, she noticed that she was no longer the "dark hole," but she was just herself again.

Note: This is an example of a successful reprocessing where the issue of "forgiving the perpetrator" was appropriate. As Cara mentioned, she was not willing or ready to give her father forgiveness at the time of his death. However, at this session she was starting to shift her understanding of her father by considering that her father was actually wounded himself. She had already started the process of forgiveness before the imagery exercise. However, the therapist made sure to validate and understand her own feelings before attempting to forgive her father. In the imagery, the therapist stated her father was sorry for what he had done which was believable since he had already asked for forgiveness. The imagery enabled her to release negative affect and put closure to a painful relationship with her father. A confirmation that a transformation occurred was her statement that she no longer was the dark hole but just herself again.

Chapter Summary

This chapter reviewed objectives for reprocessing such as completing communications, releasing perceptions of personalization, increasing a sense of power, returning to safety, and releasing negative affect. It also reviewed various techniques for reprocessing such as imaginal rescripting, fantasy, role playing, story board, emotionally connected conversation, and guided imagery techniques such as the "Catcher's mitt," and "Ghost buster machine." The chapter concluded with two examples of reprocessing sessions.

CHAPTER 14

Overcoming Barriers to Reprocessing and Building New Patterns

This chapter outlines various barriers to successful reprocessing and solutions to those barriers. It also discusses techniques for building new patterns after reprocessing. This includes how to create new life goals, and how to develop a new identity (empowered-based identity versus a victim-based identity). Testing of the new goals and identities is encouraged in a similar fashion as "behavioral experiments" used in cognitive-behavioral therapy. A technique called "counter images" is presented to prepare clients for new experiences.

Overcoming Barriers to Successful Reprocessing

There are several barriers that may prevent a successful reprocessing. Below are some possible barriers. It is recommended to acknowledge these and address them in therapy.

1. Barrier: Fear of releasing perpetrator's accountability. It is not uncommon for clients to feel that releasing their emotions (such as anger) would somehow release the culpability or accountability of their perpetrator. If they feel "okay" then it means that what happened to them was also "okay." Especially if they have a history of people minimizing, denying, or discounting their experience, clients may be defensive and afraid to relinquish their position of anger in order to hold their perpetrator accountable.

Solution: This barrier is about needing validation. It is important to acknowledge what happened to clients. They need to feel that they are believed, understood, and validated. A therapist might say, "Of course you are angry about what happened. It was a violation and betrayal." The client may need to hear this several times to feel validated. If the therapist tries to argue a client out of this position too early, such as saying, "Well, the anger is only hurting you," or "The abuse happened a long time ago, let's focus on what is happening right now in your life," then the therapist risks having an empathic failure and inadvertently reinforcing the client's position. It is more effective to acknowledge the client's feelings and then subtly suggest that when the client is ready, she will want to release the anger and move forward with her healing.

2. **Barrier: Survivor guilt.** Some clients may have survived a traumatic event while others did not. They may feel guilty, undeserving, or that it would be disrespectful if they feel better while others did not survive or fare as well from the same trauma. For example, a client and her sister were exposed to the same emotional and sexual abuse from their father. However, her sister committed suicide. The client felt she could not experience joy or success while knowing what had happened to her sister. If she was happy, then she felt she was disrespecting her sister's pain.

Solution: This barrier is actually about incomplete grief and mourning. It is not uncommon for people to confuse grief and mourning with feelings such as guilt and inappropriate personal responsibility. Therapists can help by distinguishing these issues and helping clients acknowledge their feelings of loss and sadness. They may need to get closure with the departed loved one. An imagery exercise may include the following:

1. The client imagines the departed person, and he or she is in a peaceful state.
2. The client communicates his feelings of love to the departed (e.g., "I miss you . . .").
3. The client imagines the departed person telling the client that it is okay for him to move forward in life and it is okay to be happy.
4. The client says "good-bye" and anything else that completes the conversation.

3. **Barrier: Fear of responsibility.** Some clients are afraid that if they successfully reprocess, they will have to be responsible for other aspects of their lives. They may feel pressure to do things such as going to school, getting a job, or starting to date (things they think they *should* do), but are afraid to

do them. They may have specific fears related to these endeavors or may have general concerns such as "What if I fail? What if I succeed? What if I can't think of what to do with my life?"

Solution: This barrier is about fear and having low self-confidence and low self-esteem. If there are concerns with specific tasks then these concerns can be addressed. However, the larger issue is about a lack of confidence in the ability to take on new responsibilities. It may be helpful to work with clients to create a vision of the future for themselves. How would they like to see themselves in 5 years? Interventions might include a set of counter-images, positive self-talk such as "I'm okay," "I can do this," and adopting an attitude of "one step at a time" instead of "what if-ing" or catastrophizing into the future.

4. **Barrier: Fear of facing losses.** Some clients are afraid that successful reprocessing means having to face the losses that they have incurred—loss of time, opportunities, relationships, and dreams not materialized. These thoughts lead to unproductive feelings of resentment and regret. These are labeled as "unproductive" since they promote destructive feelings rather than empowering or supportive ones. Another common fear is a sense of loss of identity. Clients have verbalized, "Who am I without this issue?" They reported feeling confused, lost, and anxious.

Solution: This barrier is about fear of not being able to accept one's circumstances and one's self. Although it may be true that if healing occurred sooner a client's circumstances might have been different, but the fact is things have already occurred as they have occurred. It is helpful to acknowledge the losses, but then move toward an attitude of acceptance. Some interventions might be practicing mindfulness, focused breathing, and a strategy of allowing things to be as they are. There may also be benefits to the way a client's life has unfolded. Finding even one benefit can make a difference. For example, Irina had many regrets after the assault she experienced while serving in the U.S. Army; it led to the premature demise of her military career. She lamented that if she had handled the situation differently, perhaps she could have continued with her military career. She stated, "I would have had 15 years this March." She had a whole possible life that she constructed from this "if only" thinking (including the possible rank she would have been, the possible finances she could have had, etc.). She also felt she could have avoided several difficult and painful experiences in her life. However, she was happy in her new relationship. The one benefit that seemed to quell these thoughts was that the circumstances of her life led to meeting her fiancée. We also discussed what she has learned, the character she has developed, and the tenderness she has gained by appreciating kindness in others.

The second part of this barrier was fear of a loss of identity. Clients can usually acknowledge that the old identity was negative and limiting, but they might retort that at least it is familiar. This item is similar to the fears presented in the previous barrier. The solution is to bolster confidence and discuss possible new identities that are more affirming.

5. Barrier: Poor foundation of coping skills. Some clients may not be able to reprocess because they are too easily overwhelmed and have a poor foundation in skills to tolerate and manage their affect. Poor coping skills coupled with an intense fear of feelings can lead to avoiding or sabotaging their therapy (e.g., not showing up for sessions, being late, filling the session with unimportant chatter, or derailing progress by having a crisis). It can also lead to dissociations dissociating in session, sabotaging other positive areas in their life, or engaging in high risk behaviors such as relapse of substance abuse or self-injury.

Solution: This barrier is about insufficient coping skills. If clients begin to sabotage their progress it may be a communication that therapy is progressing too quickly. Some clients may appear to be more advanced than they are, especially if they are highly verbal and insightful. For example, a client may be able to identify her hologram and intellectually grasp her pattern quite quickly. However, when it comes to managing and tolerating affect, she may fall apart because she needs a more secure foundation. The obvious solution is to review, practice, and learn coping skills. It may also be necessary to assess if the client is feeling stress by other life issues such as medical, financial, or relationship problems.

6. Barrier: Client's limitations. Clients may have difficulty doing reprocessing because they have difficulty keeping the observer vantage point or using imagery.

Solution: This barrier is about individual differences in abilities to do these techniques. If this is the case, there are alternative methods such as the time line technique to gather information about patterns, that can be used connected conversation, the story board technique, or role-play without imagery to reprocess.

7. Barrier: Retraumatization. If clients feel retraumatized by revisiting a scene of trauma, this would certainly interfere with the procedure. This may occur if clients have: (1) an undiagnosed or untreated co-existing psychiatric disorder, or a tendency to present well, or to minimize psychopathology or symptoms to the therapist; (2) inadequate coping skills; (3) fragmented memory of the trauma; or (4) are highly fearful of revisiting their trauma. Under these circumstances, attempting reprocessing puts them at risk for being traumatized such as feeling emotionally overwhelmed or feeling that they "failed the exercise." In response to feeling retraumatized, clients may experience increased symptoms, increased high risk behaviors, and have an increased risk of stopping therapy.

Solution: This barrier occurs when clients are not ready or able to do reprocessing. They cannot maintain enough emotional distance to successfully complete the procedure. It would not be appropriate to do reprocessing with clients who are using substances, have a history of psychosis, or are suffering from Dissociative Identity Disorder. It is important for therapists to assess for clients' ability to maintain emotional distance by using the observer vantage point and their ability to utilize coping skills. Therapists should assess if their clients have an intact memory of their trauma by discussing the event or encouraging them to write about the event. If clients are ready to proceed with reprocessing, but are still fearful, then they can practice with the pre-reprocessing induction, and can use the safety techniques such as changing the attributes of the imagery.

8. Barrier: Therapist inexperience. There are several areas where a therapist's inexperience can interfere with successful reprocessing. For example, he could not adequately assess a client's coping skills, not correctly identify the experiential hologram, choose the wrong aspect to reprocess, and either not know how to or incorrectly apply the emotional distancing or reprocessing techniques.

Solution: The solution to inexperience is, of course, more experience. One way to monitor if an intervention is effective is to observe the client's responses. Clients will let their therapist know if the therapy is working.

Building New Patterns After Reprocessing

What happens after an experiential hologram has been reprocessed? Clients may feel relieved, physically lighter, healthier, happier, more relaxed, more self-confident, and have clearer thoughts. However, for some clients these good feelings are followed by a phase of uncertainty and insecurity. They may cling to old behavior patterns even though they are aware that they are no longer necessary. Clients have stated that they know they do not need to engage in destructive behaviors anymore, but seem to continue to do them since they are familiar. Therefore, after reprocessing, there may be a period of transition from old beliefs and behaviors to new ones. This includes discussions about the impact of the reprocessing and the implications it has for the client's future including a discussion about setting new life goals and developing a new self-concept.

Setting New Life Goals

After completing reprocessing, clients may report having an improved self-worth and self-esteem. They may desire to explore new goals for their lives such as a career change, going back to school, losing weight, and leaving or starting a relationship. They may need help in problem solving, prioritizing, and strategies to seek information. It is appropriate for therapists to encourage and extend the possibilities of their dreams. For example, Ellen was a 28-year-old African American female about to complete her second year in college. She did exceptionally well, earned straight As, and was planning on getting her master's degree after completing her undergraduate work. However, all she could think of doing for a summer job was to work at the counter of a coffee stand. She stated that the job paid well and that she has experience in making coffee. We brainstormed other possible jobs including those that were relevant to her major. She stated that the options we generated never would have occurred to her. She was able to follow through and secure a better paying and more challenging job for herself.

Developing a New Self-Concept

After reprocessing, clients may change their self-perception. It is useful to discuss this change and to help them articulate their new ways of behaving. For example, Tamara always viewed herself as a pleaser. She would never say or do anything controversial or "cause waves." We discussed that this was a compensating strategy that was no longer relevant for her. She had reprocessed her experiential hologram where she was chronically taken advantage of and used by others while replicating her core violation of having her needs neglected. Pleasing others ultimately did not get her needs met, and the only way to change this pattern was to start being assertive and taking care of herself. She had promised that she would take care of the younger version of herself and now had the task of implementing that promise. We discussed what she could say to herself to encourage this change. She said, "I am important, my needs matter too." This was part of her new self-concept. Like learning any new skill, it is expected that it may be awkward at first and it may take several trials of practicing the skill before becoming comfortable with it. Tamara made it a point to voice her feelings whenever she felt something was not right. This lead to a fight with a friend, making a complaint to the dean at her school and then having to confront her teacher in a conference with the dean, and being threatened by her room-mate. For someone who spent the majority of her life pleasing others and avoiding conflicts, these were rather dramatic changes. We discussed that she was exploring her new self, but she may not be sure when to voice her opinions, or how to voice them in the most effective manner. We likened this process as going through a period of adolescence (or rebellion) to prove to herself that she can handle conflict and controversy. Having the pendu-lum swing in the opposite direction for a period of time is not uncommon when people are developing new skills. Eventually, Tamara learned that she always has the option to express herself and may or may not choose to do so. The freedom to make the choice is in itself empowering.

Counter Images

Because new behaviors are new, clients may be fearful or hesitant to try them. They may assume that they will experience a negative consequence and a negative outcome. This is the image that is generated in their head and, as the lemon exercise from chapter 8 demonstrated, the body responds to images. Thus, the following technique of "counter images" is the author's version of an experiential affirmation to help clients through the fear of trying new behaviors typical of this therapeutic phase.

1. Identify the situation or behavior.
    Sara wants to interview for a new job.
2. Identify expected fears.
    She assumes the interviewers will not like her and she will be humili-ated.
3. Identify what client really desires.
    Sara wishes she could present herself with confidence. She wants the interviewers to be impressed with her skills. She wants to get the job.
4. Create an image that counters the fear (the counter image).
    Sara imagines herself walking, talking, and moving with confidence. She imagines herself speaking about her past experiences and skills. She imagines the interviewers are impressed with her and she gets the job. She imagines feeling good. (As with all imagery, the clearer and more detailed the better.)
5. Practice the counter image.
    Sara practices the positive imagery twice a day. She rehearses what she might say in the interview. She imagines how she will present herself and imagines positive responses in return. (The imagery work can be reinforced by anchoring the positive feeling through a confident body posture.) She also practices positive self-talk (affirmations) to boost

her confidence and reconnect with the positive feeling induced by the imagery.

6. Implement the new behavior.
   Sara goes on one or more interviews and practices implementing her new behaviors.

It is important to note that the process of establishing new patterns occurs over time. It is likely that when something does not work and there is a disappointment, an old behavior may return. These are framed as "slips" and they can be predicted as a natural part of establishing new patterns. The process of reinforcement may take several trials or repeated experiences to establish the new response.

Chapter Summary

This chapter outlined several barriers to successful reprocessing and solutions to those barriers. It also reviewed techniques for establishing new life goals, new identities, such as using counter images.

CHAPTER 15

Holographic Reprocessing
in Couples Therapy

This chapter discusses how experiential holograms are often the source of miscommunication and distress in intimate relationships. Techniques on how to identify experiential holograms as they manifest in relationships, and how to resolve the resulting conflicts are discussed. This one chapter cannot comprehensively address all issues relevant to couples therapy, but rather its intention is to introduce the concept of using experiential holograms as a part of one's practice.

Case Example: Heating Up Oatmeal

This example illustrates how a seemingly insignificant incident can trigger a couple's experiential holograms. The argument revealed each member's deep unresolved emotional traumas and explained why they interacted in the manner that they did.

One Sunday morning, Jim was reheating some left-over oatmeal. He was stirring it on the stove and noticed it was too thick. So, he took the pot to the kitchen faucet and was going to add some water. Diane noticed what he was doing and quickly said, "Oh, Jim, don't do that! It will taste much better if you add some milk." She got up and moved toward the refrigerator to get the milk. Jim said he was "Fine" and proceeded to add the water. Diane got the milk and offered it to him anyway. Jim got annoyed and told Diane to leave him alone. Diane asked if he was sure, because it would be much better with the milk. Jim harshly told her to "Back off." Diane got hurt and felt rejected by Jim. She retorted by saying, "You're such a jerk." She stormed out of the kitchen. Jim yelled a few negative phrases back to her and the two avoided each other for the rest of the day.

In this incident, Jim's intention was to competently prepare his own breakfast. Diane's intention was to connect with Jim by being helpful. Both of these intentions were perfectly reasonable. There was no intention to be harmful. However, they both inadvertently triggered each other's experiential holograms. Jim's core violation was related to being criticized while Diane's core violation was related to being ignored. It is understandable how Jim would feel criticized by Diane's suggestion to add milk. It is also understandable how Diane would feel ignored by Jim's request to be left alone. They both compensated with being defensive, critical, and rejecting. Diane retreated and felt lonely and hurt. Jim felt irritated, attacked, and intruded upon. They avoided each other and avoided their own unresolved issues. They continued to blame each other instead of confronting their own deeper feelings.

This seemingly mundane incident captures a recurring dynamic of Jim and Diane's relationship. Consistent with the holographic model where the whole is evident in the parts, not only is this dynamic indicative of this one relationship, but it is also a recurring theme of several relationships throughout each of their lives. For example, Jim grew up with a physically and emotionally abusive father who constantly criticized him. Jim described him as "always putting me down" and "nothing was ever good enough for him." Jim harbors deep resentment toward his now deceased father and stated that he hates him. Jim experienced Diane's comment as a criticism, so naturally he became defensive and angry. His level of anger may have been disproportionate to Diane's words alone, but makes sense considering his years of pent up anger toward his father.

Diane grew up with neglectful parents. She described that she basically had to raise herself. In order to get attention, she would offer her help to others. Her investment in Jim's breakfast makes sense given her history. Her only means of connection was being able to help others. When Jim told her to leave him alone, Diane experienced it as if she was being neglected once again by someone she loves.

Articulating each participant's experiential hologram helped broaden the context of the couples' arguments. They had increased understanding and empathy for each other. Instead of being reactive and adversarial, they learned to help each other through the triggering of their holograms. They reported spending more time having fun together and enjoying each other's company. The shift was evident during therapy sessions. Instead, of spending the majority of the session arguing, they laughed and were more patient and complementary with each other. We agreed to end therapy with an option for a "booster session" in 4 to 6 months if the couple wanted it.

Experiential Holograms in Couples Therapy

Experiential holograms are likely to become activated in romantic relationships. Sometimes the source of attraction between two people is the compatibility of their experiential holograms. This is not always a positive dynamic, and, in fact, can be very destructive such as the union of abusers and victims. However, the relationship can serve to either reinforce the experiential holograms or it can provide an opportunity for awareness, reprocessing, and growth.

In couples therapy, facilitating understanding for each other's holograms helps foster empathy, patience, and tolerance for their differences. For example, Gina and Larry have been dating for about 17 months. Gina was diagnosed with fibromyalgia about 9 months into their relationship. Larry complained that Gina was being lazy and Gina complained that Larry was being moody and inconsiderate. She believed he was trying to sabotage their relationship. Through discussions of both participants' family history, it was revealed that both Gina and Larry had experiential holograms in play.

Gina had an experiential hologram related to her parents not taking care of her needs. This was reenacted when she needed help from Larry. When he was not available to help her she felt hurt and abandoned. She worried that he wanted to leave the relationship and assumed that she was not loved or wanted. Larry's sabotaging behaviors made Gina feel anxious and in need of more reassurance. Her anxiety increased the painful bouts of the fibromyalgia and increased the amount of time she was home in bed.

Larry also had an experiential hologram related to watching his mother care for his stepfather after he had a stroke. Gina's diagnosis triggered Larry's hologram. He was afraid of living a self-sacrificing life similar to his mother. He felt trapped and angry. However, he also had a need to "be a good person" like his "saintly" mother and did not want to be the one to break up with Gina. He felt guilty for wanting to leave the relationship. This feeling was also associated to feeling guilty for secretly wanting his stepfather to die. In response to these mixed feelings, Larry developed a coping strategy of being passive-aggressive. This was reenacted in his relationship with Gina as he sabotaged opportunities for intimacy.

The worse Gina got, the more sabotaging Larry became. The more sabotaging Larry became, the worse Gina got. This is the destructive holographic dance that was deteriorating their relationship.

The goal of this couples' therapy was to identify both participants' experiential holograms, thereby broadening the context of each other's behavior. This increased understanding lead to more empathy for each other and facilitated mutual respect and communication. They were also able to confront their own cognitive distortions and inappropriate projections that they had assumed were true for the other person and for their perceived future. This couple was able to use the experiential hologram paradigm to communicate about their hurt feelings. They were able to use the model to talk about their associations and personal meanings of the events in their lives.

Other couples may be aware of their experiential holograms but are unable to use the information to salvage their relationship. For example, Cindy had an experiential hologram that was formed when her father was unfaithful to her mother. Eventually, her parents divorced and her mother remarried. Cindy was then sexually violated by her stepbrother. These experiences made her feel distrustful and uncertain about boundaries. In response, she is easily jealous in relationships and is particularly triggered by behaviors that may be related to infidelity. Her boyfriend John stated that he enjoys looking at women and her jealousy makes him feel trapped. John carried an experiential hologram based on his experiences with his overbearing mother. He was particularly triggered by behaviors that curb his freedom. For this couple, the awareness of their holograms helped them realize that they were not a compatible match. They continued to trigger each others' holograms and the associations to these events were too distressing to live with. They agreed that the resolution would be to separate. Unless confronted and resolved, they will most likely have to confront these issues again in future relationships.

Practicing Holographic Reprocessing in Couples Therapy

1. Setting ground rules. The first step, as in individual therapy, is to establish the ground rules for the therapy. When most people start couples therapy they have a secret agenda to convince the therapist that they are right and their partner is wrong. Most people wish that the therapist will validate them and fix or change their partner. They expect that therapy is a place to safely voice everything about their partner that is irritating. This agenda and expectation is not conducive to successful therapy. Thus, clear ground rules need to be established. These rules are called "agreements" and are presented in a way so that everyone participates in and actively agrees to the rules. They have several benefits: They set a stage for basic order and containment during the therapy. They also put the therapist in a position of control and power which is important initially. Although this may sound contrary to the therapeutic stance described in chapter 6, in couples therapy the therapist has a different role. The therapist is seen as the impartial judge, umpire, and referee, as well as the expert, authority, and final word. It is necessary to take on this role at the beginning of couples therapy to help the participants surrender their polarized position of "I'm right and you're wrong." Consider the following analogy: the couple has been playing a game of tug of war and each of them is holding an end of the rope. They come into therapy tightly gripping their own end of the rope hoping that the therapist will join them and pull the other one over to their side. Instead of getting caught in this game, use of the ground rules puts the therapist in a neutral position. Following the tug of war analogy, the therapist says, "Okay, now both of you let go of your end and give me the entire rope. I'll hold it for now as your therapist. When we are further along in this process, I'll give you back the rope for you two to hold in a more cooperative manner." Taking this stance of control and power, quickly establishes rapport with the couple, and engenders confidence that the therapist is competent and can take charge of their "out of control relationship."

Some of the agreements may include:

1. The therapist is given permission by both partners to interrupt or re-direct the conversation.
2. Only the therapist can interrupt while someone is talking.
3. Everyone agrees that no swearing or name calling is permitted.
4. The therapist may sometimes ask questions or may sometimes "talk out loud" to give feedback about what is observed in the couple.
5. The therapist presents the limits of confidentiality and office policies.
6. The therapist requests that both partners consent to abide by these agreements and to engage in treatment.

2. Circular questioning to gather information. Circular questioning is an excellent technique to use in couples therapy especially if clients are adversarial.

This technique was developed by the Milan group for Systemic family therapy (see Cronen & Pearce, 1985 for a description of this method). The technique is widely used in family therapy as it allows therapists to ask indirect questions that reveal the connectedness of the members in a family. It gives participants an opportunity to hear what other people perceive about them. For example, instead of asking person A his own opinion about a situation, the therapist asks person A to state what he thinks person B's opinion is about the situation. Similarly, person B is asked what she thinks person A feels about the situation. People usually expect to tell their own opinions not what they think someone else thinks or feels. This disrupts clients' expectations and forces them to see the situation from the other person's point of view. This is particularly important in couple's therapy since most couples stop listening to each other. Although each may assert their own opinions (often repeating the same arguments in an attempt to be heard), little empathy or understanding is gained. Similar to a car stuck in mud, the wheels may turn, but the vehicle does not move. Circular questioning quickly moves the couple forward in therapy. The participants usually become highly engaged, they listen carefully to what the other person says about them, and they usually gain insight about their own behaviors and feel understood by their partner.

A further benefit of circular questioning is that the technique often reveals information about each participant's experiential hologram. For example, continuing with Diane and Jim, the couple started the conversation with an adversarial communication:

Diane: Why can't you just accept my help or nicely say, 'no thank you'?
Jim: Why can't you just let me be without interfering?

Using circular questioning, the therapist might ask:

Jim: What do you think Diane's intention was when she suggested you use milk?
Diane: What do you think Jim was feeling when he said to leave him alone?

After a few rounds of questions the therapist might reflect, summarize, or give feedback about their answers. For example:

Well, it sounds like Diane's intention was to try to help you, Jim. She really wanted you to have tasty oatmeal and was concerned about your experience. But, instead of perceiving her comments as helpful, Jim, you felt criticized and intruded upon. You just wanted to have your space and do it your own way. Diane, instead of perceiving this as his choice, you felt personally rejected and ignored because, like I said, you were just trying to help him. So, you left feeling hurt, angry, and distant from Jim. And Jim, you felt frustrated because you just wanted to eat your oatmeal in peace, and now you are upset *and* you have an upset wife. Did I get that right?

The therapist might continue with circular questioning to broaden the scope of the questions as to why Jim feels criticized and why Diane feels ignored. In this case, each knew about the other person's family history and was able to contribute examples and understanding as to why each reacted in the manner in which they did. Couples are usually surprised by how well their partners actually know them. This process helps the couple articulate their patterns and remind them of each other's context.

3. Make both members of the couple "right." Typically, couples believe only one person can be right. If both believe they are the right one, then by definition they both believe that the other one is the wrong one. This is a common trap that makes couples stuck. Even if this dynamic is not overt (e.g., when one or both members of a couple becomes passive or disengaged), it still exists. For example:

Angela: I've asked you a million times . . . why can't you fold up the paper and put it in the trash when you are done?

Dave: Why can't you just let it go? It's just a newspaper!

Angela believes Dave is a "slob" and communicates this to him almost daily. Dave believes Angela is a "control freak" and communicates this to her in return. This type of communication is ineffective and only leads to increased frustration and distance. "Making both right" means stating that it makes perfect sense why Angela wants the paper put away, and it also makes perfect sense why Dave wants the freedom to leave it out. Both points of view are valid and understandable. In fact, when it comes right down to it, these differences may be the very qualities that give the couple balance and strength. Angela's attention to detail is the perfect balance for Dave's love of spontaneity.

The therapist explains how each partner's action makes perfect sense and sets the stage for a deeper inquiry into their respective historical contexts.

4. Contextualize their experience given their life history. The next step is to broaden the context for each person. How did each grow up? What parental influences did they have and what were the formative events in their lives? There are several ways to elicit this information such as through circular questioning (as mentioned above), direct questioning, making genograms (map of each participant's extended family showing significant patterns including divorce, substance use, abuse, etc.), and experiential discovery.

Experiential discovery with couples is much the same as it is with individuals. The therapist works with one member of the couple at a time while the other member listens. The therapist might inquire about the family of origin, other romantic relationships (if appropriate), or other significant relationships such as with friends, bosses, or relatives. The idea is to gather information about their patterns including their compensating and avoidance strategies as well as what remains emotionally unresolved (i.e., their core violation and personal truth). The therapist explores what emotions are strongest regarding the conflict they are having in their relationship. When there is a felt sense or recognition that the core emotion is activated, and then the therapist can ask about other events from their lives that may be similar. The discussion is explored until the experiential hologram is revealed.

5. Identify the couple's "holographic dance." Once both members of the couple have articulated their experiential hologram, the therapist helps them identify their holographic dance. This is how their holograms interact and trigger each other. For example, when Jim feels intruded upon, he defends himself by pushing Diane away. When Diane feels pushed away, she tries harder to please Jim. The harder Diane tries to please, the further Jim pushes her away. Unless this dance is altered, the couple remains stuck regardless of each member's increased efforts. In fact, their increased efforts only render them more stuck.

The therapist can draw this dance on a piece of paper or on a board with arrows depicting the circular nature of their interaction. The visual aid helps the couple see that their actions and reactions are intertwined with each other. Although they have a unique past and set of influences, as a couple they are no longer individual people having their own responses, but have become a single interconnected unit. What affects one person, affects them both. This is an important concept that lays a foundation for the next few steps.

6. Engender empathy, understanding, and compassion. After each partner's experience is contextualized, and the holographic dance is articulated, it becomes understandable why each behaves the way they do and why the couple is having the problems they are having. Neither is a "bad" person, rather they both have needs, past hurts, and sensitivities. Couples usually find it comforting and healing to hear that their partner has empathy, understanding, and compassion for them. They like to know that their partner understands them and knows who they are. Therapists can encourage each to vocalize an understanding of the other person's experience. This exercise in and of itself can usually foster a significant increase in intimacy and satisfaction with their relationship. However, the next two steps are helpful because they establish new patterns and prevent relapses of the conflicts that brought the couple into therapy.

7. The 100% model. Most couples believe that each of them are 50% responsible for their relationship. This translates to being 50% responsible for contributing to the relationship via chores, attention, intimacy, general help, and generosity. This is an old model that sets up a business partnership, "tit-for-tat" thinking and "keeping score." These are destructive paradigms for a romantic relationship. In fact, when a relationship devolves into a 50/50 model, usually the romance is gone. A new model of 100% responsibility is introduced to the couple. In this model, each participant is 100% responsible, invested, and nurturing of the relationship. After explaining this new model, the therapist might ask, "So who is responsible for changing your holographic dance?" If they answer, "We both are," or even worse, if they point to the other person, then the therapist says, "No, try again . . . who's responsible for making the change?" The idea is for each person to say, "I am responsible for making the change." This can be a pivotal shift for the couple as it encourages each to personally take full responsibility for what they can do and how their own actions impact the relationship. It frees them from the idea that they have to wait to see what the other person does, or that they will only give as much as the other person gives. If they believe that they both are responsible for the change, then one might hold back while waiting for the other person to contribute more. The old model leads to a quick deterioration of any progress made in therapy. The new model encourages a quick restoration and strengthening of the relationship.

The therapist might write encouraging phrases on a card for the couple such as: "I am responsible for this relationship," "What I say and what I do impacts my relationship," and "What my partner feels matters to me."

8. Establish new communication patterns. The most important aspect of establishing new communication patterns is teaching the couple how to listen to each other. A frequently assigned homework is for the couple to establish a regular "talk-time." This is an agreed upon time where the couple gives each other undivided attention. That means no interruptions from children or phone calls, and no distractions such as talking over the television or eating a meal or snack. The idea is to listen or "check in" with each other about how they are feeling. When one person is talking the other person listens. At first, couples may need structure to this assignment. They may need a set amount of time such as giving each member 5 minutes of uninterrupted time to express themselves. The listening partner only responds by showing that he or she is listening (i.e., nodding). If the couple is able, they can be taught how to give a reflective, summary statement after they have listened to their partner (e.g., "It sounds like you had a really stressful day today.") The couple is encouraged to be generous with their listening and to show concern for the other person. After each has had a turn, they can ask each other "if they are complete" or if they want to go for another round. If the couple can handle the 5 minutes, then "talk time" can be expanded first by lengthening the session and then by lifting the time restriction entirely. Couples typically report that "talk time" has become a valuable ritual that they look forward to sharing.

The couple and therapist can also develop other homework assignments and strategies (e.g., as signaling when someone's experiential hologram is being triggered, or signally when someone needs a "time out"). These may seem simplistic but it helps couples from making assumptions about communicating with each other. The idea is to find strategies that best fit the couple's needs.

Chapter Summary

Holographic reprocessing in couples therapy is about broadening the context of a conflict or set of problematic behaviors as seen from the perspective of each member of a couple. The conflict is redefined in a way that makes each person "right." Their reactions are contextualized in terms of their life history and the couple is encouraged to express empathy and understanding for their partner's experience. Next the holographic dance is articulated. Once the couple can see the bigger context of how they contribute to their own conflict, they are asked to take personal responsibility to change it. The reprocessing of their mutual experiential holograms is achieved through the relationship. The relationship itself becomes the means for extinguishing old associations, creating new meanings (a response no longer has to mean what it meant in the past), and for providing ongoing corrective experiences.

CHAPTER 16

Family and Socio-Cultural Experiential Holograms

This chapter discusses how experiential holograms can be passed down through generations of a family or adopted by generations of a culture. For example, following experiences of oppression and trauma, a culture may carry forth emotional wounds that repeat themselves over time. This chapter broadens the concept of experiential holograms. The implications of these issues when conducting psychotherapy with diverse populations are discussed.

Case Example: Who Is Responding To Whom?
A Multi-Generational Analysis

This example illustrates how the understanding of family and socio-cultural holograms shifted the perceptions that perpetuated the client's personal experiential hologram. Reprocessing occurred through imaginal rescripting and connected conversation that expanded and contextualized the understanding of the problem.

Cheryl was a 38-year-old lesbian. She came to therapy to "get rid of her hurt and anger" so she could choose a better partner and have a long-term loving relationship. Cheryl described having a string of partners who were unable to commit to her. Her first girlfriend cheated on her and lied about it. Another girlfriend kept their relationship a secret, lied about Cheryl to her family, and then broke up with her after Cheryl paid off the woman's bills. In both relationships, Cheryl felt abandoned and used because she took on their problems, incurred their financial debt, and "did everything for them with nothing in return."

In the next session, we began to discuss her life history to understand the broader context of these experiences in her life. Cheryl grew up in a middle-class family with her sister and her mother. They lived in her grandparents' home. Her mother divorced their father when they were young and he was not involved in the children's lives. Her mother was a 1960s "flower-child" and believed in personal freedom. Cheryl complained of a lack of parenting from her mother. She harbored anger and resentment because her mother was permissive to the point of being neglectful. As a consequence, Cheryl lives her life being overly responsible for others (i.e., taking on projects and providing help for others sometimes at her own expense). She also highly values honesty and integrity, again as a reaction to her mother, who she felt was "slippery," "quietly dishonest," and "misleading." Cheryl was angry and stopped talking to her mother for a few years. Recently, she has reconnected with her mother because her mother was diagnosed with a cancer. However, Cheryl continues to be easily hurt, disappointed, and irritated with her mother's subtle dishonesty.

Cheryl quickly realized that she had been "dating her mother" and thus, recapitulating her experiential hologram of wanting love and intimacy but ultimately creating relationships where she was abandoned and mislead. These relationships reinforced her stance that "that nobody will take care of her" and reinforced her compensating strategy of trying harder to take care of others. To Cheryl, taking care of someone is the ultimate expression of love since this is what she was lacking from her mother. She secretly desired that someone else would love her in this way but her behaviors would not allow anyone to have that opportunity.

I listened to Cheryl's story with the intention to understand the larger context of her hologram. At this point, she could map her personal experiential hologram and could recognize how it manifests in her relationships. We could have rescripted her experiential hologram and had discussions about what kind of partnership she would like to create in her future. However, because she still had unresolved issues with her mother, I felt that we needed to continue to broaden the context of her experiential hologram. I made a choice to gather more information about her mother, grandparents, and the context of the family dynamics. It appeared that her mother had a strong set of values and a peculiar coping strategy of being dishonest. I wondered what experiential hologram her mother was reacting to and what part of a family hologram was Cheryl carrying forth?

I explained this to Cheryl and said, "We all develop coping strategies to get through life. These strategies make sense and are adaptive solutions to whatever difficulties people are confronted with. You reacted to your mother in a very reasonable manner. Of course, you were angry and hurt! You didn't get the care-taking that you needed as a child. Now, let's try to figure out why a mother would act in these ways. Could her behavior have been an adaptive solution to some other situation?" I asked her, "What do you think it was like for your mother when she was growing up? Tell me what you know about her parents?"

Cheryl stated she was very close to her grandparents who are now both deceased. Cheryl reflected on her grandmother. She stated she was particularly connected to her and said many wonderful things about "Grandma." She said she was her favorite and was essentially raised by her (i.e., her grandmother would take care of her when her mother was away). Then she started telling funny stories about how her grandfather would hide any mishaps from his wife. She told a story about how her uncle was suspended from school for 3 days. Her grandfather (his father) took him to the library everyday and made him promise not tell his mother. Cheryl laughed as she told the story and said that Grandma never found out. I asked her why it was important for her grandmother not to know these things? Cheryl was not sure, but did know that everyone was afraid of "ruffling her feathers." I said that it sounded like everyone had to be slippery and misleading around Grandma, including Cheryl's mother. We paused as she reflected on this information.

Cheryl said that her grandmother was a strict traditional Catholic who valued responsibility and morality. She saw how her mother was both rebellious and afraid of upsetting her mother. She understood that her mother's coping style of being misleading was an attempt to live her own life (contrary to her mother's) and yet avoid confrontation. Cheryl began to understand her mother's behavior in a new context. She stated that her mother must have felt trapped by her grandmother's strictness, and, as a result, she raised her own children by being permissive. Even though Cheryl felt neglected by her mother's permissiveness, she started to see a bigger picture. Who was reacting to whom? She saw that who she was being in her own relationships was not only a reaction to her relationship with her mother but was also an inadvertent reaction to her mother's relationship with her grandmother. She realized the origins of certain traits that she carried forth from both her mother and grandmother.

Cheryl had taken on an attitude of self-sufficiency, responsibility, and integrity. She identified with her grandmother who shared values of being strict and moral. Of course, she got along well with her grandmother, they were alike. And they shared a common disappointment with her mother for being independent, having a tendency to be misleading, and acting contrary to family protocol. However, through the course of the conversation, she was able to see that her mother's irritating qualities were possibly an adaptive solution given the context of her own parental issues. Whether or not Cheryl agreed with the solution her mother came up with was irrelevant. This was the solution that she came up with and it can only be understood given the context of her mother's life not Cheryl's life. The more pertinent question would be what does it mean for Cheryl? What does it mean for her future?

Cheryl was thoughtful for several minutes. She asked, "If I am overly responsible and strict like my grandmother, does that mean that my children are destined to become like my mother?" She understood the interconnected quality between her behavior and that of the past and future generations of her family. She saw that a larger experiential hologram was being reenacted through the generations and each generation was playing out opposite aspects. She also saw that she could transform the family hologram because she herself is connected to the whole. Her behaviors not only affect her life but it could also affect future generations as well. At this point in her therapy, we had the discussion that children are supposed to evolve beyond their parents. This is how the species evolves; otherwise, if parents were more evolved than their children, the species would devolve. In other words, it is healthy and normal for adult children to want to live their lives differently than their parents, and it is normal for them to want to raise their children "better." This usually engenders a shift in expectations, a broadening of context, and a greater sense of compassion toward one's parents.

Cheryl took on a new focus for therapy. She stated that her new goal was to allow people to love her and to help her. She did not want to continue living the family hologram. It would be up to her to be neither overly responsible nor overly permissive. She realized that both sides still avoided intimacy, which is what she actually wanted. We discussed how she avoided sharing about her feelings because she was too focused on attending to other people's needs. She admitted that she, like her mother, avoided sharing personal information with her grandmother that would be upsetting (i.e., she never told her grandmother that she was a lesbian).

I asked her what happened to the anger toward her mother? She stated she was "over that" and realized her mother did the best she could. Cheryl was also mature enough to realize that their differences would continue to be a source of friction between them. We discussed that it is likely that Cheryl will get triggered again by her mother's actions. We discussed that when her mother acts in ways she finds hurtful and disappointing, she has to remember the bigger picture. She stated that she found it helpful to think of her mother as a little girl trying to be independent while not upsetting Grandma. But most importantly, she realized that her mother's behavior is a reflection of her mother's own history and not about a lack of love or concern for her. This was a pivotal moment in therapy. We did a rescripting exercise where she imagined her current aged-self visiting herself as a child. She comforted her child-self with the knowledge that she is loved and her needs are important.

The rescripting helped Cheryl shift the perception of her life. She was able to construct a new meaning about her mother's permissive parenting style by viewing the behavior in a broader context. When Cheryl was freed from personalizing her mother's behavior (i.e., viewing permissiveness as lack of love), she was able to have less anger and more compassion for her mother and herself. This set the stage for her to work on her goal of increasing intimacy in her life.

This example illustrates how personal holograms exist in the context of family holograms. Understanding Cheryl as part of an ongoing multi-generational system, places her experience within a broader context. This perspective helped her free herself from recreating the family hologram. Cheryl not only altered the experiential holograms of her personal life, but also shifted the family influence on future generations.

Family Experiential Holograms

A family experiential hologram, like a personal experiential hologram, is based on an unresolved emotional issue. The experience is then reenacted by various members of a nuclear family or is passed down through generations of a family. Since experiential holograms are typically created in a context of family, it is therefore not uncommon that several members of a family either share similar personal holograms or develop holograms in response to other members of the family. Family members may play out these differences between siblings, different generations of a family (grandparent, parent, child), as well as with romantic partnerships, or in non-family relationships. Some common themes of reenactments are abuse, strict or permissive boundaries, certain fears/insecurities, and negative belief systems. As successive generations grapple with recurring family themes, often times one or more members of each generation work to resolve or heal an aspect of the family pathology. Each member is part of the whole family. Continuing with the holographic principles not only experiences the whole within, but also can influence whether the issues are resolved or perpetuated. Thus, each member of a family contributes to the collective family's evolution. Individual work on becoming aware of personal and family experiential holograms enables the current and future generations of the family to evolve. In this way, healing takes on a more complex dimension. Healing is not only limited to personal growth but includes interpersonal and intergenerational growth as well.

The following is an example of how an experiential theme is expressed through generations. A woman in her mid-20s was discussing her troubles with a custody battle with her former husband. She stated that she was served divorce papers during her pregnancy. She had just given birth to her baby a month ago, but she looked like she was never pregnant. She said she did not gain any weight because she was so angry with her husband. What was most distressing to her was that her husband "abandoned his family." She had the insight that her anger was probably related to the fact that her own father left her mother when she was young. She said, "I am probably punishing him (i.e., being uncooperative with the legal proceedings) because I really want to punish my father." (Was she reenacting her parent's relationship or was she working through her own experiential hologram of being abandoned? What experiential holograms will her daughter carry forth because of unresolved emotions in her parents and grandparents?)

Family members may carry forth experiential holograms from past generations and be completely unaware of the source of the hologram. The following example demonstrates how a simple food aversion was passed from mother to daughter without the daughter's awareness of the source of the aversion. A grown woman stated she had an aversion to eating tomatoes and made a sour face at the thought of eating one. She could not explain why, but if she put a tomato to her lips she immediately had a physical response as if she were about to eat something very bitter and distasteful. Interestingly, she admitted that because of this response, she had never really allowed herself to taste a raw tomato. She knew mother did not eat tomatoes and finally asked her why. Her mother revealed the origin of the aversion. When her mother was 4 years old she had to be hospitalized. She was served tomatoes and to this day she associates eating tomatoes with this traumatic experience. The daughter continued the aversion without having direct experience of eating tomatoes, nor even knowing about the painful association. Similarly, experiential holograms may be carried forth from one generation to another without awareness or direct personal experience of the original traumatic event.

Some family holograms are reenacted between generations where each generation alternates a certain role. For example, Jean's parents were overprotective and controlling. Although they had good intentions and wanted what was best for their only daughter, they had a tendency to make decisions for Jean and to dominate her. Jean learned to doubt herself and had a tendency to become submissive and helpless. Jean felt anxious when she had to make a decision. When she asked for help by discussing her decision with her parents (and later her boss, romantic partners, and daughter), they responded with irritation and conveyed that it was obvious what she "should" do. Jean responded by feeling confused and assumed that she was incompetent and "stupid." When Jean had her own daughter, she continued to be anxious and unsure about how to handle situations. In response, her daughter became easily frustrated with her mother and was demanding and controlling. The daughter assumed that she had to be responsible, and, like her grandparents before her, had to take care of Jean.

Implications for Family Therapy

The concept of family experiential holograms can be a useful tool for understanding the broader context for individual and couples therapy, but it is also a foundation for the practice of family therapy. In family therapy, presenting problems may be contextualized as an aspect of a broader pattern where each family member contributes to the recapitulation of an experiential hologram. The discussion could help members view their own and others' behavior within this framework, thereby decreasing blame and increasing compassion. Behaviors that may have been viewed as destructive may be reframed as avoidance or compensating strategies allowing for the surfacing of personal truths and core violations. The family is encouraged to complete unspoken communications and develop new behavioral patterns. They learn that each person's behavior influences the whole family. Through the therapy process, family members learn to see multiple truths about a situation, and learn to value and respect their interconnectedness.

Socio-Cultural Experiential Holograms

Socio-cultural experiential holograms are holograms based on a shared unresolved significantly emotional experience (e.g., following a significant event such as the Great Depression a cohort of people might share a hologram around survival), or a history of shared experiences such as oppression from a dominate group. Like other experiential holograms, socio-cultural holograms are emotional and passed down through generations. Intense experiences such as persecution or the effects of war, regardless of the origins, leave imprints that are carried forth through generations. These holographic imprints perpetuate intense emotions such as prejudice and defensiveness. Just as in the example of the food aversion, the next generation(s) may not be aware of why they hate a particular group but nonetheless have a strong emotional response. Although the original context may no longer exist, the experiential holograms linger and therefore, set the stage for recapitulation. Like other experiential holograms, socio-cultural holograms may also be triggered and reenacted. The recapitulations may occur on a group level such as ongoing wars between certain countries, group riots, institutionalized oppression, or acts of violence toward a particular group.

Like other experiential holograms, they may or may not reflect a kernel of truth from a narrow and limiting perspective. For example, people could look to the horizon for evidence of the shared belief that the world was flat. However, from a broader perspective, it was shown that indeed the world is round and the previous notion no longer had any validity. Once the experiential hologram is reprocessed, the old view no longer makes sense.

Reprocessing a socio-cultural hologram would include objectively examining the socio-cultural beliefs and extinguishing the conditioned associations, creating new meanings, and facilitating ongoing corrective experiences between members of feuding groups. Gaining a historical context may be helpful in understanding the development of a conflict. The origins of a hologram may have to do with a clash of cultural beliefs, or even more likely with economics—fighting for land, resources, and political control. One group may oppress another by generating negative associations to specific characteristics of a targeted group. Reprocessing would be a process of deconstructing false beliefs by exposing the broader truth.

However, the original event is often obscured by a complicated history of struggles rendering both groups with layers of wounds, resentments, and distrust. These events and the associated emotional impact become intertwined into the fiber of a community, and the hologram is adopted as part of the cultural identity. Of course, many complex factors contribute to the development, reenactments, and reprocessing of these holograms which is a discussion beyond the scope of this chapter. However, a few thoughts on this topic will be presented relevant to conducting psychotherapy.

In terms of psychotherapy, socio-cultural holograms are important factors to consider in their interplay and influence on a client's presenting problem. Some of these considerations would be the following: level of identification with a certain culture or group, level of acculturation, differences between the client and other generations within his family (i.e., parents or children), comparisons of himself to perceived social and family norms, and internalized oppression. What socio-cultural experiential holograms are a client carrying forth? And how are they affecting his life?

The likelihood and the intensity in which a client will relate to socio-cultural experiential holograms may be related to the degree of group identification or affiliation. Some people have a strong affiliation no matter what the social context, while others may vary in strength depending on the situation. In contexts where cultural differences are apparent, the identification with one's own culture is pushed to the foreground of one's identity. The realization of difference (in-group versus out-group) is what strengthens the awareness of embedded socio-cultural holograms. What is in the foreground for a person who is acutely aware of difference, moves into the background for a person whose cultural identity is consistent with a dominant culture. For example, a woman who chooses to work in a profession that is predominately female (such as teaching or nursing) would have a markedly different experience when working in a profession that is predominately male (such as firefighting or the military). The awareness of a minority in a group can bring forth a host of prejudices, limiting beliefs, and intense emotions regardless of the minority person's status or level of competence.

For people in a minority group position, the awareness of their difference is constant. This has the advantage of a heightened sense of cultural identity and connection to one's own history. But it also has the disadvantage of enduring social injustices. People in this group may have therapeutic tasks to resolve internalized socio-cultural holograms that perpetuate mistrust and defensiveness as well as a victim-based identity such as internalizing limiting or deprecating beliefs. A proposed model could be to acknowledge the historical context for being in the minority position, to mourn for one's ancestors, grieve for personal and family losses, to search for higher-order meanings, and to build positive internalizations.

People in the dominant group position are given certain advantages and avoid the discomfort of feeling persecuted and oppressed. They may not be aware of, or at least may not have the same sensitivity to the issues of, someone in a minority position. This, of course, perpetuates the lack of motivation for change, or worse, a defensive posturing fearing a loss of control or power. People in this group may have several therapeutic tasks including resolving socio-cultural holograms that perpetuate domination including fear of being dominated and the entitlement to dominate, as well as understanding their historical contexts (i.e., How did this group come into power?) It is also important to explore how maintaining domination and oppression of others ultimately is limiting and destructive to the well being of all.

Finally, people in the position of assimilating into a dominate group clearly have social and economic advantages, but also by definition, dilute their cultural identification and affiliation. People are left with imprints of socio-cultural holograms from their ancestors but lack experience, education, and a personal understanding to express this cultural sense. They are disconnected from their history. Thus, the only reality that exists becomes their personal reality, a reality based solely on personal experiences. With loss of a historical context, there is also a loss of a greater meaning. This can lead to confusion, a sense of isolation, a diffuse, superficial identity, self-centeredness, and lack of purpose or meaning. This is particularly evident in the American culture where many groups assimilate into the melting pot. For example, David has assimilated into the American main stream culture. He does not practice his religion and is disconnected from his heritage. However, in certain social contexts he hears prejudicial comments. In these instances, his Jewish identity is pushed to the foreground. Without any background or experience of his own culture, he not only cannot defend himself but finds himself feeling embarrassed and "not belonging" or fitting into either group.

It is in the triggering of experiential holograms that allows them to be examined. Just as in personal holograms, the reenactment sets a stage for the possibility of resolution. Unfortunately, without broadening the understanding of any hologram, reenactments, then, merely recapitulate and reinforce themselves. Practical and effective solutions are obviously needed for these difficult and complex problems.

In conclusion, all levels of experiential holograms (personal, family, and socio-cultural) can impose a limiting structure on people's lives. These limitations perpetuate themselves until they are confronted and resolved. Identifying experiential holograms and placing them in broader contexts helps alter and resolve the underlying emotional issues.

Chapter Summary

This chapter discussed the concepts of family and socio-cultural experiential holograms. Like personal holograms, these are based on unresolved emotional issues and can be triggered and reenacted. They can be carried forth through generations, even though the later generations may not have had direct experience or even an awareness of the original emotional trauma. Reprocessing these holograms means broadening the awareness of the developmental context, shifting perceptions, and implementing new affirming behaviors.

CHAPTER 17

Conclusion

This brief chapter reviews the basic concepts of the book and discusses benefits that clients have reported from engaging in HR. The author includes a final section that explores a broader context for Holographic Reprocessing. Moving from the realm of psychotherapy to that of philosophy, questions such as are there universal holograms? and what happens when all experiential holograms are resolved? are examined.

Brief Review

In review, Holographic Reprocessing is an integrative psychotherapy that draws upon the principles of Epstein's (1991, 1994, 1998) CEST. In accordance with CEST, HR utilizes techniques to reach both the cognitive and experiential systems. As Epstein states, in order for psychotherapy to effect lasting change, the experiential system must be engaged. HR uses the principles of CEST at every phase of the therapy from explaining that seemingly irrational behavior makes sense given a client's experience to facilitating retrieval of information about experiential holograms to reprocessing client's perceptions about themselves and others at the experiential level.

HR is unique in that the hologram is employed as a model to explain repeating patterns of behavior. In a hologram, the whole is contained in the parts. Similarly, in an experiential hologram, an identified theme (whole) is contained in multiple experiences (parts). The same unresolved emotional issue is repeated in various relationships and situations. An experiential hologram develops when an emotionally distressing event is poorly or not fully processed. Clients may attempt to resolve the stuck point or emotional issue by unconsciously recreating situations and relationships that simulate the original trauma. The reenactment may facilitate a healthy confrontation or may result in the reinforcement of a negative or limited perception.

Through experiential discovery, the repeating patterns are identified. This is achieved by (1) connecting with the experience, (2) identifying the feeling, and (3) free associating to images, memories, or other feelings to reveal patterns. The therapist and client work on identifying the six components of the experiential hologram. They may use the image of a pot on stove to organize and map the components. In review, the six components are: the core violation, personal truths, acquired motivation, compensating and avoiding strategies, and residual emotional state. By identifying these components, clients and therapists can understand complex behavior patterns and clarify which aspect to address in therapy.

Before reprocessing, therapists assess for the client's abilities to handle distress. Several tools were offered to help clients learn how to cope with feelings such as relaxation exercises (e.g., the Signal Breath, and the Cleansing Breath), how to detect feelings (e.g., the Body Scan/Emotional Scan, Deciphering Messages) how to tolerate feelings (e.g., Mindful Observation, Deliberate Distraction), shift through feelings (e.g., Shrinking Machine, and How to Cope with Upsets), and how to increase emotional resiliency (e.g., Maypole of Support). Also, techniques to address specific symptoms common among survivors of trauma were offered such as how to cope with nightmares, intrusive thoughts, and panic attacks (e.g., Return to safety, COPE, and the invisible negativity shield). Suggestions on how to create a "feelings plan" were also discussed.

Once the experiential hologram is identified and the client is ready (i.e., is willing to reprocess and has mastered a sufficient level of skills to manage and tolerate affect) then the therapy proceeds to reprocessing. Reprocessing may include recontextualizing the traumatic event (e.g., seeing multiple truths, age comparison, and hindsight advantage), completing undelivered communications (e.g., to the perpetrator, to the younger version of the self, or to anyone else related to the trauma), and releasing and integrating constricted affect (e.g., guilt, anger, and hurt). This is achieved by discussing the event and then revisiting the traumatic scene in a non-arousing safe manner by maintaining the observer vantage point. The client is able to imaginally rescript the scene. This may include imagining completing actions such as fighting the perpetrator, or delivering communications while the therapist may (or may not) assume the voice of one of the characters in the scene. Clients comfort the younger version of themselves and let them know they are "okay" and will be taken care of by their current aged self. Clients may gain new insights about the event such as being able to see the event in a new context.

Finally, new behaviors are encouraged to reinforce flexible and more adaptive perceptions about the self and others. One technique, counter images, helps clients develop skills by imaginally practicing how they would interact in a situation.

Reported Benefits from HR

Holographic Reprocessing has been developed and refined over the course of 10 years of clinical work. Approximately 30 interns have been trained and supervised using the techniques and over 200 clients have reported benefits. Some of these reports include the following:

1. Clients have noted that they feel validated, understood, and more "normal" and less alone and "crazy." They are relieved to know their feelings make sense.
2. Clients reported having a broader less personalized perception about their trauma. This allowed them to release constricted affected and integrate mixed feelings such as feeling disappointed but also understanding that the action was not personal.
3. After reprocessing, some clients have become more flexible and creative in their problem solving.
4. Several clients have reported feeling physically "lighter" as if a burden had been lifted from them during reprocessing (e.g., reports of feeling a release in the stomach, ears, shoulders, and reports of feeling "relieved").
5. Clients have reported that they have regained a sense of safety, feel more empowered and less afraid, and generally have improved their self-esteem.

Final Reflections

Experiential holograms have been discussed as a repeating pattern reflecting a narrow personal perception of truth. They have been discussed as patterns that recapitulate in relationships, within a family, and between generations of a family. They have also been discussed as a cultural phenomenon where a narrow perception of truth can lead to prejudice and oppression. These holograms can be confronted and dissipated by observing them and broadening their context.

Experiential holograms extend not only to contexts in the current time but are evident across time, possibly influenced by historical, political, and technological contexts. Given these more universal influences, are there such things as universal experiential holograms? Similar to Jung's (1936) concepts of a collective unconscious and archetypes, maybe everyone is also connected to universal experiential holograms that influence us but are outside of our conscious awareness.

For these influences to be experiential holograms, it suggests that there is an inherent emotional issue and a limiting perception. Maybe our concepts of "fear," "death," and "good and evil" are examples. They seem to reflect a partial awareness that if we had a larger context, our perceptions of these things might change. Using the analogy of the tissue box, if one side is "death" how would our perception change if we knew what was on the other side of the box?

Given the limitations of our awareness, and for the purpose of this reflection, what if we were able to confront every emotional issue and clear every experiential hologram? In other words, what is the ultimate goal of identifying, confronting, and clearing experiential holograms? If there were no experiential holograms, no limiting constructions, interpretations, or expectations, then what would be left? Some might say nothing. Although, in a place of nothingness lays every possibility. From that place, everything is new, fresh, clear, open, and responsive to the moment. There would be complete clarity of perception because nothing would be blocking it. If all experiential holograms are constructions, then Holographic Reprocessing is a procedure of deconstructing negative or limiting perceptions of the self, others, and the world thereby allowing for the possibility of . . . just being.

Summary of Techniques Used in HR

The following is a list of techniques discussed in this book. It is a reminder checklist for therapists to recall the techniques and concepts when practicing HR.

Step 1. Establish a therapeutic alliance

☐ Establish a good feeling
☐ Educate, normalize, and "make the client right"
☐ Address resistance, transference and counter-transference

Step 2. Ensure a foundation of coping skills

☐ *Relaxation techniques:* Signal breath, Cleansing breath, Relaxation sandwich, Counting exercise, Personal biofeedback machine
☐ *Detecting feelings:* Body scan/Emotional scan, Deciphering messages
☐ *Tolerating affect:* Mindful observation, Deliberate distraction, 5 ways to express feelings
☐ *Shifting feelings:* Shrinking machine, How to cope with upsets
☐ *Building emotional resiliency:* Maypole of support
☐ *Address symptoms such as nightmares, intrusive thoughts and panic:* COPE, Invisible negativity shield
☐ *Create a "feelings plan"*

Step 3. Engage in "experiential discovery"

☐ Connect with the experience
☐ Identify the feeling
☐ Free associate to images, memories, or other feelings

Step 4. Map the experiential hologram

☐ Pot on the stove analogy
☐ Core violation
☐ Personal truths
☐ Acquired motivation
☐ Compensating strategies
☐ Avoidance strategies
☐ Residual emotional state

Step 5. Reprocess the experiential hologram

☐ *Steps for Reprocessing:* Contextualize scene, ask for permission, induce relaxation, approach the scene, set the stage, assess for level of distress, rescript the scene, complete and debrief

☐ *Techniques to recontextualize a scene:* Hindsight advantage, Age comparison,

☐ *Techniques to ensure emotional distance:* Observer vantage point, Remaining current age, Changing attributes, therapist observes and monitors the client, therapist redirects imagery when necessary

☐ *Goals for reprocessing:* Completing communication, releasing and integrating affect, gaining a new perception, increasing power and safety

☐ *Reprocessing techniques:* Imagery rescripting, fantasy, role-playing, story board, emotionally connected conversation, guided imagery

Step 6. Establish new patterns

☐ Set new life goals
☐ Develop new self-concept
☐ Counter images

Frequently Asked Questions

FAQ: Does reprocessing cause clients to dissociate? And what should you do if a client does dissociate during the procedure?

Dissociation is a biologically mediated response to extreme stress. HR has a very low probability of inducing dissociation for the following reasons: (1) HR takes several measures to monitor and ensure that the experience is non-threatening and induces low stress, (2) clients do not "float out of one-self" but rather are instructed to remain anchored in their current body, in the here-and-now, and remain their current-aged self, and (3) reprocessing is a technique that is introduced to clients after they have some mastery of coping skills to manage and tolerate affect. However, if clients do appear disconnected or dissociated during the procedure or during any time in the therapy, for that matter, then the therapist can bring the client back to the present moment and work on staying connected and grounded.

Another related question is wondering if observing a scene "cuts people off from their feelings." As mentioned, clients remain anchored to their current aged self and continue to feel and respond to the imagery that they are viewing "as if they walked in on a scene." Most clients find reprocessing to be an emotional experience and they tend to feel tremendous relief, connection, and empathy when they are liberated from limiting perceptions.

FAQ: The relaxation seems like it is inducing a state of hypnosis. Is reprocessing a form of hypnosis?

It is true that the relaxation procedure is intended to induce relaxation. However, the intention is not to induce hypnosis, nor "trick" the client into believing that she is hypnotized, nor is the intention to induce such a deep state that the client loses consciousness. If a client falls limp, then the therapist may want to "wake up" the client. Also, because clients remain anchored in the here-and-now, they don't modify the memory of their affective or sensory experience. For example, under hypnosis, someone could recall eating a certain food and then be convinced that the food was very salty or sweet. Instead, in reprocessing, the current-aged self is not re-experiencing the event. However, because clients are in a relaxed, receptive state, therapists should take the same precautions as if all their clients were hypnotized. These precautions are not to suggest or create a memory, not to say anything that is untrue, and to carefully select who is appropriate for the procedure. Clients who do not have an intact memory, are highly dissociative, actively use substances, have a history of psychosis, or confuse fantasy with reality are not appropriate candidates for reprocessing.

FAQ: What should you do if your client does not have an intact memory of their trauma (e.g., the memory is fragmented, lacks details, is non-sequential, and has missing parts)?

The client may need to talk or write about his experience. It may be appropriate to initiate the procedure of Prolonged Exposure as this has been proven to be an effective treatment especially for clients who do not have intact memories.

FAQ: Can reprocessing be used to uncover repressed memories?

It is possible that repressed memories or repressed details may surface during a reprocessing procedure just as they may resurface during exposure procedures. As demonstrated in the example of Edward (chapter five), after recounting his experience he was able to recall a piece of his memory that helped him free a limiting personal truth. Neither reprocessing nor exposure procedures are designed to be methods to uncover repressed memories.

However, memories may spontaneously begin to surface during the course of most psychotherapies. It may be that once clients are in a safe therapeutic relationship, they are ready to remember. As difficult images, dreams, and emotions surface, the therapist can reassure the client and help them tolerate and manage the experience. The analogy of "waves coming and going" may be useful. The pain may be intense in the moment but it is temporary and it will subside. This phase of therapy may take a few sessions or it may take several months depending on the client.

FAQ: In order to do reprocessing, are all of the steps necessary and if so, do they have to be followed in the exact order as it was presented?

There is a therapeutic logic to having the six steps. It starts with establishing rapport, trust, and safety. Regardless if the therapist feels comfortable to move forward, clients need time to feel safe. Second, coping skills lay a foundation so that clients can manage and tolerate their affect. At least an assessment of coping skills is strongly recommended before proceeding. Third, correctly identifying patterns is necessary before attempting reprocessing. Otherwise, therapy runs the risk of missing the root of the problem. It is also helpful for clients to become aware of their patterns. Mapping the hologram is usually a very meaningful intervention for clients. Reprocessing helps clients shift the underlying core violation and personal truths related to a traumatic experience. Finally, the process of integration helps clients establish new patterns for their lives. Before breaking the rules of the structure and of the techniques, it is highly recommended that they are practiced as presented in this text.

Bibliography

American Psychiatric Association (1994). *Diagnostic and statistical manual of mental disorders* (4th ed.). Washington, DC.

Bandura, A. (1969). *Principles of behavior modification*. New York: Holt.

Barlow, D. H., & Craske, M. G. (1994). *Mastery of your anxiety and panic*. Albany, NY: Center for Stress and Anxiety Disorders.

Becker, C. B., & Zayfert, C. (2001). Integrating DBT-based techniques and concepts to facilitate exposure treatment in PTSD. *Cognitive & Behavioral Practice, 8*(2), 107–122.

Boal, A. (1995). *Rainbow of desire*. London: Routledge.

Bohm, D. (1980). *Wholeness and the implicit order*. London: Routledge & Kegan Paul.

Bootzin, R. R. (1997). Examining the theory and clinical utility of writing about emotional experiences. *Psychological Science, 8,* 167–169.

Briere, J. (1992). *Child abuse trauma*. Newbury Park, CA: Sage.

Brom, D., Kleber, R. J., & Defares, P. B. (1989). Brief psychotherapy for posttraumatic stress disorders. *Journal of Consulting and Clinical Psychology, 57,* 607–612.

Cardena, E., Maldonado, J., van der Hart, O., & Spiegal, D. (2000). Hypnosis. In E. B. Foa, T. M. Keane,& M. J. Friedman (Eds.), *Effective treatments for PTSD* (pp. 247–279, 350–353). New York: Guilford Press.

Catlin, G., & Epstein, S. (1992). Unforgettable experiences: The relation of life-events to basic beliefs about the self and world. *Social Cognition, 10,* 189–209.

Chemtob, C. M., Tolin, D. F., van der Kolk, B. A., & Pitman, R. K. (2000). Eye Movement Desensitization and Reprocessing. In E. B. Foa, T. M. Keane, & M. J. Friedman (Eds.), *Effective treatments for PTSD* (pp. 139–154, 333–335). New York: Guilford Press.

Cronen, V. E., & Pearce, W. B. (1985). Toward an explanation of how the Milan Method works: An invitation to a systemic epistemology and the evolution of family systems. In D. Campbell & R. Draper (Eds.), *Applications of systemic family therapy: The Milan approach* (pp. 69–84). London: Grune & Station.

Dalenberg, D. J. (2000). *Countertransference and the treatment of trauma*. Washington, DC: American Psychological Association.

Denes-Raj, V., & Epstein, S. (1994). Conflict between experiential and rational processing: When people behave against their better judgment. *Journal of Personality and Social Psychology, 66,* 819–829.

De Rios, M.D. (1997). Magical realism: A cultural intervention for traumatized Hispanic children. *Cultural Diversity and Mental Health, 3,* 159–170.

Dietrich, A. (2000). A review of visual/kinesthetic dissociation in the treatment of posttraumatic disorders: Theory, efficacy, and practice recommendations. *Traumatology, 4*(2).

Dougan, I., & Ellis, S. (1992). *The art of reflexology*. Rockport, MA: Element Books.

Elhers, A., & Clark, D. M. (2000). A cognitive model of posttraumatic stress disorder. *Behaviour Research and Therapy, 38*, 319–345.

Epstein, S. (1983). Natural healing processes of the mind: Graded stress inoculation as an inherent coping mechanism. In M Michenbaum & M. E. Jarmeko (Eds.), *Stress reduction and prevention*. New York: Plenum Press.

Epstein, S. (1991). Cognitive-experiential self-theory: An integrative theory of personality. In R. Curtis (Ed.), *The relational self: Convergences in psychoanalysis and social psychology* (pp. 111–137). New York: Guilford Press.

Epstein, S. (1994). Integration of the cognitive and the psychodynamic unconscious. *American Psychologist, 49*, 709–724.

Epstein, S. (1998). Cognitive-experiential self-theory: A dual-process personality theory with implications for diagnosis and psychotherapy. In Bornstein & Masling (Eds.), *Empirical perspectives on the psychoanalytic unconscious* (pp. 99–140). Washington, DC: American Psychological Association.

Epstein, S., & Pacini, R. (2001). The influence of imagined and unimagined verbal information on intuitive and analytical information processing. *Imagination, Cognition, and Personality, 20*, 195–216.

Epstein, S. (2003). Cognitive-experiential self-theory: An integrative psychodynamic theory of personality. In T. Millon & M. J. Lerner (Eds.), *Comprehensive handbook of psychology, Volume 5: Personality and Social*. John Wiley & Sons.

Feeny, N., Hembree, E., & Zoellner, L. (2003). Myths regarding exposure therapy for PTSD. *Cognitive and Behavioral Practice, 10*(1), 85–90.

Foa, E. (1997). Psychological processes related to recovery from a trauma and an effective treatment for PTSD. In R. Yehuda & A. C. McFarlane (Eds.), *Psychobiology of posttraumatic stress disorder* (Vol. 821, pp. 99–113). New York: Annals of the New York Academy of Sciences.

Foa, E., Keane, T., & Friedman, M. (2000). *Effective treatments for PTSD: Practice guidelines from the international society for traumatic stress studies*. New York: Guilford Press.

Foa, E., & Kozak, M. (1986). Emotional processing of fear: Exposure to corrective information. *Psychological Bulletin, 99*, 20–35.

Foa, E., Molnar, C., & Cashman, L. (1995). Change in rape narratives during exposure therapy for PTSD. *Journal of Traumatic Stress, 8*, 675–690.

Foa, E., & Riggs, D. (1993). Post-traumatic stress disorder in rape victims, In J. Oldham, M. B. Riba, & A. Tasman (Eds.), *American Psychiatric Press Teview of Psychiatry* (Vol. 12, pp. 273–303). Washington, DC: American Psychiatric Press.

Foa, E. B., & Rothbaum, B. O. (1998). *Treating the trauma of rape: Cognitive-behavior therapy for PTSD*. New York: Guilford.

Foa, E., Rothbaum, B., & Furr, J. (2003). Augmenting exposure therapy with other CBT procedures. *Psychiatric Annals, 33*(1), 47–53.

Foa, E. B., Zoellner, L. A., Feeny, N. C., Hembree, E. A., & Alvarez-Conrad, J. (2002). Does imaginal exposure exacerbate PTSD symptoms? *Journal of Consulting and Clinical Psychology, 70*(4), 1022–1028.

Frankl, V. (1959). *Man's search for meaning*. New York: Simon and Schuster.

Freedman, J., & Combs, G. (1996). *Narrative therapy: The social construction of preferred realities*. New York: W.W. Norton Company.

Friedman, M. (1997). Drug treatment for PTSD. Answers and questions. In R. Yehuda & A. C. McFarlane (Eds.), *Psychobiology of posttraumatic stress disorder* (Vol. 821; pp. 99–113). New York: Annals of the New York Academy of Sciences.

Gerbode, F. A. (1989). *Beyond psychology: An Introduction to metapsychology*. Menlo Park, CA: IRM.

Gendlin, E. (1981). *Focusing*. New York: Batam.

Greenberg, D., & Pedesky, C. A. (1994). *Mind over mood: Change the way you feel by changing the way you think*. New York: Guilford.

Greenberg, M. A., & Stone, A. A. (1992). Emotional disclosure about traumas and its relation to health: Effects of previous disclosure and trauma severity. *Journal of Personality and Social Psychology, 63*, 75–84.

Greenson, R., & Wexler, M. (1969). The non-transference relationship in the psychoanalytic situation. *International Journal of Psycho-Analysis, 50*, 27–39.

Herman, J. (1992). *Trauma and recovery.* New York: Basic Books.

Hermesh, M. (2003). Cognitive behavior therapy in anxiety disorders. *Israel Journal of Psychiatry Related Science, 40*(2). 135–144.

Horowitz, M .J. (1986). *Stress response syndromes.* Northvale, NJ: Aronson.

Horowitz, M. J. (1988). *Introduction to psychodynamics.* NJ: Basic Books.

Ironson, G., Freud, B., Strauss, J. L., & Williams, J. (2002). Comparison for two treatments for traumatic stress: A community-based study of EMDR and prolonged exposure. *Journal of Clinical Psychology, 58*, 113–128.

Janoff-Bulman, R. (1992). *Shattered assumptions.* New York: Free Press.

Jiraneck, D. (1993). Use of hypnosis in pain management in post-traumatic stress disorder. *Australian Journal of Clinical and Experimental Hypnosis*, 21, 75–84.

Jung, C. (1936). *The concept of the collective unconscious.* From the collected works of C. G. Jung, The archetypes and the collective unconscious, Part I. England: Routledge & Kegan Paul, Ltd.

Katz, L. (2001). Holographic reprocessing: A cognitive experiential psychotherapy. *Psychotherapy, 38*, 186–197.

Katz, L. (2003). Clinical coaching: A paradigm for supervision. *Psychotherapy Bulletin, 38*(1), 26–29.

Katz, L. (in press). *Fifty ways to deal with feelings.* Unpublished manuscript.

Kirkpatrick, L. A., & Epstein, S. (1992). Cognitive-experiential self-theory and subjective probability: Further evidence for two conceptual systems. *Journal of Personality and Social Psychology, 63*(4), 534–544.

Koziey, P. W., & McLeod, G. L. (1987). Visual-kinesthetic dissociation in treatment of victims of rape. *Professional Psychology: Research and Practice, 18*(3), 276–282.

Langs, R. (1982). *The psychotherapeutic conspiracy.* New York: Jason Aronson.

Laveman, L. (1994). The multi-level supervision model and the interplay between clinical supervision and psychotherapy. *The Clinical Supervisor, 12*, 75–91.

Lerner, M. (1980). *The belief in a just world.* New York: Plenum.

Linehan, M. (1995). *Treating borderline personality: The dialectical approach.* New York: Guilford Press.

Littrell, J. (1998). Is the reexperience of painful emotion therapeutic? *Clinical Psychology Review, 18*, 71–102.

McFarlane, A., & Yehuda, R. (2000). Clinical treatment of posttraumatic stress disorder: Conceptual challenges raised by recent research. *Australian and New Zealand Journal of Psychiatry, 34*, 940–953.

McFarlane, A., Yehuda, R., & Clark, C. (2002). Biologic models of traumatic memories and posttraumatic stress disorder. The role of neural networks. *The Psychiatric Clinics of North America, 25*, 253–270.

McIsaac, H., & Eich, E. (2002). Vantage point in episodic memory. *Psychonomic bulletin and review, 9*, 146–150.

McIsaac, H., & Eich, E. (2004). Vantage point in traumatic memory. *Psychological Science, 15*(4), 248–253.

Miller, D. T., & Gunasegaram, S. (1990). Temporal order and the perceived mutability of events: Implications for blame assignment. *Journal of Personality and Social Psychology, 59*, 1111–1118.

Moore, R. H. (1993). Traumatic incident reduction: a cognitive-emotive treatment of post-traumatic stress disorder. In W. Dryden & L. Hill (Eds.), *Innovations in rational-emotive therapy.* Newbury Park, CA: Sage.

Murray, J. (1993). Relationship of childhood sexual abuse to borderline personality disorder, posttraumatic stress disorder, and multiple personality disorder. *Journal of Psychology, 127*, 657–676.

Peebles, M. J. (1989). Through a glass darkly: the psychoanalytic use of hypnosis with post-traumatic stress disorder. *International Journal of Clinical Experimental Hypnosis, 37*(3), 192–206.

Pennebaker, J. W. (1997). Writing about emotional experiences as a therapeutic process. *Psychological Science, 8*, 162–166.

Pennebaker, J. W., Kiecolt-Glaser, J. K., & Glaser, R. (1988). Disclosure of traumas and immune function: Health implications for psychotherapy. *Journal of Consulting and Clinical Psychology, 56*, 239–245.

Pearlman, L., & Saakvitne, K. (1995). *Trauma and the therapist: Counter-transference and vicarious traumatization in psychotherapy with incest survivors*. New York: Norton.

Perry, J., Herman, J., van der Kolk, B., & Hoke, L. (1990). Psychotherapy and psychological trauma in borderline personality disorder. *Psychiatric Annals, 20*, 33–43.

Pietsch, P. (1981). *Shufflebrain: The quest for the hologramic mind*. Boston: Houghton Mifflin.

Potter-Enfron, R., & Potter-Enfron, P. (1989). *Letting go of shame*. New York: Hazelden.

Pribram, K. (1969). The neurophysiology of remembering. *Scientific American*, Jan., 220.

Pribram, K. (1971). *Languages of the brain*. New Jersey: Prentice-Hall.

Rachman, S. (1966). Studies in desensitization-II: Flooding. *Behavior Research and Therapy, 4*, 1–6.

Rothbaum, B. O., Meadows, E. A., Resick, P., & Foy, D. (2000). *Cognitive-behavioral Therapy*. In E. B. Foa, T. M. Keane, & M. J. Friedman (Eds.), *Effective treatments for PTSD* (pp. 60–83, 320–325. New York: Guilford Press.

Resick, P. A., & Schnicke, M. K, (1993). *Cognitive processing therapy for rape victims: A treatment manual*. London: Sage Publications.

Roine, E. (1997). *Psychodrama: Group psychotherapy as experimental theatre*. London: Jessica Kingsley Publishers.

Rothbaum, B. O., & Schwartz, A. C. (2002). Exposure therapy for posttraumatic stress disorder. *American Journal of Psychotherapy, 56*(1), 59–75.

Schnurr, P. P., Friedman, M. J., Foy, D., Shea, M. T., Hsieh, F. Y., Lavori, P. W., Glynn, S. M., Wattenberg, M., & Bernardy, N. C. (2003). Randomized trial of trauma-focused group therapy for posttraumatic stress disorder. *Archives of General Psychiatry, 60*, 481–489.

Scott, M., & Stradling, S. G. (1997). Client compliance with exposure treatment for posttraumatic stress disorder. *Journal of Traumatic Stress, 10*(3), 523–526.

Shapiro, F. (1995). *Eye movement desensitization and reprocessing: Basic principles, protocols, and procedures*. New York: Guilford Press.

Smucker, M., & Dancu, C. (1999). *Cognitive behavioral treatment for adult survivors of childhood abuse: Imaginal rescripting and reprocessing*. Northvale, NJ: Aronson.

Smucker, M., Dancu, C., Foa, E., & Niederee, J. (1995). Imagery rescripting: A new treatment for survivors of childhood sexual abuse suffering from posttraumatic stress. *Journal of Cognitive Psychotherapy, 9*, 3–17.

Smucker, M., & Niederee, J. (1995). Treating incest-related PTSD and pathogenic schemas through imaginal exposure and rescripting. *Cognitive and Behavioral Practice, 2*, 63–93.

Spiegel, D. (1989). Hypnosis in the treatment of victims of sexual abuse. *Psychiatric Clinics of North America, 12*, 295–305.

Spiegal, D. (1992). The use of hypnosis in the treatment of PTSD. *Psychiatric Medicine, 10*, 21–30.

Stampfl, T. G., & Levis, D. J. (1967). Essentials of implosive therapy: A learning-theory-based psychodynamic behavioral therapy. *Journal of Abnormal Psychology, 72*, 496–503.

Talbot, M. (1991). *The holographic universe*. New York: Harper Collins.

Tarrier, N., Hazel, P., Sommerfield, C., Faragher, B., Reynolds, M., Graham, E., & Barrowclough, C. (1999). A randomized trial of cognitive therapy and imaginal exposure in the treatment of chronic posttraumatic stress disorder. *Journal of Consulting and Clinical Psychology, 67*(1), 13–18.

Tarrier, N., & Humphreys, L. (2000). Subjective improvement in PTSD patients with treatment by imaginal exposure of cognitive therapy: Session changes. *British Journal of Clinical Psychology, 39*(1), 27–34.

van der Kolk, B. A. (1994). The body keeps the score: Memory and the evolving psychobiology of posttraumatic stress. *Harvard Review of Psychiatry, 1*, 253–265.

van der Kolk, B., Burbridge, J., & Suzuki, J. (1997). The psychobiology of traumatic memory: Clinical implication of neuroimaging studies. In R. Yehuda & A. C. McFarlane (Eds.), *Psychobiology of posttraumatic stress disorder* (Vol. 821; pp. 99–113). New York: Annals of the New York Academy of Sciences.

von Bertalanffy, L. (1968). *General systems theory*. New York: George Braziller.

Wallerstein, R. (1984). The analysis of transference: A matter of emphasis or of theory reformulation. *Psychoanalytic Inquiry, 4*(3), 325–354.

White, M., & Epston, D. (1990). *Narrative means to therapeutic ends*. New York: W.W. Norton.

Wilber, K. (Ed.) (1982). *The holographic paradigm and other paradoxes.* Boulder, CO: Shambhala.

Wilber, K. (1983). *Eye to eye: The quest for the new paradigm.* Garden City, NY: Anchor Books.

Wilson, J., & Lindy, J. (1994). *Countertransference in the treatment of PTSD.* New York: Guilford Press.

Wolpe, J. (1958). *Psychotherapy by reciprocal inhibition.* Stanford, CA: Stanford University Press.

Yahuda, R. (1997). Sensitization of the hypothalamic-pituitary-adrenal axis in posttraumatic stress disorder. In R. Yehuda & A. C. McFarlane (Eds.), *Psychobiology of posttraumatic stress disorder* (Vol. 821; pp. 99–113). New York: Annals of the New York Academy of Sciences.

Index